HARTFORD PUBLIC LI
500 MAIN STREE
HARTFORD, CT 06103
P9-DMQ-834

Peace Now!

Rhodri Jeffreys-Jones

American Society and the Ending of the Vietnam War

Yale University Press   New Haven and London

Published with assistance from the foundation established in memory of Philip Hamilton McMillan of the Class of 1894, Yale College.

Printed in the United States of America

The paper in this book meets the guidelines for permanence and durability of the Committee on Production Guidelines for Book Longevity of the Council on Library Resources.

10 9 8 7 6 5 4 3 2 1

Library of Congress Cataloging-in-Publication Data
Jeffreys-Jones, Rhodri.
Peace now! : American society and the ending of the Vietnam War / Rhodri Jeffreys-Jones.
p. cm.
Includes bibliographical references and index.
ISBN 0-300-07811-0 (alk. paper)
1. Vietnamese Conflict, 1961–1975—United States. 2. Vietnamese Conflict, 1961–1975—Protest movements—United States. 3. United States—Politics and government—1963–1969. 4. United States—Politics and government—1969–1974. 5. United States—Social conditions—1960–1980. I. Title.
DS558 J44 1999
959.704′3373—dc21 99-19725
CIP

A catalogue record for this book is available from the British Library.

Contents

Acknowledgments

Like any history book, this one has a history of its own. It stems from my experiences—unheroic and minor but still vivid for me—of social-reform movements in the 1960s: the campaigns against apartheid and nuclear weapons in Britain and against the Vietnam War in America. Hopes were then high for the introduction of greater humanity and democracy into the conduct of international relations. No doubt, the memory of such aspirations still colors my interpretation of events.

However, none of this would have resulted in a book without the advice, encouragement, and assistance of a number of people. The first person I would like to thank is Oscar Handlin, who encouraged me to apply for a postdoctoral fellowship at the Charles Warren Center for the Study of American History at Harvard University in 1971–1972. This marked the beginning of my research into the social bases of American foreign policy, leading to the present book in the wake of an earlier, companion volume, *Changing Differences: Women and the Shaping of American Foreign Policy, 1917–1994* (1995).

The period of research since 1971 has been so protracted, and the support given to me so generous and extensive, that I can give only an incomplete account of the people and institutions concerned. I would like those whom I mention, some of them now sadly deceased, to serve also as tokens for the others. To start with financial support, I am grateful to the responsible officials of the Ada E. Leeke Research Fellowship, American Philosophical Society, British Academy, Canadian Commonwealth Visiting Fellowship, Carnegie Trust for the Universities of Scotland, Charles Warren Center, Fulbright Traveling Fellowship program, John F. Kennedy-Institut für Nordamerikastudien / Stiftung Volkswagenwerk, Lyndon Baines Johnson Foundation, and Moray Fund.

Librarians and archivists have given unsparingly of their time and expertise. I would like to acknowledge the help of the following in particular: John Haynes at the Manuscript Division, Library of Congress, Washington, D.C.; William M. Joyner of the Nixon Presidential Materials Staff, National Archives and Records Administration, College Park, Maryland; Mike Parish at the Lyndon Baines Johnson Library, Austin, Texas; Carol Schwartz at the International Longshoremen's and Warehousemen's Union Library, San Francisco, California; Lenny Seigel at the Pacific Studies Center, Palo Alto, California; Diane Stalker at the Library of the State University of New York at Stony Brook; Mary-Jo Stevenson at the John P. Robarts Research Library, Toronto; Molly Sturgis at the Hoover Institution Library, Stanford, California; Jean Wassong at St. John's University Library, Jamaica, New York; and Nanci A. Young at the Seeley G. Mudd Library, Princeton, New Jersey.

Ed Larkin, one of my babysitters in the early 1950s, first stirred my interest in American history by showing me photographs of Frank and Jesse James. He made me an honorary life member of the Seafarers' International Union, of which he was an official, so I benefited for many years from regular receipt of the *Seafarers' Log*, with its detailed economic commentary on the

Vietnam War. The following scholars, politicians, and activists more recently advised me on research for my book, shared their views with me, or steered me in the direction of further information: Bella Abzug, Ron Armstead, Robert S. Bothwell, Joshua B. Freeman, Lewis Henry Gann, Godfrey Hodgson, Joan Hoff, Rob Kroes, Martin Lipset, William S. Mailliard, Charles Neu, Darryl Pinckney, Paul Robeson, Jr., Göran Rystad, Kim Salamon, George A. ("Sam") Shepperson, Barry M. Silverman, Margaret Chase Smith, Amy Swedlow, and Neil A. Wynn.

The anonymous reader engaged by Yale University Press took exceptional pains with the manuscript and made erudite and perceptive remarks. I am especially thankful, too, to a small team of specialist volunteers who subjected the manuscript to critical scrutiny: Gerard J. De Groot, Sidney Fine, Helen Laville, Robert Mason, and Robert Singh.

At Yale University Press, Charles Grench offered the kind of thoughtful, long-term support that encourages an author to continue, and Mary Pasti was a vigilant manuscript editor. My New York literary agents, Frances Goldin and Sydelle Kramer, were also a source of strength.

The hospitality extended to me in the course of research for this book was prodigious. It was a pleasure, for which I express the deepest appreciation, to stay with Jim Compton in San Francisco; Marcus and Phyllis Cunliffe and then Michael Donovan in Washington, D.C.; Buffy and Ian Manners in Austin, Texas; Catherine McCarthy on Long Island; Duncan and Susan Rice in New York City; and Nesta Selwyn in Oxford, and to be looked after in style by Provost Robert Painter and the Fellows of Trinity College, University of Toronto.

It will be for others to judge whether this book is a happy outcome of so much support and so many years of endeavor, but at least it is the product of a happy author, and for that I thank my wife, Mary, and my daughters, Gwenda and Rowena.

Peace Now!

1 Introduction

THE INCIDENT IN THE WHITE House dining room could not have been anticipated. Lady Bird Johnson's luncheon had been routine—she simply wanted to enlist fifty women in the fight against crime. The guests had been vetted; allowances had had to be made in one or two cases. One of the guests, the singer Eartha Kitt, had known the rough side of American life. She had grown up in Harlem and, in her own words, "lived in the gutters."[1] Yet Kitt's work on behalf of disadvantaged youths and her willingness to advise President Johnson's administration had marked her out as friendly. Who could possibly have imagined that she would behave so badly?

The trouble started when the president entered the dining room and mounted the podium to make a few remarks. The women listened respectfully as he told them not to expect too much of the federal government. America's mothers, the president urged, should recognize their own responsibility to combat juvenile delinquency.

Kitt interrupted Johnson. How, she demanded to know, could poor parents who were forced to go out to work assume the responsibility for fighting juvenile crime? The answer lay in day care, said the president, and he hastily left the room. His exit restored a measure of calm and allowed a number of preselected women to deliver their prepared addresses.

In the question period Kitt rose again. This time she launched an attack on the Vietnam War. She said that she spoke "as a mini-mommy of America," and, in her view, the war encouraged juvenile crime. Some young men, she said, calculated that if they had a criminal record, they would be ineligible for the Army and would escape being sent to fight in a far-off war; so "it pays to be a bad guy." These words hurt. Because of Eartha Kitt, an occasion planned as an exercise in genteel persuasion had gone wrong. The president's wife was visibly on the verge of tears.[2]

A person—a woman—from a powerless race had dared to challenge the most powerful people in the land. The White House and its allies duly retaliated. Supportive politicians rushed to condemn the ungallant abuse of Lady Bird Johnson's hospitality.

Overnight, Kitt became a bad mother, a fornicator, a user of profane language, an improper person with offensive opinions. The government dropped her as an adviser, and nightclub owners omitted her from their shows. Fittingly, Kitt was trampled down.

That, at least, was the government story. Looking back at those events in 1968, we could see Eartha Kitt as a tribune for the dispossessed. In fact, it is no novelty to suggest that a people's revolt contributed to the ending of U.S. participation in the Vietnam War.[3] What still needs elucidation, despite thousands of books and articles on the subject, is exactly how and why that revolt proved effective.[4]

The argument in this book is that the effectiveness of the revolt sprang in large measure from its serial nature. I do not seek to identify one great turning point in the politics of the era, nor do I treat President Johnson's war and President Nixon's war as significantly separate entities. Instead, I present the antiwar movement as a cumulative, repetitive series of protests running from the mid-sixties to the early seventies. I focus on four social groups—students, African Americans, women, and labor—and show how protest by each group reached a distinctive crescendo at an unpredictable moment. The result, a succession of protest peaks, gave the politicians no respite and suggested no enduring formula to apply in suppressing all forms of protest. Like American soldiers in the jungles of Vietnam, the White House had to shoot at moving and changing targets.

But if the people won, they won slowly. Although Vietnam is commonly described as America's longest war, too little attention has hitherto been devoted to that longevity's close cousin, the slow peace.[5] It is, of course, known that both the Johnson and the Nixon administrations took steps to crush the opposition—the hounding of Eartha Kitt is just one of many examples. But here I argue that the American people themselves were a prime agency for the prolongation of the war, susceptible as they were to manipulation by politicians who knew not only how to suppress opposition but how to recruit support. The four social groups chosen for special attention here gave the war solid support at its outset. In due course, students, then African Americans, then women mounted spectacular revolts against the war. Organized labor continued to support it.

It was the support of labor that gave President Nixon his opportunity. Wanting to keep America fighting so that he could achieve peace "with honor," he and his White House advisers seized on labor loyalty. They also appropriated a labor image. George Meany, president of the American Federation of Labor-Congress of Industrial Organizations (AFL-CIO), had informed his organization at a 1967 convention that prowar labor "spoke for the vast, silent majority in the nation."[6] Two years later, in November 1969, President Nixon appealed for the support of "the great silent majority" of his fellow Americans.[7] Developing the idea that a silent majority favored the war and learning lessons from prowar demonstrations mounted by hard-hat workers in Manhattan in 1970, the Republican president was able to attack the traditional power base of his Democratic opponents. In particular, as I show here, President Nixon observed, encouraged, and imitated the successful exploitation of the hard-hat demonstrations by the New York prowar senatorial candidate James Buckley and by this means was able to keep his prowar coalition afloat.

To imbue the American people indiscriminately with heroic and effective pacifism would be dewy-eyed. The prowar stances of the four selected groups have been too long neglected, as has the political exploitation of their hawkish outlook. The intention here is not to detract from the force of the cumulative opposition to the war. Indeed, even labor changed its tune toward the end, and that was ominous for the tactics that Nixon had chosen to apply.

To explore not just why peace came but why it came slowly, it is useful to examine the four social groups and their impact on foreign policy. Here are three questions to begin with, to justify this approach: Why examine the social bases of U.S. foreign policy? Why choose students, African Americans, women, and labor for special scrutiny? Did these groups have characteristics that made them prone to support or oppose the Vietnam War?

First, why examine the social bases of U.S. foreign policy?

Few historians would dispute the reverse proposition; the effects of war on society are as undeniable as they are disastrous. Generations are lost, moralities destroyed, cities flattened, and economies ruined. Nevertheless, it is possible to suggest, without challenging the truth of the formula, that it can also operate the other way. Society can have an effect on foreign policy, including the questions of war and peace. This is especially true in a democracy.

An evidential difficulty stems from the fact that elected politicians like to be thought of as the leaders of public opinion, not its followers. Wishing to project a patrician image, they are often reluctant to admit that they respond to clamor from the populace, preferring instead to give the impression that they act on principle. They tend to be reticent about their political calculations, leaving few traces for the historian to analyze.

Yet there is ample inferential evidence that presidents take voters' views into account when formulating foreign policy.[8] The White House meticulously tabulates poll data, for example, and presidents in the Vietnam era did leave other clues. Although President Johnson scribbled on a memo in June 1966 that he did not want his interest in protest groups discovered—"keep ball out of my court as much as possible"—he did tell his aide to identify the main protest groups and devise ways of winning them over.[9] President Nixon explained in May 1969 why he would not yield to the demands of the organizers of the great "Vietnam Moratorium" demonstration scheduled to take place in two days' time: "There is a clear distinction between public opinion and public demonstrations. To listen to public opinion is one thing; to be swayed by public demonstrations is another."[10] This statement is a virtual admission that Nixon listened to public opinion. A wealth of circumstantial evidence supports the view that Nixon ignored his own distinction and took heed of demonstrators, too.

Both in Hanoi, the capital of communist North Vietnam, and in Washington, there was a feeling that the opinion of the American people might prove to be a determining factor in the outcome of the war. In October 1967, President Johnson worried that domestic protest was becoming a Viet Cong asset.[11] The American historian Jeffrey Kimball has conducted oral histories in Hanoi, and the import of these, and of documents being published by the Vietnamese, is that the North Vietnamese regarded protest within the United States as part of a worldwide anti-imperialist struggle that would help them win the day.[12] So, reluctant though democratically elected leaders may be to betray their anxieties about public opinion, public opinion does influence foreign policy. The attitudes of social groups toward the Vietnam War is not just a matter of intrinsic interest but a determinant of policy.

Why focus on students, African Americans, women, and labor? They by no means exhaust the list of protesting elements; Christians and war veterans, among others, conducted significant campaigns. Businessmen were also influential, whether as hawks expecting war-related profits or as doves fearful of war-induced inflation.

The reason for the selection is that each of the groups achieved political prominence in the sixties. They were extensively discussed in the White House, in the Congress, and in the media. Society defined itself in terms of these groups and their positions for the purposes of the Vietnam War debate. Influential observers were convinced that one or another of the groups played a critical role in shaping Vietnam policy. Senator Jacob K. Javits of New York held that students had "first perceived" the "fallacies" of the Vietnam War and that "fathers and even Senators" listened to what they had to say.[13] Given such perceptions, contending factions in the Vietnam debate deemed the support of each group desirable.

To opponents of the war the groups each seemed to represent the antithesis of at least one of the defining qualities of the American ruling elite. Such an elite was assumed to exist even if the White Anglo-Saxon Protestant (WASP) was in decline.[14] The perception in the sixties was that the governing elite was a group of white, old, rich men. Antiwar activists could set a group against each aspect of this political establishment. African Americans had a defining interest in checking the exercise of white power. Students articulated the complaints of the young against the old. In spite of the high wages of some members, organized labor could, and did claim to, represent the poor against the rich. Women increasingly questioned the ascendancy of men. These dividing lines gave potency and drama to the politics of revolt. To ignore the importance of race, age, class, and sex in a discussion of the Vietnam War is to bury one's head in the sand.

What helped to give the groups their salience and therefore political importance was that they contained people who thought of themselves as different in ways that mattered where the war was concerned. The validity or otherwise of the arguments is less important than their having been proposed at all. The arguments ran as follows. Unlike the old men who conducted the war, students were of draft age and would have to fight in it. Unlike the white men who conducted the war, African Americans belonged to a racially oppressed category, like the Vietnamese they were being asked to kill. Unlike the men who conducted the war, women saw war as oppressive to their sex. Unlike those capitalists who profited from the war and protected their sons from the draft, labor paid the double price of diminishing prosperity and death of their sons in battle. Even if it was impossible to sustain all of these generalizations all of the time, in every group some members felt separated in a significant way from the white, old, rich, or male. That feeling of difference gave them their political importance and makes them worth studying now.

Did the four groups have characteristics that made them particularly prone to support or to oppose the Vietnam War? It is useful to approach this question under four headings. The first three help to explain why some members of all the groups tended in varying degrees to support or to oppose the war at different times. These headings are economic interests, immersion in local politics, and involvement in the Democratic coalition. The fourth heading is the "minority" status, real or imagined, of the chosen groups. This last heading helps to unravel the mystery of American society's early and continuing support for the Vietnam War.

Each of the selected groups had a vested economic interest in the war or in its cessation. Common to all was the diversion to the war of funds that would otherwise have been directed to help them under the Great Society program. Some women, retaining a vestigial identity as housekeepers, opposed the war because of the inflation it produced, but more commonplace was women's concern over the military appropriation of funds that might have enhanced programs for the Great Society and gender equality. In the early stages of the war, wage earners prospered from rising demand and employment, factors that encouraged labor's support for the war. But by the later stages of the war it was evident that relatively inelastic wages would not keep pace with war-induced inflation. In a further parallel with women, labor supported Great Society goals and resented the diversion of funds away from them.

All the chosen groups experienced the budgetary effects of backlash. Hawkish patriotism and populist intolerance combined to encourage a powerful fiscal reaction against those who dared to protest. As the war accelerated, university budgets at first rose because of defense contracts. But the extra money was channeled to subjects like engineering, rather than to the humanities or social sciences. Then universities had their budgets cut, and it seemed that they were being punished for spawning student protesters against the conflict. African Americans suffered from a budgetary backlash because of pent-up racism, resentment of Black Power, a desire to punish urban rioters, and their incipient criticism of the war. Some publicly funded schemes to help women never saw the light of day. Cause and effect cannot be convincingly argued in all cases—indeed, the efficacy of backlash politics was the subject of heated debate in the 1960s. But there can be no doubt that the economic dimension, however interpreted, cast its shadow over every group's association with the war.

The importance of local politics in the U.S. federal system was another factor that affected all the groups. Numerous local polls and referenda in the course of the war demonstrated the importance attached to individual regions by the press and by politicians whose constituencies were affected.[15] Defense contracts were subject to intense lobbying and to pork-barrel politics; for example, two leading hawks, Senators James Buckley and Margaret Chase Smith, fought strenuously to win or keep such contracts for New York and Maine, respectively. A lost contract meant fewer jobs, which meant fewer votes for the incumbent from the workforce and the newly unemployed. In rallying support for military programs, the Department of Defense courted legislators from constituencies where jobs depended on military-industrial contracts.[16]

The tacticians of protest also paid heed to localities. In 1970, Law Students Against the War compiled a breakdown of the attitudes of legislators toward Vietnam on a state-by-state basis and estimated the susceptibility of individual members of Congress to local pressures.[17] Students in California made a cause célèbre of the links between local community issues and what they regarded as the international crimes being committed in Vietnam. Richard M. Nixon, a Californian, was aware of such local complexities and of the problems that they could cause for any leader seeking a national consensus; well before he became president, he concluded that "Californian politics is a can of worms."[18]

As these few illustrations show, as soon as the effort is made to break society down into its constituent groups, it becomes apparent that members of these groups operated not just nationally but also within their localities and that local considerations affected their attitudes, tactics, and effectiveness. So in this book I attempt, in an exploratory manner, to fuse local, social, national, and international history. But, as ever, the historian is faced with the problem of selection: Which states and which localities should receive attention in the space of a one-volume analysis?[19] Should a state or city be selected on the basis of its typicality, its powerful position in national politics, its affinity for a political issue, or its trendsetting capacity?

Although I cover a wide variety of states and localities, I pay particular attention to New York and California. Both of these states are maritime, with a tradition of looking beyond U.S. shores, and this makes them of special interest in a discussion of foreign policy. Being maritime does not make them representative of the majority of states in the Union, yet both states were representative of America as a whole in being diverse and cosmopolitan. California and New York were, furthermore, the most populous states and therefore key prizes in presidential elections. No national politician could afford to ignore their citizens' views on Vietnam.[20] To succeed, every national politician had to be a local politician. Nixon and rivals like Ronald Reagan knew that the Berkeley students were Californians and that the Manhattan hard hats were New Yorkers.

A third factor affecting the selected groups' support for or opposition to the Vietnam War was their increasingly troubled association with the Democratic coalition, which for three decades had helped to elect Democrats to the White House and the Congress. President Franklin D. Roosevelt's Democratic administration had passed major legislation favorable to labor unions, the South, and African Americans and had turned a friendly face to women and to youth. The Democratic administrations of John F. Kennedy and Lyndon B. Johnson similarly sought to help African Americans, women, and students and expected the continuing support of these three groups and of organized labor. But the Democratic coalition had never been solid, and by the 1960s it was crumbling. Why, reasoned conservative white Southerners, should they continue to back the party responsible for the Civil Rights Act (1964) and the Voting Rights Act (1965)? Why, reasoned African American citizens, should they unswervingly support the Democrats now that, with these two acts on the statute book, loyalty was no longer at a premium? These are just two examples of the political flux that accompanied the social fragmentation of the sixties. The tantalizing durability and vulnerability of the Democratic coalition meant that both the major political parties had everything to play for. The Democrats and the Republicans competed for the loyalty of the four groups in ways that gave those groups a special position in the politics of the Vietnam War.

The four groups had a fourth and final identifiable characteristic that made them particularly prone to support the Vietnam War: their minority status. Three of the groups were literally minorities. African Americans made up around 11 percent of the population. Only about 18 percent of the workforce was organized into unions affiliated with the AFL-CIO. At the most generous estimate, the sixties generation (defined as all those who turned eighteen between 1960 and 1972, not just students) made up 22 percent of the population; those enrolled in higher education at a given time may have been as low as 2.1 percent.[21]

In contrast, women were literally in the majority, making up just over half the population of the United States.[22] But statistics do not tell the whole story about perceptions. *Webster's Collegiate Dictionary* offers two definitions of a minority that would appear to include women in spite of their numerical superiority: the first, "a group having less than the number of votes necessary for control," would apply to women in Congress, and the second, "a part of the population differing from others in some characteristics and often subjected to differential treatment," covers women at large.[23] Observers as diverse as the sociologist Gunnar Myrdal and the journalist Myra MacPherson have operated on the premise that women have a minority status.[24] Rita Hauser, a legal adviser to the Nixon administration, insisted that women should share in federal benefits like other minorities, for despite their numerical ascendancy they were truly a "social minority."[25]

The minority concept cannot, then, be too firmly tied to numerical definitions. It stems at least in part from how contemporaries chose to perceive various groups. In the 1960s it most firmly evoked racial or ethnic categories, a legacy of the post–World War I debate in Europe over the "minority problem," the fate and aspirations of certain ethnic, religious, and linguistic groups.[26] But other groups—and not just women—were labeled minorities. For example, an influential text published in 1960 revived the idea that American "labor" (blue-collar workers) formed a "permanent minority" lacking the clout to influence national politics in a significant manner. Andrew Levison's book *The Working-Class Majority* posed a numerical challenge to the assumption in 1974, arguing that there had been a miscount and that blue-collar workers still predominated in the population. But, as with women, the question is whether the workers felt and acted like an aggrieved group with only a minority voice in the shaping of national policy. Similarly, it might be argued that the significant political attribute of the student population was not its numerical inferiority but its self-perception as a tribune of the dispossessed, of those whose say in government was too small.[27] As used in this book, the word *minority* conveys not a numerical meaning but an implication of being minor in terms of power and being an outsider. Students, African Americans, women, organized labor—all these shared a self-perception of this kind: they had a minority *mentality.*

This mentality was in turn linked to a breakthrough syndrome. The syndrome affected those groups whose members and leaders wanted to break through the "glass ceilings" of American society and to gain full acceptance by their fellow citizens. It consisted of two types of symptom, each having a similar effect. The first was a tactical tendency to conform. To take one example: Should an African American leader challenge government policy at the risk of retribution for his people, or should he play a tactical game, supporting the government willy-nilly to win concessions for his followers?

The second breakthrough symptom was a psychological tendency to conform. Consciously or otherwise, members of outsider groups aspired to that mythical norm, the status of a fully accepted American. For such persons, cleavage to a foreign policy became a rite of passage. By accepting U.S. policy in Vietnam, individual outsiders sought to redefine themselves and somehow felt more American. For outsiders chasing the definitive breakthrough, the temptation to conform was very strong.

In the Vietnam era the temptation did not prevail, with the result that domestic social pressures help to account for American disengagement from the fighting. But the temptation to conform did overcome substantial numbers of people, positioning them to be receptive to the overtures of the Nixon White House. So, while the demand was for Peace Now, the ending of the Vietnam War took a long time.

2

The Social Consensus

November 1, 1965, was a reasonably good Monday for the White House press office. The front page of the *New York Times* contained three stories on the Vietnam War. The largest headline proclaimed the result of the first attack by the Viet Cong on dug-in U.S. troops. Taking only light casualties themselves, the defenders of a Marine post had killed fifty-six of the enemy attackers. The next largest headline wasn't quite so good. American planes had bombed a village, killing forty-eight innocent people. The error, however, had resulted from an accidental reversal of map coordinates by South Vietnamese military officers. The message was clear. The American fighting man was decent and skillful. Left to his own devices, he would remind the world of his awesome capabilities and win this latest war for freedom.

Tucked away near the bottom right-hand corner of the front page was another story that must have brought considerable political satisfaction to the White House: "20,000 Marchers in New York Back War." Five veteran holders of the highest U.S. military decoration, the Medal of Honor, had led this Sunday parade along Fifth Avenue. Sponsors of the march included City Councilman Matthew J. Troy, the *New York Journal-American* newspaper, and Joseph Curran of the National Maritime Union. The organizers were a little disappointed, for they had expected a turnout of 100,000, but the support was still impressive, especially if one included the 42,000 who lined the sidewalks and the hundreds who waved their support from windows. Very satisfyingly, the scale of the demonstration dwarfed the previous week's march by "pacifists" opposed to the war. The participants seemed to hold firm convictions. Indeed, as the march passed Fiftieth, Sixty-seventh, and Ninetieth Streets "burly longshoremen" left the column to impress their views on bystanders variously described as pacifists and students. According to the police, two of the bystanders subsequently received treatment in a hospital. The *New York Times* reporter Douglas Robinson noted that the parade was just one of a growing number of demonstrations in support of U.S. foreign policy and against antiwar protesters.[1]

The New York rally would in time be surpassed in scale by antiwar demonstrations, but it is still a fairly reliable guide to public opinion. There was a greater consensus in support of the Vietnam War than there had been for almost all other American wars. Because the controversies of the Vietnam War are within living memory and are easily recalled in the audiovisual age, it is all too easy to forget how much more divisive earlier struggles had been. There was strong domestic opposition to the independence movement at the outbreak of the Revolutionary War. The War of 1812 almost produced secession. The Civil War was divisive by definition. World War I, a retrospective poll indicated, was regarded with skepticism by 64 percent of Americans. Nearly the same proportion, 62 percent, believed the Korean War to have been a mistake. Going by public opinion, only World War II, with a disapproval peak of 31 percent, emerges as a clear-cut popular war. Vietnam, then, was one of the most popular American wars: 85 percent supported President Johnson's interventionist policy in 1964, and 65 percent backed Nixon's Vietnam policy at the end of 1969.[2]

The strength of popular support for the Vietnam War, the nation's longest armed conflict, had some significant consequences. It enabled America to stick to its task for many heartbreaking years. To be sure, popular support induced complacency in some politicians, and this made it difficult for them to counter protests effectively. But protracted support also gave President Nixon an opportunity to build his new Republican majority and to hold out for his "peace with honor."

It is therefore important to establish the reasons for the popularity of the war. Some reasons are to be found in the recent history of the United States. Before the intervention in Vietnam, Americans, seemingly, were bound together by the experiences of the past thirty years and were ready to make a unified effort. They had faced the great economic crisis of the 1930s together. They had overcome it with a political formula devised by a Democrat, President Roosevelt, and given bipartisan standing by a Republican, President Dwight D. Eisenhower. In World War II the American people faced and together overcame formidable foes. Then they united, once again, in opposition to the threat of Soviet imperialism. The Korean War and McCarthyism, in their different ways, cemented the American anticommunist tradition. There had developed, in the 1950s, a binding ideology about the end of ideology, centered on the idea that in opposing communism Americans were united as a nation and would not let themselves be divided by ideas about class or by racial conflict. Even the rejection of McCarthyism from the mid-1950s increased national unity in that it removed one of the nastier elements from politics without abandoning the great harmonizing spirit of anticommunism. American liberals, instead of challenging conservative ideas and policies, identified themselves—partly from conviction, partly from an instinct for self-preservation—with the crusade against international communism. Vietnam seemed to present an opportunity to stand up to a universally reviled foe, and, not surprisingly, the great majority of Americans supported the effort to do precisely that.

This recent historical background explains why a certain social process operated with a particular intensity in the sixties. This process—the tendency to norm cleavage by "minority" or "outsider" groups—had historical precedents. Thus, for example, the history of insurgent ethnic minorities in earlier crises foreshadows the roles of students, African Americans, women, and organized labor in the domestic debate over the Vietnam War. Beginning in the 1840s, with the arrival of significant numbers of immigrants first from Ireland and then from other areas of Europe, such as Italy and Poland, American minorities directed a series of conspicuous agitations at foreign countries. Irish Americans wanted independence for Ireland, and Polish Americans the reunification of Poland; in the 1920s, Italian Americans started the first antifascist movement in the world, directed against Mussolini.[3]

But these immigrant groups also shared in, indeed epitomized, the American Dream. They aspired to become indistinguishable from native-born Americans, to become acceptable politically and socially, and to ascend the economic and status ladders that formed an ineradicable part of U.S. culture. In foreign relations, leaders of the ethnic communities could see a political opportunity. They could champion a foreign cause, then, in a trade-off, they could abandon it in order to make the domestic gains that were more important for most immigrants.

Herein lay a tension between two goals, a contradiction that millions of politically conscious immigrants had to face. Should they maintain and display their separate identities by agitating for distinctive foreign policy goals, or should they forget those goals and subscribe to the normative tenets of American foreign policy, tenets that put U.S. ideals and interests first?

In the event, it must be doubted whether the ethnic influence on American foreign policy has ever been markedly strong. At the time of the debate over whether the United States should join the League of Nations, there was great agitation for Irish independence. But David I. Walsh, the first Irish-American U.S. senator from Massachusetts and a Democrat, made it clear that people in his position should be Americans by loyalty and Irish only by extraction: "Let every man of Irish blood face his duty as an American citizen in passing judgment on national and international questions—let us remember to be AMERICANS FIRST."[4] His Massachusetts colleague, the Republican Foreign Relations Committee chair Henry Cabot Lodge, had a complementary approach. He was averse to the particularization of support for his amendments to the peace treaty incorporating the League: "I have no doubt myself that . . . the great silent mass of the people want reservations to the treaty. I believe that the people of Massachusetts are in common with the people of the country."[5] Lodge's perception—that social groups who were apparently alienated yearned to join the silent mass—would be shared by some of his political successors in the sixties. The desire to conform and join, rather than to oppose and split, affected even those social groups that had something to lose from the Vietnam War.

Organized labor represented a group with a history of dissent and a tendency to conform. As its "New Left" critics pointed out in the late 1950s and early 1960s, it had become, by the Vietnam War era, a pillar of the foreign policy establishment. Its accommodationism was rooted partly in the status ambitions of its leaders, who loved to hobnob with the power elite. It sprang also from ideology: ever since the founding of the American Federation of Labor (AFL) in 1886, mainstream American labor had been anti-socialist, and its opposition to the Communists in Vietnam was consistent with this. After World War II, organized labor showed a tendency to support U.S. foreign policy for tactical reasons, for its power, as became evident, depended on government favor. In the post–World War II decades, organized labor was firmly aboard the defense gravy train. In the Indochina war of the 1960s, the welfare of many workers seemed tied to the "Vietnam Run," the provision of goods and services to the combat zone on the other side of the Pacific Ocean. This colored their judgment on the Vietnam War.

Organized labor had not always been conformist, and even if the American working class was a "permanent minority," it had shown itself capable of influencing policy. One can speak of an "age of labor," extending from the late nineteenth century to the 1930s. In this period, before the advent of "Big Labor" as a political bogeyman, many Americans saw union organizers as fighters for righteousness and justice. This created a favorable political climate in which labor was able to achieve some of its goals. The task was made easier by improved finances, the result of increasing membership; the breakthrough came in 1897–1904, when membership grew from 447,000 to 2,072,700.[6]

By the turn of the century, political respect for labor on foreign policy matters was already established. The McKinley Tariff of 1890 helped to propel its author toward a presidential career because it was presented all along as a measure to help labor; ever since the 1870s, William McKinley had promised to protect the American worker, and he continued to do so well into his presidency.[7] McKinley was president during the war with Spain in 1898, when America won Cuba, Puerto Rico, and the Philippines, and a great debate broke out on what to do with the new possessions. Under the leadership of the AFL president, Samuel Gompers, the AFL entered the lists on the side of the anti-imperialists. Labor was opposed to imperialism on principle. At the same time, American workers (especially the cigarmakers—Gompers's own union) stood to lose heavily if the Philippines was incorporated into the American economy; there would be a glut of cheap labor and cheap products in the marketplace, and living standards would fall precipitously (daily wage rates in Manila were fifteen to twenty-five cents per day, compared with top rates of three to four dollars in the United States). McKinley was by no means the only politician aware of this, and labor conducted a vigorous campaign. Former advocates of territorial imperialism, notably Henry Cabot Lodge, then the junior senator from the key industrial state of Massachusetts, received a short, sharp education. The decision was taken not to incorporate the Philippines within the U.S. tariff system.[8]

In the first two decades of the twentieth century, the Industrial Workers of the World (IWW) and the Socialist Party of America flourished briefly, and the Russian Revolution presented America with the specter of international communism. To the AFL leaders, these manifestations of socialism presented a danger—unionists might be mistaken for Communists—and a golden opportunity. Gompers and his heirs would play on employers' fears of socialism to gain concessions and recognition for themselves. By denouncing communism abroad and emphasizing its foreign nature, they hoped to overcome the disadvantages inherent in their outsider status and to gain the acceptance in America that they craved. Yet by publicizing the problem, they also fanned the fear that proletarianism might rear its unwanted head in the United States. This gave them the opportunity to present organized labor as the safe alternative and as the savior of the American way of life, at least as defined by the disseminators of business values. Passively, by serving as a potential vehicle for revolt, and more actively, through rhetoric, labor helped to give American diplomacy one of its most distinctive attributes: anticommunism.[9]

The original leader of the AFL, Gompers, remained president until his death in 1924 and set his organization on a firmly anticommunist, anti–social democrat, and "corporatist" course. Influential leaders in the mainstream labor movement continued in the collaborative tradition.[10] John L. Lewis, the dominant figure in the Congress of Industrial Organizations (CIO), the AFL's rival from the mid-1930s until the AFL-CIO merger in 1956, took a notably conservative stance. These American labor leaders opposed socialism abroad because that suited their personal conviction, because they resented challenges to their authority by domestic radicals, and because red-baiting seemed a rite of passage for American workers—indeed, one that was repeated time and time again despite repeated disappointment in the lack of recognition accorded organized labor in policymaking circles. Public opinion began to turn against Big Labor in the 1940s because a minority of unions had communist tendencies, because corruption within the labor movement was revealed, and because powerful labor leaders seemed to be able to hold the public to ransom by calling strikes. In the face of opposition, the AFL and CIO leaders took on a besieged minority mentality. They "purged" the unions of left-wing influences in order to curry favor with the power elite and regain public esteem and actively cooperated with the architects of Cold War foreign policy. Jay Lovestone, who directed the internationally active Free Trade Union Committee from 1944 to 1963 and then the International Affairs Department of the AFL-CIO, was a hard-line anti-Communist and Cold Warrior. The same was true of George Meany, president of the AFL-CIO from 1955 to 1979 and the man known as "Mr. Labor" in the period of the Vietnam War.[11]

The AFL-CIO support for the Vietnam War arose from this background. Labor's endorsement of the war was very evident at the grassroots level. Late in 1965, for example, Jerry Leopaldi, president of Local 447 of the International Union of Electrical Workers at ITT Federal Laboratories, Clifton, New York, started a labor-based Support American Servicemen in Vietnam Committee. Backed by the singer Pat Boone, he collected thousands of one-dollar donations within a year and sent the proceeds to help civilian causes in South Vietnam.[12] This local support for the war was reflected nationally: only 276 of the 3,542 delegates to the AFL-CIO annual convention in 1967 favored withdrawal from Vietnam. Not until December 1974, long after the American withdrawal from the fighting, did George Meany admit that he had been wrong to support the Vietnam policies pursued by Presidents Johnson and Nixon.[13]

Although long-term factors explain labor's general anticommunism, there were also specific reasons for its support of the Vietnam War. The way things turned out, Vietnam was fought as a working-class war, and this encouraged workers' minority mentality to become a siege mentality, for they bitterly resented criticism of the war by middle-class students who stayed at home to enjoy the privileges of their status while the sons and brothers of the less affluent shed their blood for their country. Another consideration affecting labor support for the war was political. With Kennedy and Johnson in the White House, labor was conscious of its prominent role in the Democratic coalition, of the gains to be expected from that position, and of the dangers of rocking the boat by challenging the war. A less savory factor must also be taken into consideration. Patriotism was a tactical distraction from a reputation for mobsterism that adhered to some U.S. labor unions. In an earlier age, Al Capone had claimed to be anticommunist, and with Jimmy Hoffa in prison, the Teamsters whom he had led played the same card in the Vietnam era—ineffectively as far as their reputation was concerned but in a manner that was convenient for the war's supporters.

Any war can create short-term prosperity, and American workers went along with the Vietnamese conflict when it filled order books, created full employment, and drove wages up. The importance of the economic factor may be seen in the special support given to the war by some of the workers who had the most to gain from it. Maritime workers received an economic boost from the Vietnam Run, which entailed a major sea haul across the Pacific. They benefited from goods, rather than from people. Only about 10 percent of the approximately 4 million people who crossed to and from Vietnam between 1965 and 1969 traveled by sea, but every drop of the 14 million tons of bulk petroleum needed in that period went by water, and over 95 percent of the 22 million tons of dry goods needed by the armed forces in Vietnam were transported by ship.[14] Perhaps it is easier to support a war when one transports tents and tanks, as distinct from body bags and broken people.

Paul Hall, president of the Seafarers' International Union, certainly seized on the opportunity offered. He assured President Johnson of the firmness of his anticommunist convictions and of his support for the war. At the same time, he pointed to the strategic importance of the American merchant marine, an asset that was dwindling under pressure from foreign competitors, including nations in the communist bloc, who paid their sailors a fraction of the rates negotiated by U.S. unions. Hall called for a new mercantilism; wheat exports to the Soviet Union, for example, should go on American ships. By thus preserving an American merchant fleet on the high seas, the United States would keep its military preparedness high. Thomas W. Gleason, president of the International Longshoremen's Association (a union still staggering under the impact of the anti-gangsterism film *On the Waterfront*, released in the 1956), made matching affirmations of anticommunism and promised to use his good offices to see that the maritime unions discouraged strikes that would affect the Vietnam Run.[15] Such officials received an attentive hearing at the White House, and in their demands for preferential treatment for the merchant marine as the implied price of loyalty over Vietnam, they were supported by congressmen whose districts had maritime interests.[16]

Opponents of the war complained that a powerful "military-industrial complex" boosted the position of the hawks. President Eisenhower had used the phrase in his farewell address of 1961. He criticized the way armaments industrialists and senior military figures put pressure on the government to spend money on military development, but New Left commentators like Sidney Lens argued that labor should be added to the equation.[17] More recently, a historian has complained that Eisenhower's address was simplistic: "He gave the impression that the complex was made up only of the rich and powerful, as opposed to the common people."[18] From Long Island to the Stanford Industrial Park in California, defense workers benefited financially from the Vietnam War and gave it their support. Defense contractors encouraged workers' loyalty through "every man a capitalist" programs. Lockheed Aircraft Corporation, the largest U.S. defense contractor, with ninety-three thousand workers, put up fifty cents for every dollar an employee invested in stocks or government bonds. The journalist Harry Bernstein concluded: "Earnings, profits, pay increases, dividends and jobs all ride on the defense gravy train."[19]

California prosperity was particularly dependent on the defense industry and on associated maritime activity. At the end of World War II, Samuel C. May, director of the Bureau of Public Administration at the University of California, Berkeley, noted that "California did not *convert* existing industries into war work but superimposed these huge industrial establishments on the existing economy." A smooth *reconversion* to civilian production could not therefore be expected. The postwar development of rocketry was a further threat to the military aircraft building industry; only through the intervention of the government was shipbuilding kept alive in the state through the 1950s. Little wonder that some union leaders—and the politicians who heeded them—regarded the Vietnam War as a prop to their members' way of life. California was now a key electoral state and had also produced several influential politicians: the Democratic Senator Alan Cranston played a role in the Vietnam debate, and the state was a veritable breeding ground for talented Republicans, including Earl Warren, Richard Nixon, and Ronald Reagan. For this reason, the economically induced support of so many California workers formed a significant part of the social consensus supporting the Vietnam War.[20]

The radical strain in labor's past, with its critical perspective on foreign policy, had not been forgotten in the sixties. In fact, left-wing labor history became fashionable on campus, and toward the end of the Vietnam War labor support for U.S. foreign policy did show signs of crumbling. But occasional whiffs of dissent only served to stiffen the resolve of the old guard, led by Meany, who remained strident supporters of the war throughout its course. The left proved to be amply justified in its fears. Organized labor had become, and remained, accommodationist. It supported establishment-led foreign policy—in particular, the Vietnam War.

Women, like labor, had a tendency to cling to foreign policy norms in order to advance their status. To be sure, this is a sweeping generalization. There were many shades of opinion among women and among the minority of women who were feminists. The extent to which a woman formulated her views as a woman as distinct from her other identities—as, say, a member of a blue-collar family or a clerk in a shipping office—remains moot. We all have composite political identities.

Women, or at least the feminists among them, had a tradition of alliance politics, especially with labor and African Americans, and easily collaborated with the Cold Warriors in these other groups. Like labor and like African Americans, women came to be regarded as part of the Democratic social-reform consensus of the 1960s, with a built-in inhibition about wrecking the policies of their White House benefactors (women as a whole ceased to favor the Republicans, whom they had supported in the previous decade; they distributed their votes evenly between the two major parties).[21] In the past and still in the sixties, activist women were smeared as "Reds," so they had an incentive to redeem self and gender by adopting a Cold War posture. Although women (as distinct from feminists) were a majority of the population, it could be argued that, like labor, they had an outsider status and a minority mentality that drove them toward accommodationism.

Women differed from organized labor in some respects. Unlike organized labor, which had regional strongholds as well as regions with weak support, women were a consistent proportion of the population throughout the United States. Although concentrations of feminists could be found in certain areas, including New York and northern California, women were a national lobby in the sense that they thought of themselves as representing the nation at large and did not focus on local economic issues. Another difference, though one that was being eroded, was that, compared to job-conscious male workers, they did not take quite such a producer-oriented approach to the economy. Some women at some points in history may have benefited from increased opportunities brought about by war, but women were generally less susceptible to gravy-train politics and did not support wars because of the prospects of economic gain.

Other distinctive factors did incline women to form part of the prowar consensus. According to popular conceptions, the Cold War was a conflict between the democratic values of the United States and the autocratic values of Soviet-style communism and its global offshoots, such as the North Vietnamese government in Hanoi and its Viet Cong allies in South Vietnam. This conceptualization was important to feminists, for it was a standard precept of American feminism that the use of force disadvantaged women and boosted male dominance. Soviet communism with its command structure was therefore unacceptable to feminists for a special and important reason that went beyond any distaste for socialism that they may have shared with men. In the 1950s, opinion polls had shown "liberated" women to be relatively supportive of the Korean War; it could be argued that this tendency continued in the next war against Asian communism and that the liberated/feminist trendsetters helped to ensure women's support for the Vietnam War.[22]

Against all this must be set women's historical antipathy for war. From the earliest days of the republic, women had shown a peaceful disposition. A broadsheet testified to this in the election campaign in New Jersey of 1796 (where women had the vote from 1709 to 1807):

> Now one and all proclaim
> the fall of tyrants! open wide your throats,
> And welcome in the peaceful scene
> of government in Petticoats!!![23]

Antiwar reasoning became a staple of early twentieth-century American feminism. The Nobel Peace Prize winner Emily Greene Balch argued that women should oppose war because it "tended to lower the importance and the social power of women."[24]

Yet women acquired the reputation of being pacifists in peacetime only. When it came to the crunch, they seemed to barter away their principles. Carrie Chapman Catt of the National American Women's Suffrage Association offered President Woodrow Wilson women's support for American participation in World War I in return for his endorsement of the vote for women. In the 1920s and 1930s, she and other prominent women became conspicuous in the peace movement, only to endorse American involvement in World War II. The feminist Anna Graves despairingly observed in 1942 that "Peace Societies can never have any effect when Governments *see* that when war comes they always crumble."[25] After

World War II, prominent women once again became involved in the peace movement; but if history was a guide, that was no reason to preclude their forming part of the Vietnam War consensus. Indeed, the adage holds: Moralistic reformers start moralistic wars. Peace feminists could be seen as part of that war-prone reform tradition.[26]

Whether all this matters depends on the degree to which women could be expected to have any influence whatsoever on foreign policy. Being a majority group with minority status, women had never supplied a president, vice president, chair of the Senate Foreign Relations Committee or House Foreign Affairs Committee, and were thinly represented in other foreign policy circles, such as the Congress, the foreign service, and the Departments of Defense and State (not until President Clinton's appointment of Madeleine Albright in 1997 would there be a female secretary of state). They fared badly compared with women in a number of other countries and could even be described as the "missing sisters" of the international scene.[27] From time to time, American women had shown that they could be effective both as individuals and as a collective public opinion and electoral force. Women's organizations and lobbyists had contributed to a series of international agreements in the 1920s and 1930s and had successfully demanded trade liberalization and arms embargoes—both firmly if controversially linked to the cause of peace. An American woman, Eleanor Roosevelt, had been largely responsible for the shape and adoption of the U.N. Universal Declaration of Human Rights in 1948.[28] With the approach of the second half of the twentieth century, however, women were still supplicants at the banquet of American power.

Women's political weakness was still very evident in the 1960s. Whereas 112 women had served in the German Reichstag between 1919 and 1932, only 95 served in the U.S. Congress in the fifty-year period 1926–1976.[29] The number of women in the Congress declined from 20 in 1961 to 11 in 1969—in a decade when, internationally, Ceylon produced the first woman prime minister, followed by India and Israel.[30] Senator Margaret Chase Smith's challenge for the presidency in 1964 was brave but marginal. American women were counted out of politics. To the dismay of peace-reform feminists, even within the anti-Vietnam movement, in the initial years of protest men treated women just as chauvinistically as did their antagonists in Foggy Bottom, in the White House, and on Capitol Hill.

The Johnson administration could be forgiven for believing that women were not only incapable of posing a challenge to the prowar consensus but disinclined to do so. True, Margaret Chase Smith believed that the Vietnam War was a mistake. She told her constituents in Maine in 1967: "I have repeatedly stated both publicly and privately that I did not feel that we should have become militarily involved in Vietnam."[31] But as Republican minority leader on the Armed Services Committee she saw her role as that of loyal opposition. She restricted her criticisms of administration policies to complaints that the soldiers in the field were not receiving proper support. She, like the former U.S. envoy to Rome Clare Boothe Luce, who formed Ambassadors for Nixon, proved a stalwart supporter of the Vietnam War.[32]

For some women, the war represented a career opportunity in that it permitted them to rise within the expanding armed forces—Senator Smith had fought hard and effectively for equality in this sphere. For a much larger number of women, dissent from a war whose successful outcome was important to the Democrats must have seemed foolish on tactical grounds. In 1964, when the Civil Rights Bill had been before the Congress, a Virginia congressman with sabotage in mind, not to mention an archaic sense of humor, tacked a gender clause onto the antidiscriminatory Title VII of the bill. In the words of the historians Carol Hymowitz and Michaele Weissman, "The idea that women were a 'minority' group was considered amusing."[33] Where women were concerned, not only did that legislation have serious import, but so did the Equal Pay Act of 1963, requiring fair treatment of women; the affirmative action programs required of federal contractors in President Johnson's Executive Orders 11246 (1965) and 11375 (1968); and the Age Discrimination in Employment Act of 1968, which made it easier for women to reenter the workforce after raising families.[34] Women who were concerned with their rights in the workplace had every reason to approve of the Democrats' Great Society legislation and to hope for more. Even if reform-minded women had historically overlapped with peace-minded women, their expectations left them unprepared to mount an immediate challenge to the Vietnam policy of the administration.

As the history of the Vietnam War unfolded, it became clear that the gender gap in connection with foreign policy had survived Cold War consensus and would cause problems for the hawks. But in the mid-sixties this could not have been foreseen. With the erosion of gender differences in the workplace, women, like male workers, were beginning to be aware of the gravy-train aspects of the war. They also had the tradition of peacetime pacifism, of cosmetic idealism that vanished when put to the test of war. They were anticommunist out of conviction, out of a tactical desire to join the boys in the nation's power structure, and out of a tactical appreciation of totalitarianism's special oppressiveness for women. They also appeared to have something to gain from an unembarrassed Democratic administration. As ever, the illusion of patriotism as a passport to equality proved seductive. Women seemed to have every reason to support the war in its early stages, and they did.

Many African Americans similarly believed that they would be wise to support the war, or at least to refrain from opposing it. At the beginning of the conflict, African Americans were quiescent or supportive of Johnson's Asian policy. The novelist Norman Mailer noted the paucity of black protesters even as late as October 21, 1967, the date of the great protest march on the Pentagon.[35] Like organized labor and to a greater extent than women, African Americans saw themselves as part of the liberal coalition that produced the reform impulses of the 1960s. They seemed to have a vested interest in supporting the policies of the Johnson administration with its commitment to civil rights. Another cause of African Americans' support for the war was their minority status defined in terms of power. If you were born black, you were born without power. Lacking power, African Americans were forced to sell one principle in order to achieve another. To put it bluntly, they supported and fought in racist wars in order to achieve greater dignity at home. Thus, the breakthrough syndrome operated in a tragic but effective manner for those who were born black. The African American donated his soul and his blood to the early stages of the Vietnam War and formed part of the social consensus supporting it.

In delineating African Americans' weakness and susceptibility to incorporation vis-à-vis the foreign policy process, an important distinction must be made between prejudice and influence. Racial prejudice has had an immense impact on U.S. foreign policy, from the days of warfare against the native peoples to more recent times, when Americans underestimated the fighting power of Japan because they had contempt for Asians.[36] But the direct influence of black citizens as a group has been much more limited. African Americans were powerless to prevent the enshrinement of racist imperialism at the Peace of Versailles, for instance, and in the 1930s failed to persuade the U.S. government to protect Liberia and Ethiopia, the only two countries in Africa with black leadership.[37]

Little had changed by the 1960s in spite of the civil rights crusade. According to Ron Armstead, a Vietnam War veteran and community activist, his African American brothers were partly responsible for the status quo in that they lacked historical perspective on diplomatic and military issues. He recalled that the events of the sixties ultimately awoke them to the way the white ruling elite rejected as "out of character" any black participation in foreign policy making, with the result that some African Americans at last shrugged off their foreign policy torpor.[38]

Yet the power of the breakthrough syndrome still reinforced the urge of the African American in search of social acceptance to act "in character" and support the white man's foreign policy. The confrontations of the sixties never entirely blocked the workings of that syndrome or prevented its Uncle Tom consequences. Even in a decade when Black Is Beautiful became a popular slogan, some black consumers still wished to pass for white. In the August 1968 issue of the monthly illustrated magazine *Ebony*, in the midst of an article on African Americans and the draft and right next to a photograph of two draft critics, Muhammad Ali and the late Dr. Martin Luther King, Jr., there appeared a large advertisement for "Dr. Fred Palmer's Skin Whitener."[39] The implied African American penchant for whiteness may be compared with the sometimes postulated desire of women to prove themselves by acting as aggressively as men. Black foreign-policy history may be compared with the story of women's peacetime pacifism, for black spokesmen demanded racial justice at home and abroad in peacetime but tended to endorse and fight in wars oppressive of nonwhite races rather than take the risk of being different by opposing the white majority. Past wars assumed a gloss that encouraged participation in future ones; the historian Neil Wynn notes that African Americans looked back at World War II with blinkered optimism, remembering it as a good war that advanced the cause of racial equality. As Wynn also observes, it was precisely this kind of mythology that made the black revolt against the Vietnam War such a shock to the establishment.[40] But the point to be noted here is that the mythology was in place in the early years of the war and was a vital component of the prowar consensus.

The Cold War communist attack on American values might have opened a channel for black dissent, but it did not, and served only to reinforce conformity. Certainly, the communist critique exposed America's racial divisions to public view and embarrassed the nation internationally. The Scottsboro case, the palpably unjust conviction of nine young African Americans, on a charge of rape in 1931, already ranked as an international communist cause célèbre. When African nations began to achieve their independence in the 1950s, Soviet and Chinese propagandists seized the initiative, and in the forum of world opinion the United States paid the price of its internal prejudices. Lynchings, both judicial and illegal, came in for sharp attention; the State Department agonized over such headlines as "Another Negro to Die" (*Hindustani Times*, New Delhi) and, in the more cutting communist press, "Would It Amuse You to See a Negro Killed?" (complete with gruesome photograph; *Humanité*, Paris).[41]

In practice, African Americans neither would nor could exploit these embarrassments. Racists like the FBI chief, J. Edgar Hoover, actually used the communism issue against African Americans, claiming that the civil rights crusade was a Moscow conspiracy.[42] President Johnson seems to have felt little compulsion to listen to African Americans on foreign policy matters, paying little heed to black citizens' views on Africa, let alone on Vietnam.[43] In the conduct of diplomacy, Washington was very slow to recognize the need for African American input. While wringing its hands at the excesses of Southern racists, the foreign policy establishment remained incapable of putting its own house in order. American policy toward apartheid, South Africa's equivalent of Jim Crow, remained permissive.[44] Although African Americans constituted one-ninth of the U.S. population in the early 1960s, they filled only 19 out of 3,700 foreign service posts. Those who did gain entrance to the foreign service were invariably sent to Africa; meanwhile, the few women who entered the service complained they were never sent to Africa. These policies owed much to prejudice in the recipient countries, yet the suspicion lingered that the U.S. Foreign Service had an intricate apartheid system of its own.[45] It had not been shaken out of its complacency by the communist challenge.

In any case, the Communist Party, as distinct from the right's favorite genie, the myth of the communist menace, was no longer a force in American politics; it had succumbed to FBI repression, to the defection of members, won by the more alluring and competitive appeal of liberal reform, and to contamination from association with the repulsive image of Stalinism and Russian imperialism. Nor was the Communist Party any longer equipped to respond to African American politics, which in the 1960s took a nationalist as distinct from a proletarian turn. Although the few remaining American Communists did oppose the war, their influence, never great in the black community, now dwindled to imperceptible proportions.[46]

Far from opposing the Vietnam War, the black citizen who emerged from the 1950s may have thought that fighting for America was a way of upholding civil rights. Walter Mosley's fictional character Easy Rawlins saw confusion: "Back then [in the 1940s and 1950s] we thought we knew who the enemy was. He was a white man with a foreign accent and a hatred for freedom. . . . it was Comrade Stalin and the Communists; later on,

Mao Tse-tung and the Chinese took on honorary white status. All of them bad men with evil designs on the free world."[47] Similarly, General Colin Powell recalled: "My images of going to war were formed by forties newsreels, fifties movies, and early-sixties TV documentaries, and war was always black and white." To be sure, his "arrival in Vietnam shattered all the preconceptions," but his recollection of his reasons for going there is eloquent testimony to the acceptance of the war by so many black enlistees.[48] For such soldiers, the civil rights movement and voter registration campaigns of the 1950s and early 1960s must have held forth the prospect of a fairer America worth fighting for. The Civil Rights Act passed at a remarkably expeditious moment, just in time for the presidential election of 1964. It preceded by just a month the Tonkin Gulf Resolution of the Congress, which permitted Johnson to expand the war. Politicians escalating the war could assume that African American loyalty was, and would remain, constant.[49]

Among the African American leaders, support for the war was opportunistic rather than genuine, but it was useful to the White House nonetheless. Most leaders, for example, Ralph Bunche of the U.N. Secretariat and the Harlem congressman Adam Clayton Powell, Jr., were against the war from the outset.[50] Bunche, after all, was a winner of the Nobel Peace Prize (awarded in 1950 for his work on the Palestine question), as was Martin Luther King, Jr., the outstanding American civil rights leader and upholder of nonviolent tactics who headed the Southern Christian Leadership Conference and also opposed the war from its beginning. Yet in spite of the award of the Nobel Prize in 1964, King decided not to campaign against the war in the critical period when LBJ embarked on escalation. He feared attacks from the right and did not want to jeopardize the black united front on civil rights issues. His concern on the latter point was to be amply borne out in April 1967, when he openly criticized the war, only to be upbraided by some of the most powerful figures in the black reform movement, among them Roy Wilkins and Whitney Young, leaders, respectively, of the NAACP and the National Urban League. Wilkins and Young were not war enthusiasts. They were the first to proclaim that pragmatism dictated their support for the war, support which they hoped would yield continuing government investment in the welfare of black Americans. But in a nation that lauded pragmatism, their support was no less effective for being calculated.[51]

No war can be fought without soldiers, and the African American soldier established a salient presence in the jungles and paddy fields of Vietnam. His willingness to serve reflected a reaction against past and residual discrimination affecting the black soldier, who had been routinely placed in segregated units, assigned to such menial chores as cooking and laundry, denied promotion, and refused prestigious battle opportunities. All this goaded young African Americans to go out and prove themselves. In every previous war fought by the United States, black soldiers had managed to break through the racial barriers to prove their military worth. This was a matter of pride to historically conscious African Americans at the time of the Vietnam War. Accounts abounded of the roles played by black warriors ever since the Boston Massacre of 1770, when a black sailor, Crispus Attucks, became the "first American to shed blood in the revolution that freed America from British rule." (In light of the accompanying white casualties, one historian dryly remarked that Redcoats had committed "an integrated massacre").[52] In spite of continuing discrimination, African Americans fought in the War of 1812, the Civil War (two sons of Frederick Douglass, the black abolitionist, served with the Fifty-fourth Massachusetts Colored Regiment), the Plains Wars (in the course of which, whatever the rights and wrongs of the campaign, the black "Buffalo Soldiers" proved their military worth), both world wars, and the Korean War.

By the time of Korean War, President Harry S. Truman had (in 1948) ordered the full integration of the armed services. The black labor leader A. Philip Randolph had told him, "Mr. President, the Negroes are in the mood not to bear arms for the country unless Jim Crow in the armed forces is abolished."[53] Truman's order established equality of treatment in principle, if not in practice. For black men aspiring to become soldiers, the crock of gold at the end of the rainbow had suddenly become visible—which helps to explain both initial black enthusiasm for the Vietnam War and the severity of subsequent disillusionment.

President Johnson recognized the political potentiality of black soldiers fighting for their country. He reckoned that the Army was a means of raising standards for young men from poor backgrounds, so it could be presented as an extension of the Great Society program. Approving in May 1964 a plan to counsel and help young men, "one-third of a nation" and mostly black, who could not embark on military service because they failed to meet the required medical and educational standards, he noted that the plan took "on added significance in view of the commitment of this Administration to a total and unrelenting war on poverty."[54] Here, it is important to note the claim that the armed services were a true racial melting pot. In 1963 the U.S. Commission on Human Rights reported that "Negro servicemen believe on balance that the Armed Forces offer them greater opportunities than they can find in the civilian economy." The black Vietnam War veteran Wallace Terry recalled that in early 1967 he still thought the armed forces "the most integrated institution in American Society."[55]

President Johnson's hope that black Americans would support the armed forces as a vehicle for social and racial advancement was by no means entirely disappointed, as can be seen from the files of *Ebony.* The magazine aimed to achieve a mass circulation among black people in the 1960s and therefore attempted to mirror their general opinion. Not surprisingly, given this task, it was ambivalent on some issues. In reports on the Vietnam War, *Ebony* told two narratives. The first was the story of African Americans' growing discontent. But this first story by no means supplanted the second, that of support. When Lawrence Joel of Winston-Salem, North Carolina, won the Congressional Medal of Honor for valor as a Vietnam medic in 1967, *Ebony* rejoiced with a report headlined "Dixie Town Fetes War Hero."[56] Virtually every month, there was an "Armed Services" section in the magazine, taking a supportive line and reciting similar stories.

An *Ebony* article the following year proudly noted, in a special issue on the black soldier, that "brothers are found in every part of [Vietnam]." The same issue contained an article, "Why Negroes Re-Enlist," indicating that reenlistment among African Americans eligible for discharge from the Army in 1966–1967 was

49 percent, compared with just 16 percent for whites. Its author, David Llorens, gave reasons that would have pleased LBJ: not only was reenlistment economically attractive, but it happened because there was less racism in the armed forces than in society at large. In similar vein, the magazine reported with pride, in 1970, on the advancement of Air Force Brigadier General Daniel ("Chappie") James, Jr., to be deputy assistant secretary of defense for public affairs, a job that gave him a Pentagon office with two windows, through whose "heavy, gold drapes" he could "see his gray Jaguar parked only a stone's throw away."[57] *Ebony* never gave up the dream of the military as a vehicle for black social mobility.

To sum up: although race may have been an implicit factor in American foreign policy, the direct influence of black people on U.S. diplomacy has been limited. African Americans lacked power and were apt to pass into the consensual sphere either in an effort to behave like white people and "become" them or in an attempt to barter foreign policy support for help in domestic matters, where the needs of black people were acute. Whatever the African Americans' reservations about U.S. racism at home and abroad, they had a reputation for rallying to the flag in time of war, at least to the extent that they were allowed to. This is why their threatened desertion in the sixties came as such a shock. But that is also why America at first seemed so racially united as it launched into a war against a nonwhite people in Asia.

Students, the last of the social groups to be considered here, to a large degree deserve their reputation as the vanguard of the antiwar movement. At the same time, many students supported the war, and the great majority refrained from protesting it. That only students at the more privileged institutions rebelled against the war is a myth; still, students at many tertiary education institutions, such as community colleges and church colleges, were scarcely affected by the upheavals.[58]

It does seem apparent, in retrospect, that a historically momentous event took place on the evening of March 24, 1965, when professors and students at the University of Michigan conducted the first teach-in against the Vietnam War. The university had already produced some activists in the civil rights campaign; in the fall of 1964, members of the Student Non-Violent Coordinating Committee (SNCC) were still organizing death-defying trips to the Deep South to help with voter registration, while the student newspaper, the *Michigan Daily*, boasted as one of its former editors Tom Hayden, who was to be the outstanding antiwar student of the sixties. According to one historian, in the wake of the teach-in the Ann Arbor campus "was alive with debate on Vietnam. It was impossible to avoid the controversy whether one wanted to or not."[59]

But the degree to which the Michigan students had become radicalized is all too easy to exaggerate. The pro-Goldwater organization Young American for Freedom still flourished in the fraternities. The annual football game against neighboring Michigan State University generated more enthusiasm than any political issue did. By no means everyone was interested in dissent. An example is Greg Busch, a business studies student from a poor Polish-American family in Detroit. He turned down the editorship of the *Michigan Daily* because it would delay his dreamed-of ascent by age thirty into the ranks of American millionaires. Instead, he accepted a part-time job as floor sweeper in the *Daily* building—a position that paid union rates and contributed to his starting capital.[60]

The silent student majority was by no means a peculiarity of the Ann Arbor campus. In May 1965, Beverley Anne Beisner, co-chair of the Committee for Critical Support of U.S. Policy in Vietnam at Cornell University, wrote to Senator Jacob Javits (Rep., N.Y.) enclosing a prowar petition that she thought approximated the "consensus on campus": "No doubt you are well aware of the growing unrest on campuses around our country, Cornell among them, concerning our government's foreign policy as expressed in Vietnam. It is to be regretted that the voice in support of that policy has been so quiet, even though (or perhaps because) it is a majority stand."[61]

Such observations were individual impressions, but the opinion data do seem to support them. A national opinion survey undertaken just after the 1964 elections suggested that the major support for the war came from the college-educated and better-off. Polls in 1966 and 1967 indicated that "the less education people had, the more likely they were to consider the war fruitless." In 1968 and 1969 the *Gallup Opinion Index* revealed that less-educated people had a greater disposition than others to call themselves "doves." By late 1969 the situation had reversed—dissent by the educated had come to exceed that by the uneducated. Nevertheless, it may be the case that the Vietnam War was in part sustained by the loyalty of the very college group popularly held to be against it, even in the years when student protesters were at their most effective.[62]

An appropriate question to ask is whether, by reverse logic, a distinct factor explains both the rebelliousness of certain students and the relative passivity of other social groups. Students shared some characteristics with women and labor. In that every state in the union contained one or more university systems and several other colleges, the student body was a national political entity, comparable with women. On the other hand, one might argue that the San Francisco Bay area took pride of place in terms of student protest, with New York City's Columbia University and the University of Michigan also figuring prominently. In distributive terms, then, students were like organized labor, whose strength was also concentrated; indeed, both groups were to be found in strength in California and New York.

But three characteristics did make students different. Two of these made little difference—they simply meant that students conformed in different ways. First, there was a power deficit. Through the prime period of debate on the Vietnam War, students under twenty-one lacked the vote. Not until 1971 did the Twenty-sixth Amendment lower the voting age from twenty-one to eighteen, and even then it could be argued that enfranchisement meant participation, rather than power. Lacking the vote and therefore a sense of duty toward the shaping of foreign policy, they offered the nation's leaders a silence hinting at their acquiescence.

Second, students were different in being a group without a consciously remembered history. Black leaders might complain about their fellow African Americans' ignorance of their own past, but most African Americans had a vivid political register that encompassed and placed in some kind of historical framework at least a few of the following: Africa, slavery, Uncle Tom, emancipation, Ku Klux Klan, Jim Crow, Marcus Garvey, Louis Armstrong, Paul Robeson, Jackie Robinson, and, more recently, Little Rock, Martin Luther King, Jr., and Malcolm X. In comparison, student history was a blank sheet. When students looked to the past for inspiration, they turned not to their own history but to the imagery of Frank Norris's 1901 novel *The Octopus* about the repressive policies of the Southern Pacific Railroad in California, to the struggles waged on behalf of the oppressed by the Industrial Workers of the World, and, above all, to the more recent civil rights battles conducted by African Americans.

If radical students had been more acquainted with their past, they would have found scant inspiration. In World War I (after some initial campus protest), the Harvard student newspaper *Crimson* enthusiastically supported preparedness.[63] In the 1930s some American undergraduates did develop antiwar tendencies. But in this regard they were in step with a large body of nonstudent opinion; indeed, Eleanor Roosevelt, the president's wife, lent them her support. Then, with the outbreak of the Spanish Civil War (1936–1939), the antifascist cry "*No Pasaran!*" (They shall not pass!) was heard around the nation's campuses. In conformity with the orthodoxy of the day, American students switched sides; instead of being opponents of militarism, they became supporters of a war against fascists and, later, Nazis. Campus youth may well have felt they had a stake in the Roosevelt administration and its increasingly interventionist foreign policy. At a time of great anxiety over unemployment, the National Youth Administration helped to find part-time jobs for two million students and organized training for hundreds of thousands of young people. Ominously for the peace cause, the jobs and training programs were largely in the defense industry.

Against this background, the voices of students in the 1930s remained relatively conformist, as well as being muted in comparison with the clarion cries of the New Deal and even of the minuscule Communist Party. Looking back on those days, the historian Henry May recalled "the cagey and skeptical Harvard style," and the cardinal fact that cognac could be obtained for fifteen cents in the senior common room.[64] The Great Depression politicized the nation's students only up to a point. Secretary of State Cordell Hull was alerted to the activities of pacifist students in the early years of World War II. But the inconspicuousness of students of this era contrasts sharply, one historian has suggested, to their commanding position in the 1960s.[65]

In the 1950s women and labor bent the knee to conformity, and students seemed to go along. Their mentors, the university professors, did not stand up to McCarthyism, and a wave of anti-intellectualism testified to the drop in their standing.[66] Many students were afraid of McCarthyism, fearing to put their names to even the mildest of protests. They had good cause to be nervous, as a virulent blacklist operated against those who refused to subscribe to the code of intolerance. Collectively, the students of the 1950s came to be known as the Silent Generation. They matured into the war-supportive silent majority of the sixties.[67]

President Kennedy recognized that at least part of the burgeoning teenage population of the 1960s was ready for something new. His Peace Corps, established in 1961 to allow young people to serve in a philanthropic capacity overseas, had as one of its aims the tapping of the youthful idealism that had lain buried under the materialistic values of the 1950s. It seemed to meet a long-standing demand of peace activists by supplying a glamorous activity alternative to war, and a better way of serving others than joining the armed forces. According to the legislation passed by the Congress, the Peace Corps was "to promote world peace and friendship." Thus, young people, including students, could believe that they had an idealistic stake in the Democratic administrations of the 1960s, as they had in those of the 1930s. Yet, in spite of its idealism, the Peace Corps was a Cold War instrument, designed to help wean Third World nations from dependency on the Sino-Soviet bloc. Every trainee received a pamphlet entitled *What You Must Know About Communism*. Although anticommunist ideology was the least popular aspect of Peace Corps training, the baby boomers who volunteered could still be seen as part of the Cold War consensus that underlay the Vietnam War.[68]

In the era of the Great Society, plans to expand education also promised to tie students to foreign policy norms. In 1965 the Congress passed the Elementary and Secondary Education Act "with a whoop," appropriating over a billion dollars to help poorer students. By the end of the decade, 50 percent more students were in college than in 1960, and many of them had reason to be grateful to the Democrats for the opportunity.[69]

Students, then, had a history of accommodation that was apparently about to repeat itself. Their lack of consciousness about their collective past is open to interpretation. They had forgotten about past episodes of campus revolt, such as they were, and could take no inspiration from them. Still, amnesia about an apathetic past might have been good for revolutionary morale.

The third and final way in which students were different is that, unlike labor, women, and African Americans, they did not experience a collective breakthrough syndrome. The emphasis here must be on the word *collective.* Young students are by definition developing people, susceptible to the conscious or unconscious mimicry of role models among the older generation. They tend to be ambitious and, as individuals, are under severe temptation to sacrifice ideals to personal advancement. In those senses, students are not so very different from members of other social groups.

In contrast to other groups, however, students were temporary. A woman remained a woman throughout her life, whereas a student remained a student for only a short space of time. This circumstance constituted a permanent invitation to revolt. A student generation did not survive long enough to face the temptations of incorporation. Some of the more articulate students came from privileged backgrounds and could expect to retain those privileges after having a fling in college. From that perspective, the student protest against the war could be considered a "revolt against the masses"—notably, against the mass of blue-collar workers who supported the war.[70] The transience of student generations made that revolt relatively risk-free, and their great moment arrived in the sixties.

Yet neither the threat of student revolt nor its early manifestation was a sufficient deterrent to those bent on escalating American participation in the Vietnam War. The White House had no reason to believe that students, quiescent in past wars, would fail to fall in line this time. When students rebelled in Ann Arbor and elsewhere, there was every reason to conclude that the demonstrations were the extremist actions of a transient body of protesters. The students' ethos seemed to be summed up in the philosophy of the Jack Kerouac's cult novel, *On the Road* (1957): Here today, gone tomorrow. Most students were quietly patriotic. Why worry?

The groups considered here had a mixed tradition of opposition to and support for wars. Certainly, there had been opposition to past wars, but each group also had a powerful tradition of incorporation. Labor, the best-organized of the groups, had become an arm of the Cold War national security establishment and had a vested economic interest in the Vietnam War. Women had a history of both opposing wars and accommodating to them once they had started. African Americans' protests against wars seemed to be chronically vitiated by their breakthrough syndrome: because of their dire status in American society, they had to grasp at every chance at acceptance regardless of the principles involved. Students were different in that they had no vote and no collective breakthrough syndrome, but their historical involvement in antiwar activities was slight.

All this helps to explain why America chose to fight the war in Vietnam and why it proved so tenacious in its pursuit of victory. Yet the character of each social group and its predicament in the sixties also contain clues to the crumbling of consensus and the ending of the war. That is the story now to be told, beginning with the activities of those rebels without history, the students.

3 Students

In president nixon's first term, student feelings against the Vietnam War reached a pitch of intensity summed up in the headline "Pigs Shoot to Kill—Bystanders Gunned Down," describing an incident near the University of California, Berkeley.[1] Politicians took the students seriously, especially in key electoral states. In California, U.S. Senator Alan Cranston begged the antiwar students at Stanford to campaign for the ultimately victorious candidate John Rutherford because "the race in the 14th State Senate District will have tremendous impact on the history of the world."[2] President Nixon stepped in on the other side of the debate. He made a national parable out of student disturbances in San Jose, California. In a speech broadcast over the three national television networks, he attacked the violent approach to politics that, he said, had been all too prevalent over the past decade. The Congress should give the police more money, and students should "hit the books or hit the road."[3]

The president systematically exploited the student-protest issue in his bid to destroy the antiwar movement and secure re-election in 1972. By the midterm elections of 1970, his strategy was well formed. He would appeal to blue-collar workers, normally a key element in Democratic support, playing on their dislike of middle-class students and on their patriotic aversion to draft dodgers. By this means, he was giving flesh to the political animal he had reinvented: the silent majority.

Thus, in the later stages of the Vietnam War, campus politics figured significantly in American politics—both in its own terms and on account of the vigorous White House reaction to it. Yet although campus politics was important, the real impact of the student protest movement had occurred earlier. The history of the movement can be divided into three phases. The first phase (approximately 1964–1965) was idealistic. The second (1966–1968) was more pragmatic, a period when young people characteristically protested not on principle but out of a desire not to be drafted and killed. The third phase (1969–1972) coincided with the de-Americanization of the war. Students returned to idealism and entered the sphere of legislative or "legitimate" politics.

The initial phase of student protest was the first challenge to the white, old, rich men in charge of foreign policy making and derives its special significance from that fact. In the view of a senior Republican, Senator Javits, "It was the students who first perceived acutely the fallacies, the contradictions, and the reality gap between fact and profession, of the ever-deepening American intervention in Vietnam."[4] The students' critical perception took shape during the early military escalation and later heightened the consciousness of other social groups who protested the war, with a cumulative effect on those in charge of Vietnam policy.

To appreciate the force of the student revolt, as well as some of its weaknesses, it is necessary to venture into relatively unexplored territory and to try to understand *how* it took place. Did characteristics of the revolt make it more—or less—effective? What precisely were the tactics of the student leaders? Does common sense suggest that those tactics may have been effective, and can any evidence be found to confirm that they did, in fact, have an impact? But before these questions can be tackled, some account must be given of a more familiar issue: *Why* did students rebel against the war? What motives gave their protest such intensity and in turn supplied inspiration to other social groups that embraced the peace cause?

The military and political context of the student revolt helps to explain why it developed so freely and reached such a frenetic pitch. Direct military commitment remained minor until, in August 1964, the Congress passed a resolution, in response to alleged North Vietnamese aggression against U.S. naval units in the Gulf of Tonkin, allowing President Johnson to authorize military operations without an actual declaration of war. Johnson's advisers now planned an escalation but prudently waited until after the presidential election of November 1964. On February 13, 1965, Johnson ordered the bombing campaign called Operation Rolling Thunder. On March 8, Marine units landed at Danang. In July, Johnson authorized troop levels of 175,000, approving by the end of the year another escalation to 443,000 within the next twelve months. In making these arrangements, President Johnson showed his usual sensitivity to public opinion at home, but, ironically, this very sensitivity contributed to his undoing. By not taking the risk of calling for a declaration of war, he sacrificed the right of emergency censorship. Crucially, this placed him at the mercy of his passionately articulate student critics.

The question of why students rebelled against the war can be approached through the memoirs of the preeminent student activist, Tom Hayden. Hayden recalled his motivations. World War II, after taking his father away from home, had propelled the man on the road to alcoholism and divorce—circumstances not conducive to the glorification of war. Other factors affected not just Hayden but his generation. He objected to the homogeneous architecture of his dormitory at the University of Michigan, to the absence of on-campus car-parking facilities in Ann Arbor, and to the way expanding universities like his own regarded students as mere sources of income and treated them as "unwanted orphans." He was determined to reject middle-class materialism, and he admired the ideals and courage of civil rights leaders in the South, whose struggle he joined before taking up the cudgels over Vietnam. Interviewing Edward Teller for the *Michigan Daily*, he recoiled at the atomic scientist's claim that it was "better to be dead than red." He visited Berkeley and listened to student radicals there, another source of inspiration. He claims in his autobiography that by 1960 he was already aware that the National Students' Association—the main representative body on U.S. campuses—was untrustworthy and would need to be challenged by a new organization. He soon became a prime mover in Students for a Democratic Society (SDS), founded in 1962. In short, Hayden first became a radical and then turned his attention to the Vietnam War.[5]

Hayden's recollection has echoes in Philip Altbach's account. Altbach was national chair of the Student Peace Union from its inception in 1959 until 1963, and he, too, considered campus alienation to have contributed to the sixties revolt.[6]

But individual perspectives do not necessarily explain why so many other students in America rebelled when they did. After all, war-scarred fathers have been sending their sons to universities for centuries without provoking political crises. Nor is encountering callousness at a university a uniquely American phenomenon. In 1963–1964 at Cambridge University, half a continent and an ocean away, a popular student cartoonist developed a story about a scheming professor who rid the campus not only of students but of his colleagues as well. Undergraduate "orphans" are a universal pubescent fantasy, not a peculiarity of sixties America.[7]

Other theories have similar weaknesses. One of these theories is about what William J. McGill, chancellor of the University of California, San Diego, called a "unique generational conflict."[8] In its various manifestations, the theory holds that certain characteristics apply to young people in the sixties: they held a different worldview from their parents' contemporaries, there were more of them, they were up against a generation of older men who were clinging to power, and these old men were congenital hypocrites. Let us deal with these contentions in reverse order. It is true that the old men were hypocrites. It was galling for students to hear professors extolling the virtues of New Deal liberalism while upholding conservative principles for campus government.[9] Yet people have always developed skills as they mature, which can be variously labeled tact, diplomacy, or hypocrisy; there is nothing new about it.

The "old men" theory does not apply particularly to the 1960s. In fact, the average age of secretaries of state in their last year in office in the period 1949–1973 was 62.8, only a small increase on the figure for 1892–1905, which was 61.5. Because average life expectancy in 1900 was only 47.3, compared with 69.7 in 1959, one could say that diplomacy was in the hands of old men in the early period but was conducted by men in the full vigor of late middle age in the 1960s.[10]

That there were more young people around in the 1960s is true; this factor, together with the American obsession with youth, may seem significant. Yet generational revolt over clashing worldviews is a constant. Mary McCarthy made the following observation about the Vassar graduates in her novel *The Group:* "The worst fate, they utterly agreed, would be to become like Mother and Dad, stuffy and frightened."[11] The novel is set not in the 1960s but in the 1930s.

In two senses, however, the generations theory does hold water. First, there was in the sixties a culture of unique generational conflict. McCarthy's novel was published in 1963, and, like Joseph Heller's 1961 novel, *Catch-22* (about World War II), and the film *MASH* (set in the Korean War), it was adopted as a sixties statement. In *The Group*, the Class of '33 rebelled against their parents without shocking a nation in the process. The sixties generation rebelled and did precisely that.[12]

The generations theory holds water in a second sense, too. The annual student turnover on campus meant that the student body did not hold aspirations for collective social acceptance or breakthrough. Lack of these aspirations was not unique to the sixties, but it was distinctive for students in comparison with other social groups. It meant that students collectively were not so susceptible to the blandishments of the establishment. Circumstances in the sixties ignited the campus tinderbox. Freedom from responsibility meant freedom to rebel, and this was a vital ingredient of the student revolt against the Vietnam War.

Another theory on the student revolt is that professors indoctrinated the young people in their charge. This notion was greatly exaggerated. The influence of the Marxist philosopher Herbert Marcuse at the University of California, San Diego, provoked fears that verged on the paranoid; and in a strongly nonsocialist country, few campuses could emulate Madison, Wisconsin, in boasting a whole battery of left-wing professors. Exaggeration notwithstanding, the academics of the 1960s, in teach-ins, publications, and the classroom, did impart to their students a great deal of information that could be used in criticisms of the war in Southeast Asia. Moreover, those who pitched in with outright criticism of the war tended to be the more senior professors.[13] They remembered the costs of World War II and Korea and, crucially, felt free to speak out because of the retreat of McCarthyism and Johnson's failure to seek a declaration of war or censorship. Older professors were also no doubt encouraged by having tenure, which made them unlikely to be fired for expressing their views. Students made up their own minds, but an influential minority of professors did contribute to the culture of protest and to students' confidence in their own opinions.[14]

Generational revolt and professorial radicalism help to explain student feelings and the ways they were expressed, but they do not explain why the great student revolt took place in the 1960s and over Vietnam. Short-term causes include, as noted and exemplified by Hayden, the inspiration afforded by civil rights campaigns of the 1950s and early 1960s. The Student Non-Violent Coordinating Committee, for one, impressed Hayden by its commitment to direct action to achieve racial equality in the South, and the committee itself came out against the war in 1966. SNCC's opposition came partly because it feared that conscription would deprive it of personnel essential to its civil rights activities, but for SNCC, as for other branches of the civil rights campaign, the war was also a direct affront to its principles of nonviolence.[15] If another short-term cause was the decline of McCarthyism, so was the triumph in the 1960 election of the inspirational young president John F. Kennedy. Partly because he was opposed in the Congress, partly because he harbored Cold War instincts, and finally because an assassin's bullet interceded, Kennedy left young people's aspirations frustratingly unfulfilled. The protest against the Vietnam War released some of this pent-up political idealism.

Another factor of some immediacy to students in the 1960s was the growth of the campaign against nuclear weapons in the 1950s. Nuclear anxiety and a disrespectful attitude toward the American purveyors of potential holocaust became ingrained in popular culture—for example, through the medium of such films as *Dr. Strangelove*.[16] Fears about nuclear warfare were easily transferred to the Vietnam War—and they were so transferred by performers like Joan Baez; Peter, Paul, and Mary; Buffy Sainte-Marie; Bob Dylan; and Phil Ochs, who claimed that he "was writing about Vietnam in 1962, way before the first anti-war marches."[17]

But no explanation of the student revolt would be complete that did not refer to the war itself. The war was ghastly; the belligerents on both sides committed appalling crimes; thousands of young Americans returned home in an unhinged and brutalized state of mind. The war was, in that respect, little different from any other war. Some of its features do help, nonetheless, to explain why students were so very much more vehement in their protest against the Vietnam War than previous generations of students had been against earlier conflicts. One distinctive feature of the Vietnam War was that television displayed to students, as to others, the effects of armed conflict; thanks to new technology, the gory details appeared in full color. Another distinctive feature was the sudden nature of American participation in the war. In the early 1960s, the United States had been preoccupied with other crises, in Berlin and Cuba. Although Laos was problematic, and its eastern neighbor had a long history of troubles, Vietnam impinged on American consciousness relatively late in the day. U.S. entry into World Wars I and II had, in contrast, allowed plenty of time for debate (Korea was also different, its being a plain case of enemy aggression that needed little debate). The best and most influential students have inquiring minds and thrive on discussion. Deprived of debate prior to escalation, they made up for it later, and had plenty of time do so, in the long years of the war.

Finally, the enemy was attractive to some of the protesters. North Vietnam and the Viet Cong were small-scale operators who had the courage to take on the "American Empire." In spite of Cold War propaganda about the "domino" effect, they posed no credible threat to the American homeland. Moreover, Ho Chi Minh, the North Vietnamese leader, could be represented as a nationalist first, a Communist second. His draft of the Vietnamese declaration of independence of 1945 had, after all, copied the language of the 1776 U.S. model. There seemed to be little resemblance between Ho and more serious American foes, like Hitler and Stalin. Ho seemed to have more in common with George Washington, while the American war effort was disturbingly reminiscent of the blunderings of George III.

The intensity of the student revolt and the determination of its practitioners can be understood in terms of their strong motivation. But strong motivation cannot win a campaign on its own. How the students set about their revolt and what made their rebellion effective or ineffective—these questions are rarely asked, probably because student protest was so diffuse and variegated. An answer must be sought if the impact of students on the war is to be evaluated.

One of the students' winning tactics was the use of eye-catching propaganda and evocative image making, which allowed them to rival their Madison Avenue–driven elders. The more able students were highly literate and imaginative. An example is the West Coast exploitation of octopoid imagery. This derived in part from Frank Norris's novel *The Octopus*, first published in 1901. Norris's octopus was the Southern Pacific Railroad. According to Norris, the railroad strangled every section of Californian society that threatened to compete with it, whether large-scale farmers or union-minded workers.[18] In more recent years, the image had been in frequent use in Latin America, where a despised U.S. multinational corporation, United Fruit Company, was known as *El Pulpo*, the octopus.[19]

In 1969 radical students took part in direct-action protests against the Stanford Research Institute. Located in the Industrial Park, it epitomized the activities of the military-industrial complex. The development of military research facilities at universities allegedly to the detriment of teaching and more academic research was among the students' leading grievances in the 1960s, especially at the Massachusetts Institute of Technology (dubbed "Pentagon East") and Stanford ("Pentagon West").[20] The motivations of student protesters at Stanford are illustrated in a pamphlet, *The Case Against Dillingham*. An effective piece of propaganda because it concentrated on one firm, Dillingham Corporation, this publication displayed on its cover a mid-Pacific octopus representing the multinational under attack, its tentacles extending to Indochina ("air bases for Vietnam war"), Indonesia ("resource exploitation"), the Sierra Nevada ("pollution of Lake Tahoe"), San Jose ("erection of 500 elderly low income trailer homes"), and elsewhere around the Pacific.[21] Other radical publications like *Fire and Sandstone: The Last Radical Guide to Stanford* (prepared by the Stanford Radical Caucus and the New Left Project) used similar octopoid imagery.[22]

The campus group responsible for publishing *The Case Against Dillingham* called itself Grass Roots. As used by the New Left, this term signified a need to return government to localities.[23] Thus another tentacle embraced Palo Alto Square, a hotel-and-office complex that Dillingham proposed for Stanford Industrial Park. According to Grass Roots, building the complex would push up local house rentals, bring in more automobiles to destroy the local ecology, provide jobs only for white, nonpoor workers, and draw Stanford further into the vortex of Vietnam economics.[24] The students' octopoid imagery conjured up more than a vivid image of exploitation. By depicting tentacles that spread down into the community, Grass Roots helped persuade an American public notoriously apathetic about foreign policy that their daily lives were being affected by the machinations of the military-industrial complex promoting a war in Vietnam.

One of the strengths of the student protest movement was the constant renewal of its antiestablishment mentality. At first sight, the reverse might seem to be the case. The students' defiant demeanor allied to their transience might be represented as a handicap. One doubter of students' achievements remarked: "The activist lived at a level of excitement which he could not long maintain. Activist at twenty-one, de-activated at twenty-two became a familiar pattern."[25]

When one generation of students graduated to become "proud members of a property-owning democracy," there was no guarantee that the next generation would carry on the fight.[26] Fashions changed with bewildering speed, even at high school. The historian Lewis Gann recalled his daughter's difficulties in a Palo Alto school in the late 1960s. No liberal, Gann claimed that certain antiwar students were terrorizing California college campuses, but he added that an equally pernicious group had taken over in the high schools. These were the Cowboys, the offspring of the "Okies" who had migrated to California in the Depression years. Cowboys wore cowboy hats, belts, and blue jeans. They liked rodeos, not soccer. They were not rich but would give their all for a horse. They disliked drugs and drug users, preferring alcohol instead, and they were tough. They took exception to the three other identifiable groups of schoolchildren, the Hippies (the decorative cadre of the war movement), Greasers (the motorbike brigade), and Rah-Rahs (those who cheered the high school football team). According to Gann, the Cowboy culture predominated in junior colleges as well as high schools.[27] This kind of cultural volatility and heterogeneity was a challenge not only to the nation's leaders but to the leaders of the protest movement, too.

Yet there were distinct advantages to rapid generational change. Each generation established its own voice, kept its thoughts spontaneous, and maintained outer walls relatively impenetrable by older inquisitors. One example of such a voice is the underground biweekly *San Diego Free Press*, which started publication in 1968 with the avowed intentions of challenging "the tubes [televisions] and rags [newspapers] of the Establishment," struggling "to return all power to the people," and furthering "Black Power, Chicano Power, Student Power, Hippy Power, G.I. Power, Worker Power, Rock Power, Theatre Power, and even white middle class Power—provided they do not interpret it to mean the usurpation of all other Powers mentioned."[28]

This kind of language, part stylized argot and part serious propaganda, had an appeal to young people that no parent or presidential emissary could hope to match. The young rebels acted out what Norman Mailer called "revolution by theatre and without a script."[29] Rapid changes in language, personnel, objective, place, and tactics had the further effect of confusing officials deciding how to respond to the students. Around the age of twenty-one, students entered the job market, started voting, and began to become comprehensible to the political establishment. But, by this time, they had relinquished the campuses to the ever-green anarchism of their juniors. Uninhibited by any sense of collective or cumulative sociopolitical climbing, these juniors were prepared to start the revolution all over again.

It would be a mistake to treat the student protest against the Vietnam War as a series of spontaneous events with no thought given to tactics or to the serious business of how to win the political struggle. It may be true that, in keeping with their ephemeral status, students protesting the Vietnam War had no overall, constantly applied plan. SDS national secretary Paul Booth even recalled that the antiwar students "just weren't very sophisticated about politics."[30] But Booth's retrospective judgment was probably colored by his subsequent career as a labor leader. The student rebels may have lacked a long-term plan of campaign, but that in itself appealed to a generation that was trying to reinvent anarchy, or at least gave itself an air of doing so. Apparent anarchy was sometimes just a pretense at disorder. Strategic flexibility must not be mistaken for chaos, and there is ample evidence of tactical ingenuity on the part of the campus rebels, an ingenuity that lent force to their campaign.

In 1975, the Stanford University SDS activist Lenny Siegel responded to an invitation to explain the student tactics of the sixties. As with all such attempts at retrospective rationalization, the passage of time may have colored his judgment, possibly leading him to perceive too much method in the students' madness. Yet he is quite plausible in his contention that the students had employed four successful methods of protest. First, they had used the "tantrum tactic," smashing windows on campus and wreaking other mayhem to increase the cost of the war and to force the authorities to do *something*. Second, they consciously used "child stealing," the conversion of the progeny of influential people to their point of view to put pressure on their parents. This tactic was important at elitist institutions like the Ivy League colleges and Stanford. Third, they used premeditated direct action, such as organized draft resistance and physical obstruction of installations like the Computer Center at Stanford. Last, the students had raised issues by doing more sedate things, such as organizing demonstrations. These demonstrations were effective, Siegel thought, in that they attracted media coverage.[31]

The significance of child stealing, or offspring-lobbying, might not be immediately apparent. In truth, it divided families much the way a civil war would. Some politically influential parents must have felt that their offspring had been essentially kidnapped. In some cases, the father objected and the son conformed: the high-ranking African American U.N. official Ralph Bunche told his son that the war was "totally abhorrent" to him but failed to dissuade Ralph junior from serving in Vietnam.[32] More usually, however, the quarrel was between an antiwar rebel and a parent. Daniel P. Moynihan of Harvard University told President Nixon that top business people were imbued with "hostility to the administration" over its alleged infraction of protesters' civil liberties. Why? Because they had been indoctrinated by "their children, who absorb it in the atmosphere of the elite universities."[33] Parents on the other side of the capital-labor divide also found their convictions under scrutiny. When leaders of the United Automobile Workers met for a family seder in the spring of 1967, it was only after an intergenerational agreement that there would be no discussion of Vietnam. In the event, the truce broke down, and there was a bitter intergenerational quarrel.[34]

Senator Javits noted the impact of offspring-lobbying on members of Congress: "The lesson to be drawn is not that violent civil disobedience . . . succeeds but rather that fathers and even Senators will sit up and take note when their sons hold passionate beliefs about the morality of public policy and propagate those beliefs."[35] Intergenerational conflict became a problem for executive officials in the Johnson and Nixon administrations. As Moynihan noted, the sons and daughters of top people who went to college were prone to acquire antiwar views through absorption. Although there was no organized campaign to recruit the children of top people, Siegel may well be right in his recollection that antiwar activists made a point of singling out the sons and daughters of government officials on campus and winning them over to their cause. In the period of Vietnam protest Robert McNamara, Melvin Laird, and Nicholas Katzenbach—two defense secretaries and an assistant secretary of state—had to contend not only with the harrowing daytime problems of the Pentagon and State Department but also with questions within their homes asked by a son, niece, and son, respectively, described by Siegel as "low profile active," "medium active," and "very active" in antiwar protests at Stanford University. Secretary of State Dean Rusk bore down on student protesters, whom he compared with the Hitler appeasers of the 1930s, but his son Richard, a Cornell student, opposed the war in Vietnam.

Others who had problems with their offspring over Vietnam were the Pentagon officials Paul Nitze and Paul Warnke (whose daughter traveled down from Harvard to organize a war protest from the family home), Secretary of the Army Stanley Resor,

Under Secretary of the Army Ted Beal, and National Security Adviser McGeorge Bundy. In 1978 the director of the CIA's controversial Phoenix counterinsurgency program in South Vietnam, William Colby, felt it necessary to "vehemently refute an ugly and hurtful canard that has floated about in recent years" that his daughter Catherine's death in 1973 stemmed from her father's role in Phoenix. Clearly, the child stealers gave the war leaders pause for thought.[36]

Although rebellious progeny could make life difficult for their parents, their impact on policy is a matter of conjecture. One common parental reaction to filial challenge is to retreat, shutting the mind to a viewpoint that might otherwise be acceptable. Another is to admit to fault only when the battle is over and less can be lost. McNamara waited until 1995 before publicly admitting that he had been wrong over Vietnam.[37] He was having doubts about Vietnam, expressed privately within government circles, apparently as early as the fall of 1965. In 1967 he commissioned the subsequently famous Pentagon inquiry into the decisionmaking process behind the war. He quit his job in November 1967, earlier than expected, a possible indication that he had become terminally disillusioned with the war long before America withdrew from it. Was he influenced by his son, Craig, who smashed windows in protest against the war, then took himself off to Easter Island to escape his father? McNamara's biographer Deborah Shapley offers contrary evidence to the effect that the secretary of defense never really noticed his son until the shock, one day in 1966, of seeing the Stars and Stripes upside down in Craig's room.[38] Yet it would be foolish to assume that any father is entirely deaf and blind to what is happening in his own household.

As Siegel observed, draft resistance was an important student tactic in opposing the war. This is hardly surprising: the draft was a cloud that hung over the life of every healthy male student of fighting age. The draft, seen as an instrument of democracy in nineteenth-century Europe and in the United States during World War II, had become a tool of oppression. Although 75 percent of those who served in the military in the Vietnam War years enlisted voluntarily, a far greater percentage than during

World War II and the Korean War, the figure is deceptive. Many who volunteered did so only to escape the dire consequences of being drafted. By volunteering, one could be assigned to attractive specialities or even escape Vietnam by being assigned, say, to Europe. So, in their various ways, many students demonstrated their hatred of the draft.[39]

There was a concerted assault on the principle of the draft. According to one estimate, there were as many as 570,000 draft offenders in the course of the Vietnam War, compared with 2,215,000 draftees and 8,720,000 who served in the military. Many of these were just AWOLS (absent without leave from military duty), but, according to the resistance movement, 200,000 draft offenders were serious objectors to military service.[40] Students provided a lead in publicizing and organizing draft resistance in its various forms: avoidance through such means as training for a religious calling, burning draft cards, stopping troop trains, emigration, and desertion.

The effectiveness of draft resistance as an antiwar tactic needs to be considered from several perspectives. As its critics noted, draft resistance sometimes reflected selfish or cowardly motives, and, to that extent, it was certainly a liability to the peace cause. Second, the political reaction to draft protests was uneven. Reactionary hawks tried to foment and exploit the popular backlash against draft resisters. On the other hand, from any politician's viewpoint, it is a difficult moral and political choice to commit reluctant warriors to battle. Third, in the mid-sixties there was a logistic problem in filling the draft quotas demanded by military command, and draft resistance probably did contribute to the lack. Fourth, as the war wore on, draft resistance at home came to demoralize the fighting men in Vietnam. Fifth, draft resistance was a consciousness-raising exercise of a type dear to the hearts of sixties radicals. Finally, one of the special features of American draft resistance in the Vietnam War was emigration to Canada.

Vancouver beckoned West Coast protesters and was a popular point of entry to Canada. Further to the east, draft dodgers and deserters formed refugee aid groups in Montreal, Ottawa, and Toronto, with Toronto developing into the main destination for emigrating young Americans.[41] An underground railroad developed, so called after the escape route followed by fleeing slaves before the Civil War. Because of its clandestine nature and the prohibition preventing Canadian immigration officials from asking about incomers' military status, there are no precise figures for the number of draft refugees, but the best extrapolations would suggest at least thirty thousand in Canada, with smaller concentrations in other sympathetic countries, like Sweden. The American incomers claimed to be "the best educated group of immigrants Canada has ever had," and the number of American students attending Canadian universities increased by 61 percent from 1965 to 1969.[42]

The self-justifying tone of the claim to be so well educated shows that American immigrants experienced the breakthrough syndrome in Canada. They wanted to identify themselves as Canadians, and this inhibited them from participating in the internal politics of the United States. Other factors militated against the effectiveness of the Canadian exiles. At the best of times, the American public virtually ignores Canadian affairs, and the opinions of a group within Canada who had rejected their homeland were never going to be of paramount interest. Again, it could be argued that Canada was a safety valve for discontent; if it had not existed and if the "refuseniks" had stayed at home, swelling the ranks of the greater numbers who escaped Vietnam by going underground, there might have been an even greater explosion of pent-up frustrations within the United States.

Even though the flight to Canada may have weakened the resistance movement in some ways, it did embarrass the U.S. government. The Johnson and Nixon administrations were concerned at the lack of international support for their policy in Vietnam, and the exiles were a source of bad publicity in foreign countries.

The student input into the many antiwar demonstrations of the sixties is undoubtedly significant, but a distinction must be kept in mind. As Hayden noted, the movement of the sixties was rooted in notions of "spontaneity and local initiative" deriving from the civil rights campaign in the South.[43] Students organized local demonstrations to raise consciousness about the octopoid activities of the multinational war machine and to illustrate the connections between community needs and international exploitation. But, in addition, they participated in national demonstrations—huge marches in the capital and synchronized mass meetings in several major cities. These were headline-grabbing events and gave the impression of widespread opposition to the war.

In the case of the major nationwide demonstrations, students did not act alone; they tended to cooperate with other protesting groups. Like other insurgent groups since the 1830s, notably women, African Americans, and organized labor, the students practiced alliance politics, an important part of their tactical armory, as well as an indication that the initiative in opposing the war would not reside permanently with the students. Student activists participated alongside other groups in organizing mass demonstrations and supported African Americans and Mexican Americans (Chicanos) who argued that their communities were carrying an unfair burden in the war.

The student-labor alliance was troubled, however. Although it was effective from time to time, it suffered from an important impediment: the role of labor in the antiwar movement was generally negative. Those on the left always find it tempting to see labor as the standard-bearer in radical causes. The New Left initially shared these expectations, but it was disillusioned even before Vietnam became a major issue. The Port Huron Statement, issued in 1962 at the time of the founding of the SDS, addressed the problem of "organized labor, the historic institutional representative of the exploited." It stated that labor had "succumbed to institutionalization" and become middle-class: "The House of Labor has bay windows."[44]

The student-labor relationship, in spite of this bleak outlook, could be said to have contributed to the campus protest movement. In a perverse way, the perceived corruption of labor added to the students' perception of themselves as knights in shining armor taking on the evil empire of government singlehandedly. The wicked suggestion by political reactionaries, that rich kids were snobbish about blue-collar workers anyway, cannot be dismissed—some students may have felt more comfortable in a protest movement where they could look down on proletarians, instead of associating with them.

But student radicals did not make a complete break with labor. Antiwar student leaders were encouraged by a rash of wildcat strikes to believe that the prowar AFL-CIO leadership was out of step with the rank and file. Students accordingly appeared on picket lines in the course of industrial disputes, which at least a few of them regarded as opportunities to raise consciousness on the subject of the Vietnam War. A *San Diego Free Press* contributor, Curly Marx, informed labor in the open-shop, military-production-geared city that "our common enemy is the establishment war machine that is endorsed by the Democratic union leaders."[45]

Students even cooperated with organized labor when opportunity arose. The struggle of the United Farm Workers (UFW) to organize the exploited, migrant, mainly Chicano harvesters in the western states gave them an opportunity. The grape boycott, declared in 1965 to punish anti-union growers, received solid support on campuses. When the UFW cadres shaped their movement into a broader crusade, *La Causa*, that embraced opposition to the war, the UFW leader, Cesar Chavez, became an icon in the student movement. When some longer-established unions began to have second thoughts about the war, radical students seized the moment. In August 1969 the *Free Press* described the United Auto Workers as "one of the key tools in an attempt to absorb the revolutionary potentiality of the working-class."[46] One historian has remarked that in the years before 1970 the New Left increasingly turned away from organized labor because of labor's prowar stance but that "important cross-currents" existed; the students' support for the UFW was the "best example," but there was cooperation in other enclaves across the United States, too.[47] Meanwhile, influential factions in the SDS moved away from a social-democratic–New Left position toward a revolutionary one that gave a crucial role to labor.[48] Alliance politics was on the students' agenda and proved an antiwar tactic of some importance.

The changing stance of the SDS, together with disputes over new issues—flying the Viet Cong flag, homosexuality, women's liberation, and drugs—led to fragmentation and loss of reputation. But these developments had an impact in Vietnam as well. In different ways, the campus drug culture and students' overt sympathy with the enemy undermined the morale of American troops. On the one hand, they felt betrayed at home; on the other, they began to adopt student culture by taking drugs themselves. A White House report in November 1970 indicated that the campus "drug culture" had been ineradicably planted in Vietnam. Marijuana brought indiscipline in its wake—so far in 1970, eighty-three G.I.s had tried to kill their sergeants or officers—and heroin was "becoming a serious problem."[49] Apparently, every army needs its narcotic. According to Bao Ninh, a communist soldier turned novelist, the North Vietnamese regulars smoked their own form of marijuana.[50] But that sort of comparison eluded the American students' critics, who, through the demonization of campus radicals, unwittingly made them icons, suggested that drug taking was an exclusively American problem, and contributed to the demoralization of U.S. soldiers in Vietnam.

In an article in October 1968, the International Ladies Garment Workers Union assistant president and Americans for Democratic Action activist Gus Tyler rounded on the SDS and on the recently established Youth International Party, the "Yippies." He accused the student antiwar movement of lurching in the direction of the totalitarian left and of coming close to the philosophy of the French anarcho-syndicalist philosopher Georges Sorel. This charge was only slightly less absurd than the White House's insistence that the students were falling into the communist camp. Nevertheless, the idea spread that the student antiwar leadership was losing credibility by taking an impossibilist, doctrinal approach.[51]

The "lurch to the left" hypothesis lends itself to a misrepresentation of the chronology of student protest, a chronology that owed more to the ebb and flow of idealism than to doctrinal fads. It also obscures the salient feature of the student antiwar movement: the cool and accurate judgment shown overall by its leaders in writing off labor as a radical force, even if some exceptions have to be noted. The student tactics of child stealing, draft resistance, and alliance politics were among the more effective in the antiwar movement.

It took a number of years for the full array of student tactics to appear. In the first phase of campus revolt, 1964–1965, the Johnson administration did not have to face the complete panoply of juvenile ingenuity. Yet this was the period when the student protest movement had the most impact. In particular, the president's decision in February 1965 to bomb North Vietnam and send substantial numbers of American troops overseas proved to be, according to the historian Donald Phillips, the "catalyst" for campus opposition to the war.[52] The subsequent student protest had such impact because it was the first major student revolt against foreign policy and caught the administration unawares.

The concentration of protest in electorally crucial California gave the student uprising special importance. Concentration was not immediate. The spirit of insurrection already existed in the South and throughout the nation, as the formation of SNCC in 1960 and SDS two years later showed. According to one veteran of SNCC, "Most SNCC workers opposed U.S. involvement in Vietnam as soon as they became aware of it."[53] In late December 1964, Todd Gitlin, an SDS spokesman on international issues, coined the We Won't Go slogan, and tried to persuade the National Council of the SDS to issue an immediate statement under that heading to protest U.S. intervention in Vietnam. Although he failed, he had helped to sow the seeds of the movement.[54]

The initial stages of student protest in the East were not spectacular. On March 24, 1965, the first teach-in on the Vietnam War took place at the University of Michigan. In between bomb scares, about 2,500 people attended lectures, rallies, seminars, movies, and folksinging sessions. This type of protest spread to more than a hundred campuses and to Washington, D.C., where a teach-in at the Sheraton Hotel was broadcast nationwide on radio and television. Then, on April 17, SDS and SNCC joined a coalition of groups—alliance politics in practice—to organize the first antiwar mass demonstration at the Washington Monument. This was, however, attended by a crowd of little more than 15,000 people—a mere handful compared with the 200,000 who had converged on the Lincoln Memorial in August 1963 to demand Jobs and Freedom with Martin Luther King, Jr. The nation had not yet received its massive psychological jolt.[55]

Still, other rallies followed in different cities, and over a weekend in early August, Washington once again became the focus of protest, with alliance politics a feature of interest—the Student Peace Union joined with the Mississippi Freedom Democratic Party, Women Strike for Peace, and the W. E. B. Du Bois Clubs. At this event, popular music blended with protest. The long-term effects cannot be doubted: pop with bite formed a subliminal association that helped fix the minds of a generation. As the year drew to a close, the relatively sedate National Students Union declared against the war, the SDS opened registration desks for conscientious objectors outside military induction centers, and on Veterans Day (November 11), Columbia University students organized a We Won't Go rally.[56]

Meantime, the high drama was taking place on the West Coast. By the mid-sixties California was not just politically powerful but politically volatile. It seemed to contain the ideal ingredients for an explosive challenge to the governing establishment. The post–World War II baby boom had boomed with greater intensity in California than elsewhere. The state had a higher-than-average percentage of eighteen- to twenty-year-olds, an exceptionally large proportion of young people attending college, and an apparent intermeshing of youth culture and the American Dream.[57] It boasted a radical tradition exemplified by the labor leaders Frank Roney and Harry Bridges, the social visionary Henry George, and the novelists Frank Norris, Jack London, Upton Sinclair, and John Steinbeck. The San Francisco Bay and Peninsula areas in northern California were especially freethinking—at least that was the view of the Berkeley student leader Mario Savio, a former altar boy from a working-class New York City background radicalized by the experience of helping black children in McComb, Mississippi, who on arrival in the Bay Area saw it as "one of the few places left in the United States where a history of personal involvement in radical politics was not a form of leprosy."[58]

The students at the University of California, Berkeley, took the lead. The story of their revolt forms one of the indelible images of twentieth-century U.S. history. By the mid-sixties they had already built up a head of steam. In 1957 they had formed a political party called SLATE. In the fall of 1964 this organization confronted the Regents of the university, demanding that they remove the prohibition on Communists speaking on any University of California (UC) campus. The Berkeley university president, Clark Kerr, issued a new compromise regulation, but it was too late. The Berkeley revolt began in the guise of a free speech movement (FSM). Student leaders claimed that Kerr had double-crossed them by parading his liberal pedigree and pretending to be sympathetic, but engaging in red-baiting: he had asserted that "49% of the demonstrators are followers of the Castro-Maoist line." Berkeley students now released *Joy to UC*, a record of "free speech carols," the tone of which indicated that the Kennedy-inspired honeymoon between the liberal establishment and youth was over: "Oh, come, all ye mindless / Conceptless and spineless."[59]

The California student struggle now took a turn that helped to define the coming polarization of American society over the Vietnam War. In March 1965 the radical FSM sympathizer John Thomson was arrested by the Berkeley police for displaying a piece of paper bearing the word *fuck*. His detention galvanized libertarians who, in the wake of the McCarthy era, were hypersensitive to any suppression of freedom of expression. To the radical students, his arrest furthermore symbolized the hypocrisy of a system that turned a blind eye to fraternity gambols—for example, a contemporary Ugly Man Contest won by Miss Pussy Galore.[60] The radical students now shunned the codes of respectability to which earlier protest movements had clung. They sympathized with a spectrum of anti-authoritarian symbols, from bad language to D. H. Lawrence to American Communists. The FSM, for example, claimed the active participation of Bettina

Aptheker, Margaret Lima, and Lee Goldblatt, the daughters of leading Communists: Herbert Aptheker the historian, Albert J. Lima the Northern California Communist Party chair, and Louis Goldblatt, secretary-treasurer of the Longshoremen's union.[61]

Bettina actively pursued a left-wing agenda. (Question: "What's a nice girl like you doing mixed up with communism?" Putative reply: "Who says I'm a nice girl?")[62] Yet the protest movement was intractably chaotic, unlike the old left. This may have been its charm as far as students were concerned, but its anarchistic tendency alienated the Cold War cadres of the Communist Party. The party opposed the activities of the Vietnam Day Committee (VDC) at Berkeley: communist discipline required control, the VDC was uncontrollable, and the party recalled its member participants. Similarly in SDS, the standard quip about the Communists was "They can't take us over because they can't find us."[63] One result of this absence of party control was that the protest movement retained its attraction for young people who would certainly have been repelled by party discipline, just as they were by parental and other forms of control. Another result was that the FBI lost track of what was going on. Over many years, the bureau had slipped into a rut, imagining that the key to all domestic countersubversion lay in watching the Communists. (The CIA's attempt to find out about student protest, aptly code-named Operation CHAOS, fared no better.) The FBI proved unequal to its new task and was inefficient both in its attempts to inform the White House about the protest movement and in its efforts to disrupt it.[64]

The May 21–22 Berkeley teach-in against the Vietnam War was by no means the first such event, but it captivated the media because of its style and location. Jerry Rubin and Stephen Smale had set up the VDC to organize the event, and they showed considerable flair. Lasting thirty-six hours, the sit-in attracted thirty thousand participants. They devoted rapt attention to a star cast, among them Phil Ochs, the household-name pediatric author Benjamin Spock, the veteran socialist leader Norman Thomas, SNCC leader Bob Moses, the novelist Norman Mailer, and, winner of the greatest ovation, the independent editorialist I. F. Stone. These people not only had big names but were charismatic, providing a draw that the prowar forces would be unable to match. Here, the Berkeley students set a precedent that the antiwar movement as a whole was to follow.

Nor did the Berkeley rebellion stop there. By early August students were obstructing troop trains running through the neighboring flatlands to the nearby Oakland Army Base. Groups of students would sit down on the tracks. As a train approached, they would typically get up at the last moment and run away. But the tactic was disruptive and newsworthy. Given the start of the Vietnam Run on the West Coast, California students were exceptionally well positioned to protest in this way, but they also set a direct-action example that students elsewhere followed.[65]

On August 13 the *Berkeley Barb* started publication. It was not the first underground counterculture paper, and there were many others, but it became one of the best and most respected. This was no surprise to scholars all over the country, who were acclaiming Berkeley as the leading academic institution in the United States—another factor that made its troubles awesome. In all, the Berkeley students had succeeded in their goal of issuing a challenge to the establishment and its tubes and rags. Dazed and bewitched, the press responded by devoting a disproportionate amount of attention to events in California.[66]

The student revolt in 1965 raised consciousness about the war and was the first of a cumulative series of blows against it. But the immediate effect on Washington was mixed. Did the students achieve leverage in the U.S. Senate, the legislative body charged with foreign policy powers? William Fulbright of Arkansas, chair of the Foreign Relations Committee, was by late July having doubts about the war. But he does not appear to have been influenced by student protest and, in spite of his strong academic credentials, was considered to be too aloof and too reactionary on racial matters to be a rallying point for campus antiwar protesters. Up to a point, Senator Javits of New York was more sensitive to student opinion. Encouraged by this, a constituent complained to him about an inquiry, by the Judiciary Committee's Subcommittee on Internal Security, into his protest activities against the Vietnam War at the University of Wisconsin. But Javits treated the matter as one of patronage, not principle, and merely secured an assurance that the investigation of that particular student would be taken no further. The judiciary subcommittee duly produced, in October, its report on the teach-ins. It paid the protesters a backhanded tribute: "By sheer noise and persistence and clever propaganda, the sponsors of the anti-Vietnam movement have succeeded in creating the impression that they speak for the better part of the American academic community." But the authors of the report further observed that the leaders of the movement had failed to "demarcate their position" from that of the Communists or block communist participation in the movement. Evidence suggests that collectively the Senate was worried by, but far from sympathetic to, student protest.[67]

Although the student revolt did not convert the white, old, rich men in charge of the country, it did catch them by surprise. The unprepared authorities were unable to nip the antiwar movement in the bud, and that allowed the movement to develop a propaganda momentum. To be sure, Mario Savio and other leaders of the FSM's sit-in were arrested, charged, prosecuted, and sent to prison on trespass charges, but this was a local event that only created an opportunity for another batch of student leaders to emerge from the ever-fecund bowers of Berkeley to lead the VDC campaign.[68] Nationally, there was not yet any systematic plan for the suppression of the movement. In April 1965, President Johnson and FBI director J. Edgar Hoover, who met to discuss SDS and the antiwar movement, agreed that Communists were responsible for the trouble. Hoover confirmed his view in a subsequent report, and the FBI was instructed to make a special study of SDS. The episode illustrates White House concern, but deciding on effective action was another matter.[69]

As the realization dawned that a serious revolt was under way, the Johnson administration did take some belated steps to remedy the situation. Bombing pauses and peace initiatives were aimed not just at the North Vietnamese but also at public opinion and protesting students at home. They were intended to show that LBJ was a reasonable man. Convinced that a "vocal minority" was behind the protest, White House officials organized a panel of speakers to visit campuses. To deny the protesters credibility, the officials would attend teach-ins as individuals, not official representatives, but would still state the administration's case. The task of the war apologist was, however, a daunting one. William Bundy, LBJ's assistant on Asian affairs, refused an invitation to attend Berkeley's VDC teach-in. The political scientist Robert A. Scalapino and the novelist Eugene Burdick withdrew at the last moment from the teach-in, claiming it was rigged. The withdrawal inspired the local dish "chicken Scalapino," but its namesake was just being prudent. As Senate investigators noted, "At many of the teach-ins, spokesmen for the administration's policy were subjected to booing and hissing and catcalling, so that it was impossible for them to make a coherent presentation of their case."[70] It may be concluded that the protesting students of 1965 had administered a shock to the White House, forced some confidence-sapping policy modifications, and given heart to the Communists and nationalists in Vietnam. Yet the young radicals were not subjected to serious harassment nor forced to deal with countertactics, an omission that contributed to their success and enabled them to protest for several more years, even if their clamor was later eclipsed by that of other social groups.

The second phase of student protest, 1966–1968, was a time of diminishing momentum and power. But student protest against the war continued to be significant in three ways. First, the protesters persisted in offering intelligent criticism of the war. Second, alliance tactics came into play, and the students were an important presence at protests and demonstrations conducted jointly with other groups, even if African Americans and women developed a more prominent role in opposing the war. Third, the image of student protest, kept alive by the ongoing activities of campus radicals, formed an essential part of the antiminority mindset that came to characterize the outlook of many Americans and of the White House. The compound silent majority mentality that helped to prolong the war stemmed, in part, from a negative attitude toward students.

The second phase of student protest had certain characteristics. First, antiwar students associated with the SDS moved to the left. Although the move involved only a tiny minority of antiwar students and was sufficiently unpopular to result in the collapse of SDS in 1969, it lent itself to distortion. It allowed conservatives and hawks to vilify student protest and gave the Build, Not Burn element in the protest movement the backdrop against which they could define their contrasting, respectable credentials.[71] Second, the draft became the main issue of student protest, so self-preservation or self-interest powerfully supplemented idealism as a motivating factor, even if plenty of idealism remained.[72] Third, the protest movement became a mass phenomenon, even though student input was diluted. Fourth, student action provoked responses from senior politicians, ranging from the Democrats' Mayor Richard Daley and President Johnson to the Republicans' Governor Reagan and President Nixon.

The remaining three years of LBJ's presidency were a time of more fighting, more casualties, more draft demands, and more student recruitment into the armed services. Although Vietnam remained predominantly a working-class war, the number of middle-class students required to fight was rising. The student exemption rules were tightened in 1967, and the draft threat now embraced the more affluent and cast its shadow over an entire generation. In 1969, in a surveyed group of high-school graduates 75 percent identified the draft and Vietnam when asked to name "the problems young men your age worry about most"; in 1966, when polled as sophomores, only 7 percent of the same sample had given the same reply.[73] Against the background of these changes, students used their ingenuity to avoid military service in Vietnam and demonstrated against the war in impressive numbers.

The idealists among them were still hard at work. Sheer humanity caused students to protest the output of a napalm factory in Coyote, seventy miles south of San Francisco. The antiwar periodical *Opposition West* (jointly edited by Marc Sapir of Stanford University and Bill Miller of Berkeley) advocated, in June 1966, a boycott of all Dow Chemical Company products because Dow made polystyrene, which accounted for 50 percent of the "new, improved, more adhesive Napalm-B."[74] Idealism notwithstanding, hundreds of thousands of students were now joining the movement for reasons that could be interpreted as fear of the draft and of military action. Potentially, the apparent departure from idealism represented a point of weakness in the antiwar campaign. The student movement remained formidable, but it was less compelling than before, and no longer the unchallenged moral leader of the antiwar movement.

This was no great consolation to LBJ, for whom the war was a catalog of woe. No matter how much he deluded himself or the American public, it showed no sign of ending. At home, there seemed to be no prospect of neutralizing the minority of student troublemakers or of preventing the spread of the contagion to other groups. Another monster lurked in the political wings. The midterm election of 1966 threw up a new, conservative threat: the prowar, antistudent challenger for the governorship of California, Ronald Reagan. Johnson now had no way to position himself to advantage vis-à-vis the student-war problem. If he outhawked Reagan, he alienated the students, but if he inclined to the students, he risked defeat by a rejuvenated Republican Party playing the patriotic card.

In 1966 the protest against the war began to follow a two-track format, those who were prepared to break the law supplying the background that made the legitimate protesters look respectable. Events at the Port Chicago Naval Weapons Center in California illustrate this in cameo. On the one hand, peaceful picketing protested the use of the facility that, according to its critics, supplied more than 90 percent of the ammunition and explosives used in Vietnam by American forces. On the other hand, a printed leaflet issued by the Berkeley-based Contra Costa Citizens Against the War in Vietnam instructed "those citizens who are prepared to risk arrest" to separate themselves "from the main body and continue to interrupt the munitions traffic by stopping explosives and napalm trucks as they arrive."[75]

Older problems intermingled with the new. The experiences of Herbert Aptheker indicate, for example, that the free speech issue of 1964 continued to color antiwar protest through 1965 and into 1966. In May 1965 the authorities at the Ohio State University had barred Aptheker from speaking on campus. He turned up but remained silent while sympathetic faculty members read excerpts from his speeches to the gathered crowd of students and newspaper journalists. The inconsistency was plain: Whereas Russian or Polish communist leaders with dubious human rights records were welcomed and listened to attentively in the United States in the interest of keeping the nuclear peace, American Communists—just like anticommunist dissidents in Russia and Poland—were refused free speech rights. The inconsistency also affected some of the opponents of the Vietnam War. When the Yale professor Staughton Lynd received an invitation to visit Hanoi in company with Hayden and Aptheker, he was reluctant to travel with an American Communist (although he ultimately did so). Controversy caused by the inconsistencies of the establishment was even greater because the establishment was automatically in the firing line; campus protesters regarded the Aptheker case as a means of putting establishment hypocrites to the sword.[76]

Free speech was still an issue at Harvard in the spring of 1966, when a student was threatened with expulsion for inviting Aptheker to speak on campus (according to Aptheker, this was the first visit by an American Communist since the McCarthy era). A compromise was struck whereby Aptheker flew up from New York but gave a lecture on black slave revolts. True to the agreement, he kept his hosts out of trouble by steadfastly refusing to answer questions about his recent visit to North Vietnam. Then in November, after the university had refused an SDS demand for a right to reply when Robert McNamara spoke on campus, a crowd of student demonstrators surrounded the defense secretary's automobile and shouted slogans at him. Rattled, he mounted the hood of a nearby car and shouted abuse back. To him and his Washington colleagues, it seemed as if the universities had been infected with an ineradicable virus.[77]

It could be argued that the increase in mass protests was linked to old tactics. In the final days of 1966, two hundred young opponents of the war met in Chicago at the instigation of Bettina Aptheker. Bettina had an unreconstructed old left faith in the potentialities of the American working class. She wanted a national student strike supported by labor: "If the Longshoremen refused to unload ships or load ships, if workers would pull work stoppages, that was the most directly effective and powerful mechanism that you had."[78] The conference rejected her idea but formed the Student Mobilization Committee, which lent its support to the notion of mass demonstrations, recently mooted by the Spring Mobilization Committee, a hitherto ineffective group dominated by the youth branch of the Socialist Workers Party (SWP).

The SWP was anti-Stalinist, and this may account in some small measure for the rising appeal of the Mobe idea. But other, and more important, factors explain why students swelled the ranks of the mass antiwar demonstrations. Escalation of the ground war in Vietnam was leading to more draft calls. In 1966 the Senate Foreign Relations Committee commenced hearings on the war at the instigation of Senator Fulbright, giving a respectable forum to its critics and a feeling of legitimacy to students who might otherwise have been deterred from undertaking seemingly unpatriotic protests.

Illustrative of the distrust between government and campus was the revelation, in February 1967, that the CIA had been secretly subsidizing the activities of the National Students' Association (NSA). Responsible for the exposé was *Ramparts*, the radical Catholic magazine published in California, but the story received immense publicity in the major newspapers, too. Students were already upset at government manipulation of universities through lucrative defense research contracts, which was giving rise to the phrase *military-industrial-university complex*, and were repelled by this further instance of Big Government undermining academic independence. Students were further outraged by the disclosure that the U.S. Selective Service director, General Lewis Hershey, used his deferment powers as a political weapon to help the supporters of the war and injure its foes. In vain did government officials protest that LBJ was unaware of such practices and that previous presidents had been responsible for the suborning of the main student organization in the country. The Democratic administration, which was overseeing a huge expansion in higher education, had incurred the unwavering distrust of students, the very group it sought to help.[79]

Students participated in growing numbers in mass demonstrations supported by a widening coalition of protesters. Large crowds attended the Spring Mobe demonstrations of April 15, 1967, in Washington, San Francisco, and New York, where public draft-card burnings took place. Spring Mobe having renamed itself the National Mobilization Committee, the students and their allies organized a demonstration on October 21 that laid siege to the Pentagon. Norman Mailer, who was arrested on that occasion, paid tribute to the residual idealism of the student demonstrators at that event, who "did not care if they were overheard [by the FBI], photographed, mapped, clocked, or even admired."[80]

The number of student demonstrations involving at least thirty-five students was on the increase, according to statistics collected later by the NSA. There were 71 demonstrations on 62 campuses in the first half of the 1967–1968 academic year, but 221 on 101 campuses in the second half. Nineteen sixty-eight was an alarming year, for students were in revolt internationally; France in particular was shaken by student-labor demonstrations that brought the country to the brink of revolution. Two events that shook the United States to the core were the student occupation of Columbia University in April 1968—it started as a "community" demonstration in support of black inhabitants of nearby Harlem and ended as an antiwar protest—and the late August demonstrations outside the Democratic convention in Chicago.[81]

But what did all this mean in terms of political impact? If direct impact is the criterion, student protest against the Vietnam War could be seen as declining in potency with the passage of time. But indirect political impact of student protest was powerful and complex and sometimes contradictory. For the Berkeley rebels, hard truths began at home. The popularity of Reagan's antistudent rhetoric in the 1966 elections in California cruelly exposed their shortcomings. More than this, they presaged the doom of the Democrats locally and nationally and, in projecting Reagan onto the political scene, warned the Republicans that they would have to field a conservative, pro-order, prowar candidate in the 1968 presidential election.

The war was, by mid-1966, a source of division and weakness for California's Democrats. Antiwar feeling existed even in the more conservative southern part of the state—the mayor of Los Angeles, Sam Yorty, had counseled against escalation as early as January 1964. Yorty and other leading Democrats, like State Controller Alan Cranston, held their fire out of loyalty to the Democratic administration. So did Governor Pat Brown. When he ran for reelection in 1966 against the hawkish Reagan, he refused to come out against the war in spite of having formerly been a supporter of Berkeley's young radicals.[82] But his silence could not disguise a deep rift in the Democratic ranks. One person who commented on this was Frederick Dutton, a lawyer and World War II veteran who had been a senior figure in the 1960 and 1964 Kennedy and Johnson election campaigns. Dutton warned the White House press secretary Bill Moyers that the Democrats were "increasingly disunited in California." Vietnam was "a fierce symbol and ulcer eating away at local level support for moderate Democrats like Brown and the President. The strength of feeling over it, both ways, overrides any public issue or political tie in the state at the present."[83]

Student activism over the war damaged the Democrats. To be sure, antiwar students set out with the best of intentions. In principle, student participation in local political agitation was a means of achieving two objectives: education and the creation of those political preconditions necessary to congressional insistence upon withdrawal from Vietnam. One politician who offered a tactical opportunity of the kind appreciated by antiwar students was Edward M. Keating. Editor in chief of *Ramparts*, Keating was in 1966 a candidate in the Democratic congressional primaries for San Mateo County, Republican territory consisting of San Francisco's southern suburbs. His campaign literature reflected the students' tactic of stressing local issues to generate interest in foreign policy. His propaganda issues were listed under the headings "San Mateo County," "Foreign Policy," and "National," in that order. He recommended "de-escalation of the war, not unilateral withdrawal." He described as "hopeless" the third-party plans then being discussed within the student and labor movements. Inflation and the collapse of the Great Society program occasioned by military spending would ultimately undermine support for the Vietnam War; in the meantime, "we must do whatever can be done within the parties." Questioned by a *Redwood City Tribune* journalist, Keating, a disorganized candidate who failed in his primary bid, said that he regarded his campaign as educational. From President Johnson's viewpoint, its results were not so much educational as politically divisive. As for the antiwar students who supported Keating, they were damaging one enemy, the Democratic administration, only at the cost of strengthening another, the Republican hawks.[84]

The Republicans had another, more personal factor operating in their favor in their bid to combat the Democrats in a key electoral state. Reagan was good-looking, charismatic, a gifted communicator. He was a candidate who could appeal both to the right and—as a former leader of the Hollywood labor union the Screen Actors' Guild—to workers who might otherwise stay with the labor-Democratic coalition. The riots in the Watts district of Los Angeles in August 1965 and March 1966 (the latter was the first of forty-three race riots across the nation that year) played strongly into the hands of a law-and-order candidate like Reagan. But so did the student protest movement, especially in its more anarchic aspects, which lent themselves to purple passages in the press about promiscuity and drug taking. Reagan kept files on activists like Bettina Aptheker. In correspondence he denounced the soft line of the Berkeley administration toward student dissent. In public he declaimed: "The preservation of free speech does not justify letting beatniks, and advocates of sexual orgies, drug usage and filthy speech disrupt the academic community and interfere with our universities' purpose."[85]

Reagan was categorical in his denunciation of the Berkeley students' opposition to the war: "When some Americans are fighting and dying for their country, free speech must stop short of lending comfort and aid to the enemy." In the election year of

1966, newspapers like the *San Francisco Examiner* helped Reagan's cause by giving extensive coverage to the communism-on-campus issue.[86] Reagan's friends and opponents agreed that the Berkeley issue provided the turning point in his political career and helped the former movie actor to win the gubernatorial election in 1966.[87]

Both student protest and Reagan's exploitation of it had an impact on the Democrats. To ignore the growing protest was impossible. A contemporary analyst, Jerome Skolnick, noted that "the size of demonstrations varies directly with the popular opposition to the war during the period 1965 to 1968."[88] But which affected which? Politicians could not ignore the possibility that the demonstrators were winning over opinion.

The student protesters had some impact in Washington, even if legislators continued to support the war until the 1970s. Senator Fulbright's Foreign Affairs Committee hearings on the war between January 28 and February 18, 1966, are a case in point. Fulbright was no hero of the student left. Nevertheless, on a speaking tour a little later, the Arkansas Democrat praised the "courage, decency, and patriotism" of the protest movement of students, professors, clergy, and others. In April and May he chose an academic audience—the occasion was the Christian A. Herter Lectures at the Johns Hopkins University in Baltimore—to deliver his famous thesis that the war could be blamed on the "arrogance of power" affecting the judgment of the mandarins in Washington.[89]

The superimposition of Reagan's triumphal rise on the apparent success of the protesters worsened the Democrats' disarray. In the summer of 1967, Joseph Rauh tried to address the problem of how to satisfy the peace lobby while securing the reelection of a Democratic president. A former New Dealer and chair of Americans for Democratic Action and now a Washington lawyer active in the civil rights cause, Rauh was a respected liberal strategist. He rejected the "Dump Johnson" movement that was gaining ground as the presidential primaries approached, proposing instead the organization of a "Peace Democrats" caucus in time for the Democratic convention the following year. But Cranston and a member of the Democratic National Committee, Eugene Wyman of Beverly Hills, were lukewarm, feeling that even this move would be divisive in California. There was no way out of the impasse, no way to prevent the widening of the rift in the Democratic Party.[90]

The Johnson administration responded in four ways to the dual challenge of student protest and Reagan's exploitation of it. The administration tried to win the war outright, to remove the moral sting from student discontent by reforming the draft, to discredit student protest, and, finally, to de-Americanize the war. Let us begin with the first. The administration's most hoped-for response to Reagan was to win a politically preemptive victory, thus clipping the wings of the right-wing superhawks. The pressing political need to achieve this goal blinded the policymakers to what cooler analysts were already saying, that the war was not winnable. In this roundabout and indirect sense, the students, by giving Reagan a drum to beat, unintentionally contributed to the blinkered escalation of hostilities.

The second way in which the Johnson administration responded to student protest was to introduce draft reform in a manner that made it appear sensitive to the inequities of which the student radicals were complaining, yet firm in the face of draft resistance. Reform had been in the air since the Kennedy administration, and in 1966, President Johnson had established the National Advisory Commission on Selective Service. He appointed a further task force in March 1967, after Reagan's election. It defended the current system, but in the summer General Hershey began to clarify and change draft deferment provisions. All undergraduate students would be entitled to draft deferment, but deferments for graduate students would disappear, with the exception of certain categories, like health professionals, that were deemed "critical" by the National Security Council, the president's advisory committee. In a further move a few days after the October demonstration at the Pentagon, Hershey tried to show that he was firm and evenhanded: he directed local draft boards to abolish deferments for draft resisters.[91]

The political results of these changes were unsatisfactory from the standpoint of the administration. The perceived victimization of draft resisters ensured the continuation of principled opposition, while the removal of the graduate-school escape hatch made the war unpopular among large numbers of students who might otherwise have been apathetic. But the motives behind the reforms are also of interest, for they reveal the ways antiwar activity was affecting government thinking. On the one hand, the reforms were designed to answer the complaints of the idealistic minority who objected to their own privileges. On the other hand, the draft modifications were an effort to silence the troublesome minority by intimidating, punishing, and deterring draft resisters. It was perhaps hoped that, thus pilloried, the resisters would become objects of derision to the American majority.

The administration's resort to the security services is further evidence of the seriousness with which it took student protest—and the Republican challenge. Reagan, in his 1966 gubernatorial campaign, had promised to appoint John McCone, former head of the CIA, to conduct an investigation into student unrest.[92] In the same vein, the White House began to collect intelligence on the protesters.

The task confronting intelligence gatherers had always been complex and was becoming impossible. The White House staffer Dick Moose revealed the heterogeneity of the protesters in describing a delegation from the Spring Mobilization Committee whom the president refused to see in May 1967: "A member of the group, who introduced himself as a professor, . . . presented a well-balanced slate of 3-minute speakers, leading off with a representative of the Women's Strike for Peace, followed by a long-haired blonde, an American Indian (who invoked Indian treaty rights), a draft-age youth 'representing half-a-million students,' a female journalist, who has visited North Vietnam, a Negro Vietnam veteran, a labor representative ('Local 65'), an aged Negro farm worker from Mississippi (carrying a bundle of cotton and a rambling complaint about cotton allegedly taken from him), another potential draft evader, and a goateed Washington Negro interested in D.C. home rule."[93]

But where a more detached person might have seen complexity, the president saw a problem that would resolve itself by application of a simple formula. In August 1967, Johnson authorized the setting up of a special operations group within the CIA with the object of determining the degree to which the protest movement was part of an international conspiracy run by Soviet, Chinese, and Cuban Communists. Fifty-two CIA employees took part in Operation CHAOS, and they compiled files on 7,200 U.S. citizens. By the fall, Army intelligence and the FBI had joined in the effort to find out about and discredit the plans of the Mobe organizers—few details of the Pentagon demonstration were not known to the administration in advance.

The results were disappointing to the president. In November the CIA director, Richard Helms, reported that in spite of having access to FBI files as well as his own, he found himself "woefully short of information on the day-to-day activities and itineraries" of the peace campaigners, who were "highly mobile and sometimes difficult even to identify." He concluded, however, that there was no evidence of external sponsorship and enclosed a report on Hayden and the other main antiwar leaders in which, in describing them as "tireless, peripatetic, full time crusaders," he implied that they were self-motivated.[94]

It is a measure of the administration's obsession with antiwar protest that, regardless of the paucity of evidence and even after the Tet offensive of January–February 1968 had pricked the illusion of impending U.S. victory, Johnson continued to authorize the investigation and harassment of domestic protest groups. In the wake of the Columbia University occupation, the FBI launched its COINTELPRO, or investigation-with-dirty-tricks, against what it termed the "New Left." The program was unfocused, for Hoover's men still did not know whom, exactly, they were up against, but its operatives did apply on campuses some of the techniques honed in earlier COINTELPROs against the Communist Party of the United States of America, white hate groups like the Ku Klux Klan, and black nationalists. For example, the FBI collected information with a view to discrediting a few dozen student leaders in Antioch College, Ohio, who had been active in the antiwar campaign. Hoover authorized the local FBI to leak information to the *Cincinnati Inquirer* purporting to show that the protesters were harming the academic prospects of Antioch students; the FBI then arranged for the clippings to be sent to worried parents, who, it was hoped, would persuade the college authorities to keep the radicals in line.[95]

President Johnson's final response to student protest came in the aftermath of the Tet offensive. The American armed forces launched a crippling counteroffensive after that surprise attack, inflicting heavy losses on the Vietnamese Communists in February 1968. The vigor of the communist assault, however, shook the president. Evidently, U.S. strategy was not working as well as Johnson's military advisers pretended. When General William C. Westmoreland, commander of the American forces in Vietnam, asked for a further 206,000 troops, there was a fierce debate within the administration. The "Wise Men," senior policy advisers, who had previously supported the war, met with Johnson on March 25 and advised him to disengage. The president said no to Westmoreland's request. The process known as de-Americanization began. On March 31, in a nationally televised address, President Johnson announced a bombing pause and a new peace initiative and said that he would not be running for reelection. To say that the protesting students were responsible for all this would be a distortion, but they had stimulated his paranoid fears of dissent and in this way had an effect on policy out of proportion to their numbers and actual power.

For a fleeting moment, the protesting students could imagine having won a remarkable victory that would slow the draft and end the war. But hostilities dragged on, Johnson and Hoover continued to bear down on campus radicals, and it soon became clear that the protesters had nowhere to go politically. To be sure, the political strategist Allard Lowenstein had organized a "reform from within" movement among the Democrats, inspiring support from student activists. For a short time, antiwar students had a champion in the Democratic primary candidate Senator Eugene McCarthy. Students swung into action in their thousands in the New Hampshire primary. They shaved their beards to be Neat and Clean for Gene and were the harbingers of a new move toward "legitimacy" in student antiwar campaigning, but in 1968 they were doomed to disappointment. The vagaries of the voters put

McCarthy out of the running. Then, Senator Robert F. Kennedy fell to an assassin's bullet just when he seemed to offer hope of a rather more potent antiwar candidacy. In the end, the Democrats ran Vice President Hubert Humphrey for president. Lowenstein rallied to his cause, but Humphrey went down to defeat in a campaign weakened by the administration's failings.[96]

Long before this, backlash politics had come to town. A phenomenon that owed much to reactions against student protest, it more than counteracted the achievements of the peace crusaders. Both the Columbia and the Chicago demonstrations met with physically vigorous police responses, and students were prosecuted. Notably, the trial of the Chicago Eight—Tom Hayden and seven other "conspirators" allegedly behind the violent antiwar protest—became a cause célèbre. Newspapers and television conveyed images of working-class policemen attempting to discipline middle-class students. Mayor Richard Daley of Chicago, who had ordered the police in, received 100,000 letters on the riot of which 95 percent favored his tough stand. Here, plainly, was an issue ready for exploitation by conservatives and by prowar politicians.[97]

Daley was a Democratic mayor "defending" a Democratic convention. But the war-related law-and-order issue was custom-made for Republicans. Richard Nixon was aware that it could also be used *within* the Republican Party, and he took care to outflank Reagan as the candidate who could be seen as tough on students. Strongly challenged by the Californian in the crucial New York Republican primary, Nixon called for the expulsion from Columbia University of "the anarchic students" whose goal was to "seize the universities of this country" and foment a revolution.[98] When Nixon won the election, antiwar students seemed to have lost the chance of having a sympathetic hearing in the White House and even the prospect of assured de-escalation of the war.

Yet Nixon was a politician. He knew the antiwar protesters were in the minority, but he was aware that minorities can grow and that majorities can be made up of coalitions of minorities. As one of the few presidents to have come from a genuinely poor background, he was also capable of appreciating the antiestablishment mindset. He took the younger generation seriously. Like the architects of the Reform Act of 1832 in Britain, he hoped that by extending the vote (in this case, to eighteen-year-olds), he would win the loyalty of its grateful recipients. More immediately for the purpose of winning the Republican nomination and the ensuing election, Nixon endorsed the de-Americanization of the war even as he made belligerent and patriotic noises to deflate the Reaganite right. He could thus represent himself as a peaceful man on the stump.

On accepting the Republican nomination on August 3, 1968, Nixon demonstrated his flexibility. He outlined his Vietnam policy to the platform committee: the South Vietnamese were to be equipped and trained to fight for themselves, and American troops would be "phased out."[99] Then, in a radio broadcast on October 16, 1968, the Republican candidate appealed to youth, advocating the vote at eighteen, a greater student voice in campus government, and a volunteer army upon the passing of the Vietnam crisis. Later in the campaign, the journalist Robert B. Semple, Jr., advanced a "Two Nixons" hypothesis, to wit, that Nixon in this radio mode was a different person from Nixon on the campaign trail. At any rate, de-Americanization was now definitely a bipartisan policy.[100] Thus student protesters (along with others) could claim to have influenced both political parties. For the more idealistic students, however, the victory was of the wrong sort. It would permit the war to continue by other means and would irrigate the myth that a silent majority supported a military solution.

The third and last phase of student protest against the Vietnam war (1969–1972) was in some ways a depressing one for those involved. The student movement, never less than heterogeneous, fragmented even further. The SDS impaled itself on the sword of Marxist sectarianism. Other students gravitated to a variety of causes, leading to dissipated effort and diluted impact in the antiwar crusade. On the other hand, with de-Americanization the draft issue diminished in importance, and this left the field clear for the return of the idealists, with their power to inspire and to command respect. Another promising development from the viewpoint of the protesters was the recourse of some students to the politics of legitimacy, with an emphasis on achieving peace goals through the established legislative process.

Student opponents of the war thus kept the pot simmering, if not constantly on the boil, and there were some sensational incidents to remind America of the discontent of its youth. Yet in historical significance, all this is overshadowed by the politics of the silent majority. Far more important than student protest was the *issue* of student protest or—to use the language of the conservatives—student disorder. The idea of rallying majority opinion against a pilloried minority was by no means new in American political history, and it had already been toyed with in connection with the Vietnam war. But the articulation, adoption, and propagation of the notion of the silent majority as a slogan and as a populist philosophy occurred in the first two years of the Nixon administration. Protesting students played an objectivized role in the politics of the period. In spite of their active protests, their main significance came through their passive role as an object observed, vilified, and manipulated for political ends. It is chiefly from this perspective that the story of the years 1969–1972 needs to be examined.

The Nixon policy was, however, by no means entirely a matter of student bashing. He complemented his policy of attacking the minority within the minority, the students blamed for civil disturbances, by appealing to the majority within the minority, students presumed to be potential supporters of the war. To popularize this appeal, Nixon consolidated Johnson's program of reducing students' liability to military service in Vietnam. In principle, class and racial bias had been removed from the selective service system. In practice, the reform was on paper only, and the change spared the lives of middle-class youth. Why? Because the democratization of military service was accompanied by a reduction in the need for it. In June 1969, Nixon announced the first troop reductions—25,000 of the 550,000 in Vietnam were to be brought home. This eased the pressure for manpower, and the government was able to introduce a draft lottery and move toward greater theoretical democracy in recruitment for the armed services without actually calling up more students who would serve in Vietnam.[101]

Here, domestic political priorities were not the only influences on presidential policy. In times of war, the White House operates within a framework of unyielding military constraints. De-Americanization reflected, in part, a change from one military doctrine to another. American troops had not won the war, so there seemed to be a case for equipping the South Vietnamese to see if they could finish the job. This also met the objection that the South Vietnamese were becoming too dependent on America for their own good. De-Americanization represented as well a return to counterinsurgency doctrine, the idea that it was vital to win the hearts and minds of indigenous peoples in the war against communism. Rather than bombing indiscriminately and using such inhumane weapons as napalm, it would be better to win trust and to trust the local people in turn. Some of these assumptions were inherent in the president's enunciation of the "Nixon Doctrine" in July 25, 1969; he called for self-sufficiency and less American commitment in East Asia as a whole, not just in Vietnam.[102]

While the politicians talked in public of grand strategy, they privately entertained motives to which they were loath to admit. In the early months of the Nixon administration, Secretary of State William Rogers and Secretary of Defense Melvin Laird were chiefly responsible for pushing Nixon and his national security adviser, Henry Kissinger, to implement de-Americanization. It was not just that Laird's son and niece had been ideologically child-stolen by the campus antiwar movement; even his mother came out against the war. The defense secretary coined the word *Vietnamization* to replace *de-Americanization*, implying a positive strategy rather than a flight before family pressures or public opinion, but, like Rogers, he was deeply concerned about the ebbing of support for the war at home; interviewed in August 1969, he showed himself to be acutely concerned about what might happen on the campuses that fall.[103]

Laird was justified in his apprehension. In the fall of 1969, there began a series of "moratorium" protests against the war.

Unlike earlier mass demonstrations, which concentrated in two or three major cities, these took place all over the United States. On November 15, New Mobe organized spectacular demonstrations in Washington and San Francisco. Hundreds of thousands participated. One historian puts the total attendance at "millions," and another describes the combined demonstrations as "the most potent and widespread antiwar protests ever mounted in a western democracy."[104]

These demonstrations were not exclusively or even predominantly student affairs, which may have helped them to achieve their goal of making a point with dignity and responsibility. The restrained tone of the demonstrations may have encouraged the president to make his definitive, televised Silent Majority broadcast on November 3, 1969, in which he appealed to "the great silent majority of my fellow-Americans" to support the war as a means to securing a proper peace. Perhaps he recognized a threat to his control of the middle ground in American politics. Challenging him from the conservative side of the political spectrum in a speech in San Francisco on June 13, Governor Reagan had appealed to "the great silent majority" to rally with him against "a tiny minority" of faculty and students who sought to disrupt the even tenor of American life.

Nixon's memoirs reflect his alarm that the moratorium of October 15 had attracted 250,000 protesters to Washington. With the new decorum the antiwar movement potentially appealed to an even wider audience. Unwilling as ever to admit to being influenced by demonstrations, Nixon said that his aim in making the broadcast was to demonstrate to Hanoi that Vietnamese Communists could not fish "in our troubled domestic waters." Later, he described the speech as one of the "very few" to have actually influenced "the course of history." It is perfectly true that the Silent Majority broadcast was an important policy statement, if not for the reason Nixon stated. Intentionally or otherwise, it inaugurated an effective foreign-policy strategy.[105]

Although students in the Nixon years were more important as the objects of political rhetoric than as active agents of political change, their activities remain significant. After all, the administration's imprecations would have lacked credibility had there not been some evidence of fire beneath the smoke. Student protest remained formidable, especially to those who would crush it, because it remained so changeable, various, and impermeable to the efforts of hostile intelligence gatherers.

In 1969 the antiwar movement presented the administration with a moving target. In April the Harvard SDS demanded the abolition of the Reserve Officer Training Corps (ROTC), an oblique reference to the war, but it also raised other issues, such as the need for a black studies program on campus. There was similar movement and diversification of demands at Berkeley, the University of Chicago, and the City College of New York.[106] In 1969 the Urban Research Corporation of Chicago surveyed 232 campuses and found that the draft was the major issue in less than 1 percent of protests. Whereas antimilitarism was a main issue in 25 percent of cases, two other issues counted for more: racial issues, at 59 percent, and student power, at 42 percent.[107] There were also efforts to bridge the campus-community gap. The *Berkeley Barb*, for example, supported resistance to the attempt of public authorities to appropriate a local park for commercial development—counter-appropriated by the students, it became the "people's park." This protest, like others of the period, shifted to encompass the issue of police brutality. Other issues ephemerally boosted in Berkeley included injustices to Chicanos, Indians, and African Americans and the institution of courses in Afro-American studies.[108] These various issues were connected to the war by a number of threads. For example, an arrested student who was put on probation would be ineligible for the draft while on probation, regardless of the issue he had been protesting while committing the alleged offense; in this way, a challenge to authority over, say, Black Studies programs might also imply opposition to the war. Yet it is clear that the diversity of new issues had, in the eyes of many student journalists, achieved a significance of its own.

In June the SDS met in national convention in Chicago, but the meeting was its swan song, thus removing one of the FBI's more identifiable targets. With the demise of the SDS, there was no shortage of other focal points for opposition to the war. Sam

Brown, a leading light in the moratorium campaign, came from the Young Republicans, the NSA, and the Gene McCarthy campaign team and received financial support from the Boston envelope manufacturer Jerome Grossman. The New Mobe committee consisted of a "cross section of independent leftists, radical pacifists, Trotskyists and various liberals." These circumstances puzzled and confused the older men in charge of the nation and its intelligence services and ensured that they would continue to be troubled.[109]

While extremism and experimentalism tinged some sections of the student movement in 1969, the peace movement itself reverted to a more idealistic hue. With the draft threat receding, antiwar students could no longer be thought of as merely out to save their own skins. The military-industrial-university complexes came under renewed attack. The initiative lay with faculty at MIT, where forty-eight professors signed a manifesto against the militarization of American science, eliciting praise from the *New Republic* for having "the courage to bite the hand that has been feeding them."[110] In Stanford, students tried in May 1969 to disrupt production in the Industrial Park, a major research, development, and production center for Vietnam weaponry. The innocuous-sounding Food Machinery and Chemical Corporation undertook research on antipersonnel fragmentation bombs, and GTE Sylvania produced unattended sensors for deployment along the Ho Chi Minh Trail. Stanford University itself received many millions of dollars in weapons research contracts; one of its trustees, David Packard, had a stake in Hewlett-Packard, a local firm of defense contractors; he was also U.S. undersecretary for defense. It took an extra 150 policemen from San Jose to bring the students under control when they invaded the park in 1969. Three years later, protesters were still compiling information on the alleged malpractices of thirteen major primary contractors selling from the park to the Defense Department.[111]

The white, old, rich men were thus morally challenged. The Nixon administration had a further, parallel problem: when it tried to represent itself as the party of law and order, it had to contend with the public image of the authorities' propensity to use violence against protesters. In May 1970, when students protested nationwide against the extension of the war to Cambodia, National Guardsmen shot four of them dead at Kent State University in Ohio. Two more students died at the hands of the police at Jackson State College, Mississippi. These events provoked student demonstrations across the nation and cast doubt on the proposition that the authorities were reliable purveyors of peace and quiet.

A complementary worry, from the viewpoint of the government scaremongers, was the growth on campus of legitimate protest. According to White House figures, violent campus "incidents" declined from 425 in 1968 to 245 the following year and dropped to 195 in 1970.[112] This was good news in one way, but it also threw into embarrassing relief the overreactive conduct of some local authorities, for it became increasingly evident that students no longer insisted on direct action to the exclusion of parliamentary activity, and politicians, for their part, were beginning to join the antiwar movement. The White House aide Bud Krogh estimated that 25 senators and 52 House members attended moratorium demonstrations in the fall of 1969 and spring of 1970.[113]

Law Students Against the War pledged to work "within the traditional political process." It favored the Hatfield-McGovern amendment cutting off funds for further Vietnam and Cambodian "escapades," and to this end lobbied Secretary of State Rogers, Attorney General Mitchell, and National Security Adviser Kissinger and interviewed 86 senators and 113 representatives. In preparation for the 1970 midterm elections, it took a leaf out of organized labor's book on traditional lobbying tactics and compiled a "friends and enemies" list of candidates in every state to enable students to support doves and oppose hawks in an informed manner. This lobby was small but well organized. Against the background of increasing activities of this kind, the White House had to outlegitimize the legitimists.[114]

However, the case for making scapegoats of campus protesters was bolstered by some convincing evidence to show how little would be lost by taking a tough stand, for public opinion had turned against students. Bills against campus extremism were introduced in forty state legislatures in 1969 and 1970, the strongest of them in states that had experienced major demonstrations: New York, Wisconsin, Ohio, and California.[115] In California, Governor Reagan shut down all twenty-eight campuses of the state college and university systems for four days following the Kent State tragedy and local student strikes. Elsewhere, governors made similar political calculations: they sent the National Guard into campuses in Kentucky, South Carolina, Illinois, and Wisconsin even though, in the later verdict of the President's Commission on Campus Unrest, students "on campus after campus" had sought "politically viable alternatives to violent action."[116] Gallup indicated in June 1970 that 82 percent of a sample of Americans polled disapproved of "college students going on strike as a way to protest the way things are run in this country."[117] The president calculated that he could usefully appeal to the antistudent sentiments thus reflected: "When students on university campuses burn buildings, when they engage in violence, when they break up furniture, when they terrorize their fellow students and terrorize the faculty, then I think 'bums' is perhaps too kind a word to apply to that kind of person."[118]

This kind of rhetoric was potentially dangerous in that it could alienate not just the minority of student activists but most students. White House evaluations of campus opinion suggested, however, that little would be lost by attacking students, because they were against Nixon anyway. A group of White House interns who surveyed their nationwide contacts claimed in April 1970 that the campuses were moving against the president: the eastern "liberal" campuses were experiencing "profoundly pervasive anti-war, anti-establishment currents" and were "nearly completely gone" as prospective sources of Republican support. In California, "Reagan no longer goes to campuses," and the West was if anything surpassing the East in its hostility; only in the Middle West and the South did the "apathetic moderates" give the administration an edge, and that seemed likely to disappear. A year later, the president read an assessment of the "18–20 year old vote" in which his political adviser listed the draft and the war as the issues of major concern and said that "young people feel that we have rejected their generation."[119]

There was also some evidence that the student fashion for legitimacy might not pose a real political threat. A national campus referendum in April 1970 produced a 43,000 to 25,000 vote in favor of the immediate withdrawal of U.S. troops from Vietnam. But poll data on youthful attitudes as a whole showed opinion to be more evenly divided between proponents of withdrawal and escalation. The White House aide and former Californian cosmetics executive Jeb Magruder took heart from the fact that the campus referendum represented "less than 2% of the college student population of the United States."[120]

Some students, depressed by their failure to stop the war, showed signs of apathy as the 1970 midterm elections approached, and a few joined the conservative cause. According to Harvard's *Crimson*, "What used to be frustration is now just total desolation. The great majority just don't see anything they can do that can have any effect. They'd rather do nothing." Campus opinion polls showed that a small and declining minority of students intended to campaign for candidates of their choice in the midterms. White House Chief of Staff Bob Haldeman did his best to ensure that they would be on Nixon's side. In the spring he mobilized the right-wing Young Americans for Freedom (YAF) to counter antiwar, anti-administration activities. With White House help the YAF distributed 400,000 pieces of literature and sponsored pro-Nixon students to speak on campuses, radio programs, and television; in April one of its officers claimed to have "defused" the Vietnam issue. On the eve of the election the *New York Times* detected only a few flickers of life in the campus debate on Vietnam, and these vital signs emanated not from protesters but from students supporting the right-wing, prowar senatorial candidates James L. Buckley (N.Y.) and George Murphy (Calif.).[121]

Perhaps the nation's students were not after all a lost cause, and most hawks were careful to distinguish between the militant minority and the students who supported the war. But in 1970 as in 1968, the public opinion backlash against students in revolt made the politics of intransigence more attractive than the politics of propitiation, and the Nixon administration took a tough line. The intelligence services continued their work against the student protest movement.[122] In June 1970, when Nixon established the President's Commission on Campus Unrest, he charged it with "identifying the principal causes of campus violence" and protecting "academic freedom."[123] He meant the violence of students and the freedom of conservatives to state their views on campus, not police brutality and student free speech.

Reagan maintained his profile as a potential presidential candidate who would be congenial to hawks, a circumstance that Nixon was unable to ignore. Unconstrained by any sense of evidential responsibility, the California governor claimed that student demonstrations were unpatriotic and directed by supporters of the Viet Cong or by politicians behind the Iron Curtain.[124] Nixon waited impatiently for the evidence to come in on such allegations but in the meantime felt obliged to exploit student protest to the full in the 1970 midterm elections, a move that protected his right flank. In California he wished to neutralize Reagan, but he also wanted the reelection of the governor because the Republicans would need to carry the state in the presidential election of 1972. He tried to achieve both ends by making a visible contribution to Reagan's reelection and, a more challenging task, attempting to prevent, if possible, the defeat of Republican Senator George Murphy. In a speech broadcast over the three national television networks after students had allegedly thrown a rock at the presidential limousine in San Jose, Nixon attacked the violent approach to politics that, he said, had been all too prevalent over the past decade. He stated that the Congress should appropriate more money to the police effort, and he told students to "hit the books or hit the road."[125]

The election results of 1970 were uninspiring for the Republicans. Murphy went down to a resounding defeat at the hands of John V. Tunney. Governor Reagan said it was time to "get it over with" and to silence the demonstrators, even if "it takes a bloodbath."[126] But his gubernatorial challenger Jesse M. Unruh gave low priority to the problem of student violence and halved the incumbent's majority. Although the Republicans had taken control of the Californian state legislature in 1968, they lost both houses in 1970 and with them the right to reapportion the legislative and congressional lines in the state. Outside California the Democrats captured several governorships from the Republicans. Even allowing for midterm anti-administration swings, a wily politician like Nixon could find justification for a new policy emphasis if he wanted to.[127]

To some extent, he did find justification. The White House was aware that the problem of student disenchantment with the administration would "become more significant politically with the passage of the 18 year old vote" in time for the next presidential election, in 1972.[128] The following year, Nixon asked his staff to start presenting him as a president who stood for youth and change, possibly using the forthcoming White House Conference on Youth for that purpose.[129] He wanted more opportunities to meet those "who support us in Vietnam" and fewer confrontations with opponents of the war. Yet, in spite of expressing strong feelings on this point (according to his aide Bob Finch), the president played a restrained hand.[130] He had shown an awareness that public opinion is divided into constituent parts, and knew that students composed one of them. He toned down his antiyouth rhetoric once Reagan and student radicalism seemed to be receding as threats.

In the 1972 campaign it was prudent for Nixon to avoid alienating students, because his Democratic opponent George McGovern was appealing to them. McGovern made a specific plea to youth in a primary campaign speech at Hunter College, New York, and continued in the same vein into the later stages of his presidential campaign. The chosen forum for his address attacking "the immorality of the war" on October 11, 1972, was Wheaton Methodist College, Illinois.[131] By this time, Nixon's antistudent rhetoric had served its purpose. Not only had Reagan been dispatched, but also, as will be demonstrated in Chapter 6, Nixon had used the specter of student protest to whip up anti intellectualism and recruit a significant portion of organized labor. The labor defection had dealt such a blow to the Democrats that Nixon no longer needed to attack students but could appeal to them instead.

Student rebellion against the Vietnam War came from a group with a penchant for direct action uninhibited by any tradition of compromise in the interest of collective status promotion. The students shocked the nation in 1965 by puncturing the American Dream at its most iridescent point, California—which happened also to be a key state logistically and politically, being at the eastern end of the Vietnam Run and holding a large chunk of votes in the electoral college.

While shocking the nation in this manner was an achievement, the student movement against the Vietnam War suffered from several weaknesses. The greatest of these did not inhere in the movement itself. Rather, the movement became a passive vehicle for the politics of the silent majority. This was the dominant political feature of the student movement by 1970, and, under the guidance of President Nixon,the silent majority tactic had far-reaching consequences.

Although the student campaign against the draft contributed significantly to the Vietnamization decision, the force of its impact should be gauged with caution. First, Vietnamization was not a step toward peace or even, at first, toward American withdrawal, for American bombing and fighting continued to the end of 1972. Second, although student agitation was a cause of Vietnamization, it was not the only cause. Setbacks in conventional warfare in Vietnam suggested a pressing need for the adoption of a new doctrine, and domestically, the students were by 1967 no longer alone in agitating for draft reform. They first shared and then yielded the limelight to Americans of African descent.

The Old Liberal Alliance—Walter Reuther, president of the United Automobile Workers, is to the left of President Johnson, and Clark Kerr, president of the University of California, Berkeley, is to Johnson's right. By the time this photograph was taken in November 1968, Johnson and Kerr had resigned their respective presidencies. Both were casualties of the fracturing effects of the Vietnam War. (Yoichi A. Okamoto, LBJ Library Collection.)

Warriors Together—George Meany, president of the AFL-CIO, gave his unstinting support to Johnson's war. (Frank Wolfe, LBJ Library Collection.)

The Loyal Opposition—Margaret Chase Smith, Republican minority leader on the Senate Armed Services Committee, thought the war was a mistake but, out of loyalty to the commander in chief and the fighting men, gave it her solid support. (Yoichi A. Okamoto, LBJ Library Collection.)

Loyalty at a Price—When this photograph was taken in March 1966, the civil rights leader Martin Luther King, Jr., was still struggling to remain loyal to the president despite his deep moral objections to the war. (Yoichi A. Okamoto, LBJ Library Collection.)

March on the Pentagon— Norman Mailer noted the shortage of African Americans in this demonstration of October 21, 1967, but they were not entirely absent. (Frank Wolfe, LBJ Library Collection.)

Women Against the War— These and other women on the Pentagon march of 1967 heralded a political breakthrough for their sex and contributed to the ending of American participation in the Vietnam War. (Frank Wolfe, LBJ Library Collection.)

Eartha Kitt at the White House—The singer has just attacked the president's social policies and is about to denounce the Vietnam War. Lady Bird Johnson is at the far left. (LBJ Library Collection.)

The Few or the Many?—This demonstration of support took place on February 6, 1968, in the immediate wake of the Tet offensive. The Silent Majority slogan, coined before the Nixon administration took it up, was ingenious. It indicated that the majority of Americans supported the war but rarely attended demonstrations. So less meant more. (Jack Kightlinger, LBJ Library Collection.)

The Hard-Hat Reception—After the hard-hat demonstration in favor of the war in Manhattan in 1970, Nixon invited its organizers to Washington, and the White House photographer took some staged photographs. Presenting the hat to the president is Peter J. Brennan, president of the Building and Construction Trades Council of Greater New York and New York State (BCTCNY), who became Nixon's secretary of labor. To his right in the front row are Thomas Gleason, president of the International Longshoremen's Association; Thomas Tobin, secretary-treasurer of the BCTCNY; an unidentified African American (perhaps included to soften the unprogressive image of the white labor leaders); and George Daly, representing the Steamfitters Union, Local 638. In the photograph but unidentified is Michael Donovan of the Bricklayers Union, Local 3, whose son had been killed in action. (Ollie Atkins, Nixon Presidential Materials Project.)

The New Majority—Nixon wanted to win an election as well as a war, so he was greatly taken by this particular hard hat worn during the New York demonstration, because it indicated support for a Republican president from a normally Democratic quarter: organized labor. The president kept the hat after it had been presented by the man who wore it, George Daly. Also in the frame are Brennan and, wearing spectacles, Charles Johnson, Jr., vice president of the BCTCNY. Chuck Colson identified Johnson, Brennan, Gleason, and Tobin as the "prime movers" in the hard-hat parade. (Ollie Atkins, Nixon Presidential Materials Project.)

4 African Americans

On April 28, 1967, Muhammad Ali attended the Houston, Texas, induction center. The lieutenant on duty told him to step forward to be admitted into the armed forces of the United States. But Ali did not move. "Who is this white man, . . . to order a descendant of slaves to fight other people in their own country?" When he remembered that fateful day, another incident, too, stood out in Ali's mind. As he departed, an old white woman whose son was serving in Vietnam accosted him: "I hope you rot in jail. I hope they throw away the key." [1] Before the day was out, Ali was stripped of his world heavyweight boxing championship and barred from fighting professionally in the United States. Official retribution did not stop there: he was sentenced to five years in prison, a punishment that hung over him until 1971, when the Supreme Court reversed his conviction.

Ali's account illustrates two aspects of the African Americans' revolt against the Vietnam War. One is the drama and shock of that rebellion. Just three weeks earlier, Dr. Martin Luther King, Jr., had condemned the war, shattering the racial consensus upon which rested the edifice of Democratic liberal politics. Now Ali, the witty and poetic idol of sports fans throughout the world, had refused to serve. The African American revolt made it seem—in the words of the Vietnam veteran Ron Armstead—that black people were acting "out of character." [2] Two years after rebellious students in Berkeley had administered a slap to the complacent face of the political establishment, the African American had landed an equally discomfiting blow that ensured the sting would not fade.

The heavyweight champion's account throws light on a second aspect of the African American revolt: the reaction that it engendered. The woman's reaction was characteristic of the silent majority upon whom Richard Nixon was to base his political strategy. Other key phrases in his team's electoral approach were "law and order" and "Southern strategy"; the intention was to target radical blacks as a focus for white resentment, pulling in votes for the Republicans in the process.

If the African American revolt against the war resembled the student rebellion, there were nevertheless differences. Whereas students fought for the right of Communists to speak on campus, African Americans were disillusioned with the Communist Party in spite of its past campaigns on their behalf.[3] Black radicals fashioned their own ideology in criticizing the Vietnam War, an ideology that borrowed from socialist ideas on the iniquity of imperialism but was more deeply rooted in notions of racial solidarity with Third World nonwhites.

African Americans differed from students, in fact, in being more firmly imbued with a minority mentality. In contrast to students but in common with other groups for whom social breakthrough was important, the African Americans produced spokespersons who saw conformity as the road to elevation. Leaders of the National Association for the Advancement of Colored People (NAACP) and National Urban League (NUL), as well as the only black U.S. senator, Edward Brooke of Massachusetts, were too circumspect to come out firmly against the war. More than this, the majority of African Americans gave the war their wholehearted support, especially in its early stages.

African Americans may be said to have had a triple accelerator effect on the politics of the Vietnam War. In the early stages of the war, they boosted support for a popular war. In 1967 they gave a powerful fillip to the antiwar movement. After that, and here their role was entirely involuntary, they stimulated the tide of reaction that allowed the Nixon administration to prolong the war.

The Vietnam War was deeply objectionable from the African American point of view. Their perspective was complex. The historian Robert W. Mullen has suggested that black protesters against the Vietnam War had three approaches: revolutionary, assimilationist, and separatist.[4] These approaches merit attention, for they help to explain the strength of feeling among African Americans, even as they illuminate the weakening divisiveness of black politics.

Adherents of the revolutionary approach maintained that the white capitalist class in America was oppressing people of color both at home and in the Third World. Exponents of this view included Huey Newton, Bobby Seale, Stokely Carmichael, and

Eldridge Cleaver, who wrote his influential book *Soul on Ice* in prison. Cleaver warned that spineless leaders had sold out the black people of the United States. Black Americans had been tricked into supporting the Vietnam War, but once they had delivered that support, they would soon resume their role as the white man's "longtime punching bag."[5] It would be easy to dismiss Cleaver and his like as extreme and unrepresentative radicals and even criminals. They had a claim, however, to being the tribunes of the dispossessed masses who were responsible for the urban race riots of the mid-1960s. To be sure, the riots could be regarded as exhibitions of lawlessness or as a form of aggression-displacement, absorbing energies that might otherwise have been more constructively devoted to respectable political activity—including a more serious revolt against the Vietnam War. But it is just as plausible to portray the riots as the protorevolutionary actions of an American racial underclass that was disgusted with the war.

Adherents of the assimilationist approach, dominated by King, perceived links between oppression in Selma and oppression in Saigon, but took a Christian view of the brotherhood of man and operated within a multiracial social-reform framework that included white American liberals. Riots were morally unacceptable to King and his supporters, who believed in nonviolence, even if, in practice, urban disorder formed an accidental backdrop that lent comparative respectability to their peaceful black protests.

The advocates of separatism were more sanguine about black riots—to their minds, a justifiable way of resisting white oppression. They emphasized the solidarity of people of color and rejected cooperation with the untrustworthy whites. This attitude extended to the Army: at home, separatists usually opposed the induction of African Americans into the white oppressors' armed forces; once inside the military, the same sentiment led black soldiers to agitate for black rights, recognition of black identity, and, in some cases, rebellion against the war. Separatists like Malcolm X shared with the revolutionaries and the assimilationists the belief that people of color both at home and in Vietnam should unite in brotherly resistance to the white "agents of imperialism."[6]

Mullen, in assessing protesters' views, singles out three causes of the black revolt against the war. One was a fear of genocide being practiced by white Americans against African Americans. It may seem surprising that Mullen singled out a concept that smacks of hyperbole, but talk of genocide did touch some raw nerves within the black community. In support of the genocide theory, a 1967 article in the magazine *Liberator* cited the imposition of birth control on ghetto blacks, discriminatory living conditions that shortened the black lifespan, the narcotics problem in the ghetto, and the wasting of young black lives in Vietnam.[7] Stokely Carmichael, King, and Malcolm X all expressed views consistent with the genocide theory, which meshed with contemporary perceptions that there were disproportionately high black casualties in Vietnam. A second motive for black opposition to the war was the perceived inconsistency of fighting for freedom in South Vietnam at a time when African Americans were not yet free at home. Rarely, indeed, did any African American discuss the war without showing an awareness of its racial hypocrisy. Finally, Mullen points to the African Americans' conceptualization of the war as a racial conflict, fought with the goal of oppressing colored people. Here, too, abundant evidence supports this view. Black commentators variously noted that the French had already used African soldiers from Senegal to impose their will in Vietnam, that racists from the Deep South were among the most prominent hawks, and that African Americans had more in common with the peoples of the Third World than with the white inhabitants of the United States.[8] Recalling his days as a token Negro in the Johnson administration, the journalist Roger Wilkins wrote that "it would be hard to find a serious black in the United States who does not believe that the war was profoundly racist."[9]

Mullen lists profound objections to the war, yet they by no means exhaust the fund of African Americans' grievances against it. They complained that the conflict was an economic disaster. Once the war was costing an extra $30 billion each year on top of an already bloated defense budget, African Americans protested strenuously that it should be discontinued, for it was sapping expenditure on the Johnson administration's campaign against poverty. Help to the poor would have been of special benefit to Americans of color, the dispossessed of the nation. King lamented: "The Great Society has been shot down on the battlefields of Vietnam."[10] Shirley Chisholm, a Democrat from Brooklyn, New York, and the first black woman to enter the Congress, gave low priority to the war issue until she realized that the Nixon administration, too, intended to spend on guns, not butter. Then she made it her top cause, and she attacked the war in her maiden speech in the House in 1969: "I could not vote for money for war while funds were being denied to feed, house, and school Americans."[11]

Johnson's decision to concentrate on war instead of welfare revived suspicions that he was not fully committed to African Americans. Certainly, the Johnson administration may be defended. Johnson, a Texas liberal, was relatively tolerant in racial matters. His willingness to spend on the military instead of on social programs was by no means unusual. Defense, especially in times of war, has always attracted more government money than domestic reform; New Deal reform expenditure, for example, was minuscule compared with the federal spending of World War II. It could also be argued that by 1965, when Johnson switched Vice President Humphrey from a job coordinating civil rights to a post connected with oversight of Vietnam, the civil rights campaign had already run its course.[12] If the campaign was in its terminal stages, Johnson's emphasis on other matters did not necessarily fly in the face of black opinion.

Herein lay a danger. With the civil rights issue receding, black leaders like Whitney M. Young, Jr., of the National Urban League warmed to the Johnson administration's antipoverty program as the African American's next step forward. The new economic emphasis was bipartisan. Henry Ford II and Richard Nixon offered "Black Capitalism" as a nostrum to satisfy the increasingly economic aspirations of black America.[13] Johnson could abandon civil rights in favor of antipoverty because black leaders were already headed that way, but he could not abandon both—and get away with it—in order to fight a war. The civil rights official James Farmer, founder of the Congress of Racial Equality (CORE) back in 1942, was sympathetic to Johnson and credited him with sincere sympathy for African Americans. Yet he noted that "about '65 the President changed not his feelings, but his priorities."[14] The shift was to prove costly in terms of African American support.

Roger Wilkins was not the only disaffected black man inside the administration. Clifford Alexander, chair of the Equal Employment Opportunity Commission, who performed an ambivalent role as purveyor of presidential truths and adviser on African American affairs, was disillusioned at the end. To him, it was significant that Secretary of State Dean Rusk was "a southerner by background." For dispelling "the old club atmosphere" in the foreign service, "there was no real help from the top." Hoover of the FBI (a ruthless opponent of the civil rights campaign) had poisoned the well of race relations in the Johnson administration. Asked about the American Dream that anyone could become president, he replied, "Yes, but to a black it's a nightmare."[15]

Nor did matters improve in the Nixon administration. In 1971 the thirteen members of the Congressional Black Caucus (CBC) expressed concern that only 19 of the 320 top positions in the State Department were held by African Americans and blamed the Vietnam War for hampering positive social developments and relegating "minority citizens . . . to lower-echelon positions."[16] In the Johnson administration, black leaders already saw the war as a running sore on the body of their people, but under Nixon they came to view the administration as racist and undeserving of loyalty on any issue, war included.

As if this were not enough, African Americans were angry over issues concerning the black soldier. They felt that there had always been discrimination against black soldiers and that when they were allowed to fight, their sacrifices were not appreciated by white people. Writing in 1969 of World War II but with contemporary issues in mind, the novelist Maya Angelou told of the unobservant white woman who refused to sit beside a black man in a San Francisco streetcar. Explaining her refusal, the woman told the man that he must be a draft dodger and that he should be out there fighting, like her son in Iwo Jima. The man replied: "Then ask your son to look around for my arm, which I left over there."[17]

According to the African American litany of complaints, black soldiers were still treated with contempt at home, even though they were now expected to perform an exceptional role in the Vietnam War. As befitted a servile race, they would do so in a subordinate capacity; after all, officer training tended to take place on campus, and relatively few African Americans could afford to go to college. Educational disadvantage, however, was not allowed to keep black men out of the lower ranks. According to a *New York Times* report in 1966, two-thirds of black eighteen-year-olds failed the selective service examination compared with less than one-fifth of the whites tested, yet African Americans were drafted and sent to the front in Vietnam in disproportionately high numbers. Local draft boards decided who would be drafted, and there was virtually no black representation on those boards, especially in the South.[18]

In some areas in the South, National Guard slots were reserved for otherwise draftable sons of white families—families that might have turned against the war if their progeny had not by this device been able to avoid the trip to Vietnam. Young African Americans could not avail themselves of that route, and the inescapable draft angered a significant number of them. African Americans were further offended when on occasion the draft was used as an instrument of oppression. For example, James Joliff was an epileptic graded 4-F and unfit for military service until he became president of the NAACP chapter in his Mississippi county, when he miraculously became I-A and fit to fight. Against this background, significant numbers of young African Americans developed the conviction that they were being used as cannon fodder and that the draft was a form of racial control. The list of black objections to the war was thus formidable and gave a special intensity to the African American rebellion.[19]

Strong motivation can help to ensure success but does not guarantee it. The effectiveness of black protest depended on more than the deeply held convictions of certain leaders and participants; it also depended on the numbers of protesters involved and on the tactics employed by successive administrations, tactics that could have deflated the antiwar crusade through conciliation, manipulation, or just outright opposition.

There can be little doubt that African American disenchantment with the war was widespread. Deckle McLean, writing for *Ebony* in 1968, found that "there are few black voices supporting Negro participation in the war."[20] According to a *Newsweek* poll in 1969, African Americans believed seven to one that the war squeezed out the campaign against poverty.[21] Black leaders and personalities were just as critical of the war as the broad mass of their brothers and sisters. According to a biographer, Ralph Bunche, U.N. undersecretary-general and civil rights activist, had opposed U.S. involvement in Indochina "from the very beginning."[22] The veteran Harlem Democratic congressman Adam Clayton Powell complained in March 1966 that America was treating its own citizens with "heartless stinginess" while spending "uncountable billions of dollars to pursue a victory-less war."[23] The Congressional Black Caucus opposed the war, as did African Americans as diverse as King, Ali, and the singers Eartha Kitt and Harry Belafonte.

Yet disenchantment did not always translate into outright opposition. African Americans had other pressing concerns and sometimes did not feel inspired to join white-led protests whose main focus was not on black affairs. Such tactical considerations affected several African American leaders. Farmer explained why he urged CORE not to adopt an anti-Vietnam war platform in 1965: it would just have been an opportunist way of uniting the organization, which was split over civil rights tactics, and would have opened the door to "Communist infiltration." Like Bunche, Farmer was personally opposed to the war but remained circumspect in his public statements.[24]

Rank-and-file African Americans were similarly reluctant to express their misgivings about the war in public. The mass demonstration against the war in New York on April 15, 1967, took place in the wake of exhortations to protest by King and Stokely Carmichael, but few African Americans participated in it—just five hundred, according to a witness who visited the staging area in Harlem.[25] Later in the year, Norman Mailer noted that African Americans had left the march on the Pentagon "en masse."[26] As far as the African American was concerned, Vietnam was not the only pressing item on the racial agenda. Politically demoralized and given a less than firm lead, African Americans tended to stay away from demonstrations, preferring to nurse their grievances in private or with a few friends.

Black support for the antiwar cause was therefore often unexpressed, even if it was prevalent. Yet the makings of black dissent are discernible well before 1967, the year when it peaked. Discontent is evident in the riots of the mid-sixties, the direct criticisms by organizations and individuals, and the gathering revolt over the treatment of black soldiers.

If the mid-sixties riots expressed political discontent, they did so in no uncertain terms. Thirty-four people died in the Watts, Los Angeles, uprising of 1965; the following year Chicago, Cleveland, and forty other cities were rocked by serious racial disturbances; and in 1967, Newark (New Jersey) and Detroit were badly hit by race riots. These riots stemmed largely from frustrated ambitions. Yet to the extent that the demands of the war on the Treasury were responsible for restrictions on government expenditure, and these in turn for continuing poverty, events in Vietnam could be, and were, denounced as contributing to the framework within which the riots occurred. That does not mean that the riots were conscious expressions of hostility to the war. But discontent with the war, a consciousness of its racial hypocrisy, and an indignation at the affront to black people represented in spending priorities cannot be ruled out as ambient factors in the revolt on the streets.

Rioters seldom leave a written record of their thoughts, but they are not always inarticulate. In the wake of the 1967 riots, a federal commission on civil disorders asked some questions of the rioters and compared their answers with a control group of nonrioters. Although the responses reflect the heightened consciousness of war issues that obtained in 1967, they may well be an indication of earlier feelings, too. According to the commission's report: "Perhaps the most revealing and disturbing measure of the rioters' anger at the social and political system was their response to a question asking whether they thought 'the country was worth fighting for in a major war.' . . . 39.4 percent in Detroit and 52.8 percent in Newark shared the view that it was not. By contrast, 15.5 percent of the noninvolved in Detroit and 27.8 percent of the noninvolved in Newark shared this sentiment." A typical "not worth fighting for" reason given by an interviewee was "because my husband came back from Vietnam and nothing has changed."[27]

Clearer indications of early African American opposition to the war come from the positions adopted by organizations and by an inspirational minority of individuals. Malcolm X at the time of his assassination on February 21, 1965, was a leader of growing moral stature. He commanded a strong following among young black men and, as a Muslim, compared with the Christian, King, was considered to cut through the hypocrisy of organized religion. His denunciation of the Vietnam War on December 13, 1964, was therefore ominous for the Johnson administration.[28]

Malcolm X commanded respect within SNCC, an organization for whose members the Vietnam War was distasteful from the outset. By the end of 1964 two of SNCC's most inspiring leaders had already turned against the war. James Forman, its executive secretary, publicly denounced the administration for intervening in Vietnam while taking no action at home to help civil rights workers in the South. Bob Moses, a pioneer of direct-action civil rights tactics in McComb County, Mississippi, voiced similar sentiments early on, and the SNCC executive committee came out against the war in the spring of 1965. There was a fight within SNCC on the ground that the organization should concentrate on civil rights, not foreign policy, but, following the fatal shooting of the SNCC voter-registration worker Sammy Younge on January 3, 1966, as he attempted to use a "white" restroom in Tuskegee, Alabama, the executive committee reiterated its opposition to the war, denouncing once again the hypocrisy of America's fight for "freedom" in Southeast Asia. By this time, young African Americans were setting up a multiplicity of antiwar organizations, mostly evanescent but collectively ominous for the war effort; examples are the Black Anti-Draft Union and Afro-Americans Against the War in Vietnam.[29]

Prominent African Americans who denounced the war before 1967 included, in addition to Muhammad Ali and Adam Clayton Powell, Dick Gregory, John Lewis, and Julian Bond.[30] Perhaps the most frightening dissent came from the Black Panther Party. In contrast to the Southern-based students of SNCC, the Panthers drew support from the Northern and Western underclasses. Led by Huey Newton, Bobby Seale, and Eldridge Cleaver, they offered a radical challenge to the pacifist tactics of SNCC. Their advocacy of the right of black people to arm and defend themselves within the United States merely mirrored the arguments of white-racist extollers of the Second Amendment, but to whites made nervous by the race riots of the mid-sixties, such advocacy seemed threatening. In October 1966, the Panthers' platform declared: "We believe that Black people should not be forced to fight in the military service to defend a racist government that does not protect us. We will not fight and kill other people of color in the world who, like black people, are being victimized by the white racist government in America."[31]

Military service and the injustices of the draft system had become a major grievance for African Americans by the end of 1966. It was not just a question of racist draft boards. There was also a fundamental discrepancy between justice in theory and the realities of induction. In theory, college exemptions from the draft worked evenhandedly for the different races. In practice, many black Americans were too poor to enter college or too poor to stay there once admitted. In August 1965, Congressman Charles A. Vanik (Dem., Ohio) complained to the president's assistant Jack Valenti of numerous and "distressing" draft problems: "For example, I have several young men of minority groups who have made their way into first-rate colleges as exemplary students who were drafted because they dropped out of college for a semester in order to raise money for the next semester."[32] The distressing nature of the problem was all too evident to the African Americans affected and to their families. Harold ("Light Bulb") Bryant served as a combat engineer in Vietnam from February 1966 to February 1967. His father "was not too hot" about his son's military service because he had himself suffered from racial discrimination when a soldier in Europe in World War II. As Harold recalled in explaining his reluctant soldiering in Vietnam, he had had to drop out of Southern Illinois University because "the expenses had gotten too much for my family," and he could find no means of escape.[33]

Discriminatory practices had a cumulative effect. According to figures released by the Department of Defense in January 1967, the "percentage of Negroes in the Armed Forces" had been "steadily rising" since 1962. Of the enlisted men in the Army, 14.5 percent were now black, well above the proportion of blacks in the U.S. population (11 percent in 1960). An even higher proportion of black men was to be found in the forward units that did the fighting. In the twenty-three-month period ending on November 30, 1966, African Americans made up 22.4 percent of battle fatalities. According to the same Defense Department figures, only 3.8 percent of the officers serving in Vietnam were black.[34] Educational and class differences lay at the root of some of these problems. But the racism and self-preservation instincts of the white officers in control were widely suspected to be the reasons why, in the words of one infantryman, "it seemed like more blacks in the field than in the rear."[35]

The black American press eventually recognized the discontent of the black soldier and ventilated the disturbing statistics. The author of an *Ebony* article bleakly observed in 1968: "There are 1,342 admirals and generals in the U.S. military. But only two are Negro. That is to say, the nation's top brass is .149 per cent 'integrated.'"[36] This changing civilian perception both reflected and nurtured feelings of injustice within the armed forces.[37]

African American complaints against racism in the military went beyond draft and battle statistics. The problem was endemic and had many manifestations—for example, unfair disciplinary procedures. "If I had been white, I would never have went to jail for fighting," said a rifleman, Reginald Edwards, convicted of assaulting a fellow Marine during a riot sparked by "profanity in front of some sisters."[38] Black enlisted men complained that their achievements were ignored. "'The brothers aren't getting any stripes" and "we aren't getting our share of the medals" were two of their complaints. No doubt opportunism motivated some of the racial charges. But even the best-intentioned top brass betrayed set views on the proper standing of black people in the professional pecking order. Brigadier General Donald H. McGovern, chief of personnel at Saigon headquarters, claimed that he did not "give a damn what color a man is," offering as proof the fact that "my own personal secretary, Sgt. Vance, is a Negro."[39]

Various arguments were advanced to exculpate the armed forces: the Army was more fully integrated than civilian society; the high proportion of black soldiers reflected the lower median age of the black population and thus its relative susceptibility to the draft; lower promotion rates reflected poor black performance in Army aptitude tests; the inequities in the draft system reflected inequities in society and could not be blamed on the Army; higher rates of black volunteering and reenlistment were beyond the control of the Army; African Americans chose not to avail themselves of a standard way of avoiding service in Vietnam—volunteering for the National Guard. This option was available to them outside the South, but, according to the civil rights leader Marion Barry, they did not want to shoot their "brothers" in urban riots policed by the state militias. None of these arguments entirely exonerated the military, which sent African Americans into battle zones at a higher rate than whites even in cases where they had scored well in aptitude tests. Even if the arguments partially rehabilitated the military, they hardly placed the Johnson administration and its war effort in a good light. Lower black life expectancy and education levels, together with the inner city riots, suggested the failure of reform and a need to step up the war on poverty rather than spend more money on a foreign war.[40] The administration's discomfiture persisted, and the issue of the black soldier joined the remorseless flow of the great river of African American discontent.

From the early stages of the war, the Johnson administration was alert to the need to respond to its racial dimensions. Well before Dr. King's major attack on the war in April 1967, the president and his advisers paid heed to the problem of African American vexation in a manner that reflected their concern about the seriousness of a potential black revolt. But the resolution of the "American dilemma" in a way consistent with contemporary foreign-policy goals required sudden answers to a centuries-old problem. These answers were not forthcoming

From the outset, debate on the problem of the black soldier featured acrid exchanges. In March 1965, Senator Margaret Chase Smith of Maine demanded information on the progress of integration in the National Guard, a pressing problem at home as well as one that affected the racial composition of the armed forces in Vietnam. Secretary of Defense McNamara replied: "There are no segregated State Guards today." But Smith, a longtime equal rights advocate who rarely accepted a McNamara statement at face value, wanted to see the figures. When she finally received them, she noted that at the end of 1966, only 1.15 percent of the Army National Guard and 0.6 percent of the Air National Guard were African Americans and that "there were no Negro officers in the Army National Guard in any of the southern States." On this basis, she declared that the secretary had not been "honest in his statement." When the press reported her reaction in 1967, McNamara wrote her a pained letter saying that he was "seeking to determine whether it is possible to establish a relationship with the ranking Republican member of the Senate Armed Services Committee which will permit me to fulfill my responsibilities as Secretary of Defense."[41]

Clifford Alexander did his best to save the administration from further embarrassments, especially from the damaging effects of attacks from the SNCC and King, who was already grumbling about the war even if he was not yet in full attack mode. In January 1966 the SNCC urged young people to work in the civil rights movement as a "valid alternative to the draft," so Alexander reported to the president on ways to counter this kind of opposition. He was already prodding the NAACP's Roy Wilkins and the NUL's Whitney Young, Jr., to dissociate themselves from the SNCC statement. After the application of pressure, he now expected the Negro Publishers Association to "strongly denounce the SNCC statements in their editorial columns." King's reaction would be "the most difficult part of the equation," but Alexander was taking steps to persuade his organization, the Southern Christian Leadership Conference (SCLC), that opposition to the war would be harmful to the civil rights movement.[42]

Alexander told the president that elected legislators were better representatives of African American opinion than the SNCC leader John Lewis and suggested that it might therefore be a good idea "to have the six Negro Congressmen issue a statement expressing the wholehearted support of the Negro people for our actions in Vietnam." But the mood in the Congress was changing. In February, Charles C. Diggs, an African American from Michigan who served on the House Foreign Affairs Committee, challenged the director of the selective service, Lewis Hershey, to respond to newspaper revelations that the all-white Southern draft boards were sending disproportionate numbers of African Americans to Vietnam and were making sure that the civil rights activists among them were first in line. Diggs was especially upset that Hershey could not document the matter one way or the other.[43]

Thus, there was already a slightly desperate air to the administration's attempts to create a groundswell of public support for its policies. In mid-1966 it took two actions that were meant to assuage black discontent, both of which reveal the extent of official anxiety. The first happened in June, when the White House hosted a conference on civil rights. President Johnson made sure that King, the nation's leading civil rights personality, was marginalized at this conference in retribution for King's early grumblings about the war.[44]

The same summer Secretary McNamara launched Project 100,000 (or Project One Hundred Thousand: POHT), a recruitment drive that would meet a manpower shortfall in the armed forces while saving President Johnson from the unpopularity of calling up the Reserves or ending college deferments. Although it served the purpose of keeping white America on his side, it could also be dressed up as a measure that would benefit the economically and racially oppressed. The project addressed the problem that so many poor people, among whom African Americans were heavily represented, failed the Armed Forces Qualification Test (AFQT). It aimed to lower the entry standards for the armed forces and to supply remedial training to those who scored low on the AFQT. McNamara explained: "The poor of America . . . have not had the opportunity to earn their fair share of this nation's abundance, but they can be given an opportunity to serve in their country's defense and . . . to return to civilian life with skills and aptitudes which for them and their families will reverse the downward spiral of decay."[45] As the name suggests, the goal of POHT was to find 100,000 additional recruits per annum. Logistically successful, it was the instrument of recruitment between October 1966 and June 1969 for 246,000 "New Standards Men."[46]

Although POHT was a key element in Johnson's Vietnam policy, its origins lay in earlier thinking and in pilot schemes stretching back to the Kennedy administration; indeed, the idea of "one-third of a nation ill-housed, ill-clad, ill-nourished" needing special economic intervention by the government went back to the presidency of an earlier reforming Democrat, Franklin D. Roosevelt.[47] What was new about the Kennedy-Johnson initiatives was the suggestion that the armed forces might serve as a vehicle for combating domestic poverty. As ever, the Congress had dragged its heels when called on to authorize a peacetime expenditure high enough to make a difference for the nation's poor. The reforming Democrats of the 1960s tried to turn to their advantage the double standard: the willingness to spend on the military but not on "wasteful" peaceful programs. They asked themselves, Why not dress up social reform as military expenditure? The POHT drive promised further benefits, too, by rectifying the *under*representation of African Americans in the armed forces. In theory, it was a means of correcting a social blemish at home when international communists were accusing America of racism, just as it was a means of demonstrating that the fight against communism in Vietnam and elsewhere was not an exercise in racist neocolonialism but a politically correct crusade undertaken with a multiracial and fully integrated military machine.

To the critics of POHT, the statistics told a different story. In 1966, with the lowering of admissions standards, 30.2 percent of African Americans who registered for selective service were drafted, compared with 18.8 percent of whites. Of the entire POHT intake, 1966–1968, a large proportion—41 percent—were black, most of them poor and not well educated. Because they lacked the skills to enter specialist units, 40 percent of the New Standards Men found themselves in combat units, and in the Army and Marines 50 percent of the New Standards Men went to Vietnam. One objective of POHT was to inject pride into the black male, making him a better father figure and revitalizing the allegedly sick African American family. But, in the event, only 7.5 percent of the New Standards Men were taught remedial skills. The majority returned to society just as disadvantaged as before, some as physical or psychological cripples, and others did not return at all, leaving the administration open to the charge that it had sacrificed black lives.[48]

POHT mirrored the Johnson administration as a whole. It started with high intentions but subsided into failure and tragedy. Johnson and his advisers made a political misjudgment. They failed to distinguish between, on the one hand, African Americans' demand for equality in the armed forces in general terms and, on the other, a demand for equality in the armed forces at any price, including a slavish loyalty to a war against people of color in the Third World and the acceptance of a disproportionate casualty rate. Because of the miscalculation, LBJ's team sent into battle in Vietnam a stream of men who saw themselves less as pioneers of integration than as the latest victims of racism and who contributed to the further demoralization of a force already suffering from crumbling morale. It also laid in store for itself political problems with African Americans at home.

On April 4, 1967, Dr. Martin Luther King, Jr., shook America with a speech against the war delivered before three thousand people at the Riverside Church, New York. According to the historian Melvin Small, this was the start of "bad news for Johnson on the antiwar front in 1967."[49] King called for an end to the bombing, a unilateral cease-fire, negotiations with the National Liberation Front (the South Vietnamese Communists), and the setting of a date by which all foreign troops would be removed from Vietnam.[50] The impact of the address came in part from King's stature in the civil rights movement. But this was not his first attack on the war, of which he had been publicly, if discreetly, critical since March 1965. The historical significance of the Riverside speech lies, rather, in its nature and timing: the rebuke was not only public but heavily publicized. For the first time, the leading advocate of nonviolence as a civil rights tactic systematically criticized the international violence used by his former allies in the Democratic administration. The address was intended to be the first blast in a renewed, organized campaign against the war, and it coincided with an attempt to commit the SCLC officially to that campaign. Finally, the timing of the attack was discouraging for the White House, where hitherto the hope had been that the worst of the student protests was over and that an American victory would soon end the war. According to Carl T. Rowan, who had headed the United States Information Agency, President Johnson "flushed with anger" when he read wire service reports of the Riverside speech.[51]

The timing of King's attack has attracted some speculation. In an unfriendly vein, Rowan and others have suggested that by the mid-sixties, King's halo was slipping. His civil rights achievements were behind him, the young men involved in the Black Power movement regarded him as too soft, and the NAACP and Urban League thought he was tactically played out and dispensable—so King had to invent a new role for himself.[52] A different theory holds that he waited until the time was propitious, speaking out only when he was sure he stood a chance of gaining substantial support in the African American community. The race riots of the mid-sixties appear to have been yet another factor encouraging his decision: by 1967 he felt that he could no longer speak out against urban thugs and looters with any credibility unless he also condemned the actions in Vietnam of "the greatest purveyor of violence in the world today—my own government." According to King, his politically dictated discretion prior to 1967 weighed heavily on his conscience; he believed that, as the recipient of the Nobel Peace Prize in 1964, he had a duty to speak out on Vietnam.

At last, on reading an account of napalm injuries to Vietnamese children in the January 1967 issue of *Ramparts*, he found that he could no longer keep quiet.[53]

In reality, King attacked in April 1967 not so much because he had changed as because Lyndon Johnson had changed. Confronted by an invidious choice, King had thus far conditionally condoned the Vietnam War for reasons suggested in a telegram that he sent the president in January 1966: "May I commend you for your eloquent comprehensive and far-reaching state of the union address. It was reassuring to hear you emphatically affirm that the administration will not allow the continued existence of the war in Viet Nam to cause a letup in the great domestic and welfare programs that you have so creatively generated through your concepts of the Great Society."[54] At first, King did not want to rock the Great Society boat, but, as the year wore on, Johnson began to neglect his social-reform objectives. The president seemed psychologically and politically distracted from domestic issues. He neglected his black supporters, seeing fewer of them. The war seemed to be taking away resources that could have been used at home. Johnson did not press the Congress hard for legislation friendly to African Americans, such as that barring housing discrimination. Midterm election reverses for the Democrats in 1966 and the fear of white backlash were constraining factors here. But Johnson and his close observers agreed on a further culprit, the attention-consuming war and the need to drum up support for it. This view coincided with King's perception. "The heart of the administration is in that war in Vietnam," he told a journalist just before his Riverside speech. King knew that African Americans could not lose the president by opposing the war, because the president was already lost. So it was timely and not imprudent to denounce the discrepancy between $80 billion spent on defense and "a pittance here and there for social uplift."[55]

The timing of King's attack on the Vietnam War was at least partly dictated by the domestic needs of black people. Did his linkage of civil rights and foreign policy impair the efficacy of the attack? According to one student of the domestic repercussions of the war, King's Riverside address was effective in one way:

it was a turning point for the "liberal wing of the Democratic Party," which "took nothing more seriously than the long struggle for black rights."[56] But a number of black leaders, believing that African Americans paid a price for the great crusader's candor, obstructed and weakened his attack on the war.

King's critics accused him of endangering the African American cause by associating it with the controversial antiwar movement, fatally undermining the consensus behind the racially liberal Great Society program. His antiwar stance split the black leadership, so it could also be argued that he weakened the Democratic coalition, driving the wounded Johnson toward what his literary namesake termed "the last refuge of a scoundrel"—patriotism—and toward continued war as a desperate means of recouping prestige and electoral credibility.

King had taken a risk with public opinion. A Harris poll on May 22, 1967, indicated that 25 percent of African Americans supported his stand, with 34 percent believing his campaign would hurt the civil rights movement. The poll did suggest racial differences—only 9 percent of the population at large agreed with his objections to the war, whereas 60 percent thought his outspokenness would harm the civil rights movement—but even among the black people polled, there was clearly a less than wholehearted mandate to join cause with opponents of the war. Then, in June, a Gallup poll showed only 2 percent of Americans declaring their support for King's touted third-party peace candidacy, although King's reluctance to run for the presidency may have been a factor here.[57] Such evidence may well have helped to persuade Joe Rauh, the antiwar Democratic liberal tactician, to drop his Dump Johnson approach and seek instead to form a peace caucus at the Democratic National Convention in 1968. Noting in October 1967 that Wilkins, Young, and a "large segment" of black leadership supported Johnson, he counseled: "The 'dump Johnson' movement would fracture the liberal-labor-Negro coalition that has elected every liberal President and made possible every liberal advance since the 1930s. The Vietnam war and black power have split the coalition badly enough; this would complete the process. . . . To split the liberals from their natural labor and

Negro allies will not only weaken efforts toward de-escalation and peace in Vietnam, but will also shatter hope for progress at home."[58] Whatever else King may have achieved through his antiwar comments, he did not inspire a rush of public support for or mass defections from the Democrats, or even from Johnson.

There was unfavorable reaction to King's new cause among black journalists. The former baseball great Jackie Robinson, now a columnist, said he had supported King in the past and still thought he was "one of the most magnificent mass movement leaders who has ever lived." But Robinson was now "distressed" at his neglect of the civil rights issue and his stand on Vietnam. The *Amsterdam News*, one of the largest and most influential black weeklies in the United States, said that King had a "heroic" past but claimed that Johnson deserved black support because he had righted more wrongs for African Americans than any other president—apparently including Lincoln. The *News* was impressed that the black senator Edward Brooke of Massachusetts had gone to visit Vietnam in a critical frame of mind and had come back a convert to Johnson's war policy.[59]

King's critics had relatively good access to the president's ear. Clifford Alexander recalled that Johnson's "relationship with King was a formal one. I don't think there was any love lost." But the president "counseled a good deal" with Whitney Young, Jr., of the Urban League and with Roy Wilkins of the NAACP. These favored leaders were not entirely uncritical of Johnson's foreign policy but tended to be supportive. Young, for example, visited Vietnam and came back, not to denounce the war, but to tell a sympathetic president that there should be more African American generals.[60]

Wilkins and the NAACP were the major critics of King's antiwar stance. The NAACP has had a history of radicalism and of courageous opposition to racism ever since its foundation in 1909. But in dealing with post–World War II foreign policy, its leaders gave the impression of being in active pursuit of tactical retreat. In 1952, the NAACP secretary Walter White consulted Cord Meyer of the CIA about the position the association should adopt toward Asia. Six years later, his successor Wilkins disclaimed any sympathy with the current "international anti-white crusade," the origins of which he perceived in black resentment at the Italian invasion of Ethiopia and in the dropping of the atomic bomb on Japan, a "colored" nation. Not all nonwhite victims of Caucasian aggression were necessarily friends of the African American. What, he asked, had the Ethiopians or the Japanese ever done for African Americans? But, Wilkins warned, President Eisenhower would have to "assume moral leadership in the school integration fight" if he wished his foreign policy to prevail. The reference here was to the battle for Third World opinion, but with the suggestion, too, that African Americans would not support U.S. Cold War policy unless they were better treated at home, or, to put it another way, they were prepared to fall in line diplomatically in exchange for domestic concessions.[61]

In 1962, with the wind of change blowing through Africa, Wilkins joined King, Young, Farmer, and the labor leader A. Philip Randolph on the committee that established and guided the American Negro Leadership Conference on Africa (ANLCA). But, according to the *New York Times*, the NAACP secretary "indicated to the [founding] conference that it was necessary not to overstep the terms of reference set for the conference and unwittingly involve the United States in embarrassing situations." Subsequently, Wilkins and the ANLCA director Theodore E. Brown went out of their way to endorse President Kennedy's policy in the Congo, a policy that favored white interests and may have encouraged the January 17, 1961, assassination of Prime Minister Patrice Lumumba.[62]

This desire to please continued during Johnson's Vietnam War. Wilkins, for instance, cooperated with General Hershey in trying to calm Congressman Diggs's fears: "We do not know of any complaint that any Negro has been singled out for drafting by reason of his civil rights activity although it is always possible that this might occur in some isolated instances."[63]

Well before the Riverside speech, NAACP officials were alert to the danger (as they saw it) that King would imperil the civil rights movement. In April 1966, King maintained that the war propped up a "bankrupt government" in Saigon, distracted attention from the civil rights campaign, and threatened the right to dissent. Reacting to his statement, Gloster B. Current, director of NAACP branches and field administration, warned Wilkins: "The Harris Poll has already borne out our surmise that getting tied to this issue will not help the civil rights programs we espouse and adds support to the [wrongheaded] John Birch position that civil rights organizations are a tool of the international Communist conspiracy."[64]

The NAACP's position sprang from its desire to be pragmatic rather than from genuine enthusiasm for U.S. policy in Vietnam. In fact, Wilkins disapproved of the war. His 1972 claim that American withdrawal from the Vietnam War had "long been integral to NAACP policies and programs" may have been an exaggeration, but he did have deep private reservations about the conflict.[65] In May 1966 he drafted a petition to Johnson urging him to take a firmer stand in opposing white supremacists in Rhodesia. The black majority in Rhodesia could be helped "at a far less cost" than the Vietnamese, on whose behalf America was "expending precious lives and billions of dollars." Obeying the dictates of prudence, Wilkins dropped the last observation from the final draft of the petition. He continued to be circumspect even many years later; in his 1982 autobiography he hardly mentioned the Vietnam War, merely noting that LBJ lost his "common touch" because of it.[66]

Evincing the breakthrough mentality of a minority-group leader, Wilkins thought it worth sacrificing foreign policy principles on the altar of racial acceptance and progress. The Riverside speech encouraged him to distance himself from King. A few days after Riverside, his assistant Current attended the Spring Mobe rally and sent him a memorandum on the antiwar speeches by King, Stokely Carmichael, and others. Wilkins now publicly asserted that King was knifing heroic American soldiers in the back and insisted that the Viet Cong were not the brothers of African Americans, for there had never been any suggestion of reciprocal fraternity. In June, when a member of the NAACP board pressed Wilkins to take a pro-Israel and anti–Vietnam War stance, Wilkins presented his policy as one of neutral statecraft: "The better plan is to stick with the civil rights issue and leave foreign policy to individuals who feel a strong urge and to organizations working in that field."[67]

In the short term, King did alienate supporters of the African American cause. Yet the King-Wilkins confrontation can also be viewed from a different perspective. King's rebellion was less risky than his critics claimed. By 1967 he could afford to offend the Johnson administration because it had already abandoned the African American. Similarly, there was no need to please Wilkins, Young, and their supporters because they had written him off as a reliable ally. He had nothing to lose.

Furthermore, there was less to lose than it might appear, because the NAACP was weak and getting weaker. Although some journalists were bitingly critical of King's stance, others agreed with him that the NAACP and the Urban League had become middle-class, stand-pat organizations with large treasuries that they were unwilling to disburse in defense of poor people's causes. NAACP members resigned in significant numbers on learning that its directors had on April 10, 1967, unanimously condemned King's Riverside speech. One supporter of twenty-seven years' standing immediately tore up his membership card and put it in an ashtray; others returned their cards or wrote angrily to Wilkins.[68]

Black Americans were turning against the war and making their views known. One indication is to be found in the reactions of politically sensitive legislators. In the second half of Johnson's presidency, the credibility of the myth of a racial consensus regarding the war rapidly deteriorated. In the fall of 1967, Edward Brooke, with all the authority of the first African American member of the Senate since 1881, said that "if the Vietnamese would not fight, we shouldn't help them." In February 1968, following the government's call for a federal surtax to cope with increasing financial problems, Senator Javits—another Republican stalwart of the loyal opposition—criticized "the Administration's refusal to declare the economic emergency to be due to the Vietnam War" and called for a tax to help the ghettos.[69]

Racially oriented criticisms of the war poured forth. Perhaps most worrying from the military viewpoint was the trouble in the

Army. If 1967 was the year of the King protest, it was also the time when Americans witnessed the stirrings of resistance from the black soldier. By 1968 there was serious African American discontent within the Army as well as resistance to induction.

The attitude within the Army undoubtedly changed. The African American journalist Wallace Terry noted the deterioration in morale that had taken place between his visit to Vietnam in May 1967—when he reported for *Time* magazine that most black soldiers still supported the war—and his return later the same year. Draftees, many of them fresh from civil rights demonstrations or ghetto riots, were replacing the military careerists. They spoke out against Army discrimination; they retaliated against white soldiers' taunts, cross burnings, and Confederate flag displays; and, contributing a new word to the lexicon of black militancy, they called themselves "Bloods."[70] In Vietnam, the African American soldier could not be relied on to give the military salute, but he did give the Black Power salute to his brothers. In extreme cases, black soldiers expressed their discontent by shooting white officers in combat or attacking them on base. The term *fragging* derived from the practice of throwing fragmentation grenades into the tents of medal-hungry officers. When an enlisted man saw no reason to risk his life to satisfy the combat ambitions of a promotion-hungry commander, it was tempting to take such direct action. It is known that explosive-device assaults killed at least eighty-six commissioned and noncommissioned officers in Vietnam between 1969 and 1972. The practice was not confined to black soldiers, but African Americans' known sense of grievance did render them men to be feared. According to one historian, "Officers in Vietnam began to develop a paranoiac fear of giving direct orders to Afro-American GIs for fear of getting 'fragged.'"[71]

The conspiracy of silence that surrounded fragging made it all the more frightening and destructive of military morale; at the same time, it kept fragging from becoming a major political issue. Racial rioting on military bases was, however, more difficult to conceal. There had always been violent intimidation of black soldiers in the Army, but in 1968 black soldiers began to hit back. The Pentagon was aware that racial disturbances were an "explosive problem" in Vietnam, and General Westmoreland commissioned a black officer to conduct a secret investigation. In August, President Johnson sent his top national security adviser, Walt Rostow, to investigate a riot in Long Binh, fifteen miles northeast of Saigon. In the course of this disturbance, African American detainees angered by bad conditions had rebelled in the prison compound, burning several buildings. Inmates bashed out protest rhythms on oil drums. Terrified psychiatrists quizzed the prisoners through the barbed wire fence. The riot resulted in one death and several injuries. Rostow reported on the containment action by the predominantly white military police, but—revealing how the Johnson administration was losing touch—said nothing about the black prisoners' grievances.[72]

By this time it was too late to prevent further outbreaks, and racial clashes occurred in Germany and at home, as well as in Vietnam. Preparations in Fort Hood, Texas, to use soldiers to police urban riots led to disturbances, after which forty-three were court-martialed. Early in 1969, Joe Miles, a black Trotskyist, established G.I.s United Against the War in Vietnam at the base in Fort Jackson, South Carolina; in this case, court-martial proceedings were dropped after a national outcry at the arrest of the eight black soldiers involved. Brawling black Marines at Camp Lejeune, North Carolina, likewise commanded sympathy. *Ebony* noted that the elite Marine Corps had delayed integration until 1960 and that the "New Breed" African American recruit now refused to put up with a continuation of indignities, such as the ban on soul music in service clubs.[73] From the military point of view, all this amounted to a disastrous collapse in morale.

Resistance to military service did not come easily to the African American, who lacked the more affluent white student's advantage of having a well-versed lawyer at his elbow. Nevertheless, in August 1968, *Ebony* raised the issue of the black deserter in exile. One of these deserters was a Marine, Terry Whitmore. After he was badly wounded toward the end of 1967, President Johnson visited him in the hospital and placed an array of gallantry medals on his pillow. But then the authorities told Whitmore that he would have to return to Vietnam once he had recovered. With help from Soviet agents, the decorated hero fled to Sweden, where other black refugees had banded together to form the Afro-American Deserters' Committee. Whitmore had a distinctly racial perspective. He praised the "colored" Japanese who had helped him escape. Perhaps influenced by Hanoi Hannah, the collective nickname given to communist radio hostesses who asked black soldiers why they were fighting the Viet Cong instead of their real enemy back home, Whitmore believed that "Charlie" (the Viet Cong soldier) had tried to avoid killing him and other African Americans. He was suspicious of the motives of the Russians who had helped him, and thought the Swedes were cold. But he attacked American foreign policy and called LBJ a "turd." Whitmore became an icon for protesters in a country already predisposed to attack the U.S. policy in Vietnam.[74]

The number of black deserters or draft evaders living in exile was limited. In mid-1968, there were only eighty American deserters in Sweden all told, of whom fourteen were black—a small number, even if larger than the ratio of blacks to whites in the U.S. population. No figures are available for the number of African Americans who made their way to Tangiers, the destination favored by Eldridge Cleaver. Only between five hundred and one thousand black draft avoiders, supplemented by an even smaller number of deserters, ended up in Canada. African Americans who wished to escape the military rarely had the necessary literacy and the know-how of the whites who followed the exile route. Also, blacks found Canada, the major exile destination, unattractive. It had been the northern terminus of the underground railway for escaping slaves in the nineteenth century and still had its long-established black community of U.S. origin, as well as a more recent West Indian influx. But a cultural gap separated Americans of African descent from both the West Indians and their distant U.S.-origin cousins, whom they regarded in much the same way as the Canadians regarded "Newfies," the much-abused Newfoundlanders, accused of being innately boring and noncosmopolitan. Canada supplied no compelling attraction for African Americans. The progeny of one involuntary diaspora, they had no special desire to participate in another.[75]

In two respects, however, the question of Canadian exile did play a role in the black protest movement. First, African Americans were well placed to embarrass those who presided over U.S. foreign policy. When Eusi Ndugu exchanged his native Mississippi for Toronto and established the organization African-American Draft Resisters in Canada, he declared that he was not a draft dodger but a refugee from slavery. The mere existence of such organizations was embarrassing to the U.S. government; whereas white military exiles could be described as unpatriotic, black ones could claim that they had never been full U.S. citizens in the first place. Second, the very shortage of black exiles was significant for the protest movement. Jim Russell of the Black Refugee Organization (BRO) advised, "It's not that easy for blacks in Canada so I would say to brothers on the other side of the border to stay there if it is at all possible—do what you can to resist there." In other words, Canada placed U.S. foreign policy in double jeopardy: it was a place of racial embarrassment, yet failed to serve as a safety valve for black discontent.[76]

If the number of African American protesters remained small, the publicity that they generated was nevertheless considerable. Slavery weighed too heavily on the conscience of white America for the black predicament to be ignored, and the dramatic events of 1968—the Tet offensive, followed by the assassination of Dr. Martin Luther King, Jr., on April 3—heightened awareness. The ABC television commentator Howard K. Smith expressed the resentment that supporters of the war felt at the attention given to black radicals. Smith, who had joined the administration-sponsored Citizens Committee for Peace with Freedom in Vietnam, complained even before King's death that the press was lavishing a disproportionate amount of attention on rebels like Stokely Carmichael and H. Rap Brown and promoting a "one-eyed view of the war in Viet Nam."[77]

In fixing on such individuals, the press may have been making a mountain out of a molehill. What people think or are led to believe is important nonetheless. Politics is about mentalities, and the White House was developing a siege mentality in response to the racially defined mentality of the African American. President Johnson believed, just as his successor in the White House believed, that black criticism of the war was an aspect of an evil international communist conspiracy. In fact, the Soviets, though wary of the destabilizing effects of the Vietnam War, were aware that they needed to be seen to be helping the social protest within America if they were to sustain their leadership at the head of the communist world. Propaganda and encouragement were fairly risk-free activities, and African American agitation gave them an opportunity. Just after the King assassination, the Central Committee of the Communist Party of the Soviet Union secretly instructed Soviet ambassadors and other officials to encourage all social and political movements with which they had contact to agitate for a peace favorable to Hanoi.[78] Both Washington and Moscow, then, derived political advantage from the idea that there was an international communist conspiracy to boost the black antiwar movement. The potency of the movement therefore increased out of proportion to its size.

Rightly or wrongly, the "Bloods" were an omnipervasive topic for debate by mid-1968. The publication of David Parks's *G.I. Diary* fanned the controversy. Parks observed that the racist system corrupted even good white men: his commanding officer's patience snapped when Parks expressed admiration for King's denunciation of the war. Parks confirmed the doubly genocidal nature of the war. His entry for January 31, 1967, noted that the job of the patrolling forward officer was particularly hazardous, but so far Sergeant Paulson had "fingered only Negroes and Puerto Ricans" for the task.[79] Newspapers rushed to report on the black soldier. Before King's death, Sol Stern had warned *New York Times* readers that POHT was a racist sham and that "the returning black Viet vet is a potential source of leadership and tactical know-how in helping the black community organize for what they expect to be a savage summer of military repression."[80] In May the *Washington Star* sent Paul Hathaway to Vietnam to write a five-article series. He found no shortage of black hawks and found that some black soldiers were just as callous toward the Vietnamese as their white comrades were. But he also found black soldiers who were afraid that "chuck" [white] officers were sending them on suicide missions, and others who were convinced that the "gooks" (Vietnamese) liked to kill white men and let the "Bloods" escape alive.[81]

Thomas Johnson sent a three-part series to the *New York Times* and contributed to a special issue of *Ebony* devoted to the African American soldier. The black monthly *Sepia* had published letters and articles on the African American soldier since 1969, initially (like *Ebony*) "to salute our fighting men," but by the summer of 1968 its correspondents were condemning white foreign-policy racism, worrying about equality of treatment for their families back home, and speculating about "who my enemy really is." Periodicals ranging from the liberal *Progressive* to the mainstream *Newsweek* ran articles on the black soldier in Vietnam, and Cleaver's antiwar *Soul on Ice* came out to acclaim in 1968. Thus, the press in its different forms dressed up '68 as a year when revolutionary ideas were stirring Americans of African descent.[82] If King's attack on the war in 1967 represented a peak in black protest, the focus on antimilitarism in 1968 was almost as serious.

Black antimilitarism was a problem for President Johnson in terms of both winning the war and winning the 1968 presidential election. Johnson and his officials had no solution. They had always been aware of the threat posed by King's radicalism but thought that surveillance, disruption, and counterpropaganda provided a sufficient response. Even before King's antiwar campaign, the FBI had sought to discredit him by exposing real or imaginary details about his sex life and alleged communist associations.[83] King's Riverside speech and his involvement in Spring Mobe in 1967—episodes anxiously monitored by administration officials—persuaded FBI director Hoover and Johnson to step up surveillance and harassment by the bureau. The FBI already had an informer, an SCLC accountant named James A. Harrison, in a key position. The bureau now resumed its wiretaps "to obtain racial intelligence information" and attempted to block government and private financial support for the SCLC; it also smeared King by attributing the phrase "traitor to his country and race" to the black press and planting it in the white media.[84]

LBJ's hostile approach to King stemmed in part from his perception that he had more to fear from a white backlash than from African Americans. At the same time, Johnson tried to hang on to the African American vote through a program of overtures and propaganda. In May 1967 the press officer Fred Panzer warned the president of Harris poll indications that a King endorsement would deliver between one-third and one-half of African American votes to a candidate of his choice, and that candidate was "unlikely to be LBJ." A few days later, LBJ and Secretary of Housing and Urban Development Robert Weaver, the first-ever African American cabinet member, were among leading administration officials who wooed the national convention of Democratic black legislators and government officials, a pioneering initiative held in Washington, D.C. Press reporters noted that it took place with the Carmichael and King attacks on Vietnam policy in the background and amid rumors of massive black defections from the Democratic Party. There were even rumblings of a third-party candidacy, including a possible bid by King himself. Indeed, the purpose of the convention was to plan ways of shoring up black support for Johnson in the 1968 presidential election.[85]

Troubled by the potential political effects of King's allegation that the needs of war were gaining ascendancy over those of the Great Society, the administration charged the Department of Defense with answering the question "Have the Great Society programs in education, anti-poverty, urban renewal, and civil rights been sacrificed to the war?" A defense systems analyst replied that there had been a 35 percent reduction in "availability of funds," amounting to a projected $4 billion reduction for fiscal year 1968. He added that on account of the transferability of skills, increased defense expenditure had come largely at a cost to the space program. Defense expenditure, he said, was good for the economy because it had "a greater initial multiplier effect than non-defense spending." Approved in due course by the director of the Bureau of the Budget, Charles L. Schultze, the report gave the administration a cosmetic gloss to place on its spending priorities.[86]

The administration tried to defuse black discontent over the draft—as it had student discontent—by ending some of the more glaring inequities in the selective service system, such as graduate school deferment. It also put pressure on the white South to include African Americans on local draft boards. But it did not want to go too far. The segregationist governor of Alabama, George C. Wallace, was waiting in the wings as a "white backlash" challenger. As the 1968 election results would show—Wallace took nearly ten million votes running as an independent—Democratic candidates were right to fear him. Wallace had already done well in Wisconsin, Maryland, and Indiana in the 1964 Democratic primaries. In June 1967, Panzer reported to the president that judging from Gallup poll data, he thought "Wallace is a bigger threat—more than five times bigger—than a peace party headed by Martin Luther King."[87]

Wallace's proven appeal outside the South was a menacing consideration, and one reinforced by the attitude of that stalwart ally of the Democrats, the labor movement. AFL-CIO president George Meany told the president in a ten-page letter, dated December 29, 1967, what he would like to see in the State of the Union message. His first point was that "nothing is more important than the war in Viet Nam." He concluded by warning about "the left" in terms that alerted the president to a white-patriot, working-class impatience with the black community: "They infiltrate the ghettos, and segments of the civil rights movement, transforming the rightful quest for the redress of ancient grievances into violent social disorders."[88]

Although African American opposition to the Vietnam War presented Johnson with a choice between stopping the war and alienating black America, his problem did not stop there. Black antiwar agitation helped provoke a white backlash in the hitherto solidly Democratic South, as well as elsewhere in the nation. Johnson—himself at daggers drawn with the black radicals—was in no position to call on Dixie's illiberal Democrats to exercise restraint in commenting on such people. This situation was custom-made for Nixon and his fellow campaigners for the presidency in 1968, for they were able to play the patriotism and law and order cards, the latter a thinly disguised appeal to the white backlashers. The hapless Johnson thus lost with either response to the racial dilemma. The war had broken what had always been a fragile accommodation within the Democratic Party between the racial liberals and the Dixie diehards. Johnson's reaction was an admission of political as well as foreign policy failure: on March 31, 1968, just days before King's death, he withdrew from the presidential race. To his replacement as the Democratic candidate, Hubert Humphrey, he left an agenda for defeat. To his Republican White House successor he left the following foreign policy messages: it was opportune to continue the war; it was prudent to talk of peace; and, in order to survive politically, it would be wise to massage certain key social groups at the heart of what remained of the Vietnam war consensus.

President Nixon's first term in office was marked by a lessening in the density of African American protest against the war and, in consequence of King's assassination, a deterioration in the quality of mass leadership in the antiwar cause. In terms of dramatizing a great issue, then, King's Riverside speech was a peak beyond which lay decline.

In the late sixties, black demands were diluted through proliferation. Campus protesters, for example, were in some conspicuous cases more concerned to establish Afro-American studies programs in their respective universities than to protest the war. Divisiveness plagued the black radicals, and they also fell out with some old allies. King's death was a blow to the friendly pact that had existed between African American and Jewish liberals.[89] Black anti-Semitic tendencies surfaced in the looting of Jewish stores, in anti-Israeli postures adopted by pro-Arab Black Muslims, and in hostility to Jewish professors who questioned the automatic hiring of black instructors to teach black studies.

Political circumstances further weakened the hand of African American war protesters. Presidential elections normally afford an opportunity to present a case, but, with the Republicans' "Southern strategy," the 1968 contest had become a showcase not for black protest but for subliminal white racism. Following the voter registration drive in the South, the political emergence of the black citizen had seemed imminent, but the thrust of the election campaign suggested that, on the contrary, the African American's moment had passed. If black activists, to restore their ailing political fortunes, looked for an ally in the weightiest white critic of the war, they perceived an unpromising spectacle: Senator Fulbright (Dem., Ark.) had not shaken off his 1950s reputation as a white supremacist. Finally, President Nixon took steps to recruit some African American support. His attempt to recruit black voters indicates his belief in the possibility of denting black enthusiasm for the Democrats. Such was the state of Democratic disarray that his overtures seemed less implausible than they might have.[90]

In the Nixon years, black antiwar protest led to some dramatic incidents, such as the fatal shooting two unarmed students at Jackson State College, Mississippi, in May 1970 by Mississippi highway patrolmen and Jackson City policemen. Yet, on the whole, African Americans continued to be conspicuous by their absence from the antiwar mass demonstrations. One historian has even speculated that because the media tended automatically to associate black radicalism with the Panthers and black nationalists, the absence of African American demonstrators may have "redounded to the benefit of the [antiwar] movement."[91]

Black resistance to Vietnam policy did continue, and its strength may be appreciated in two areas in particular. One was the continuing racial bitterness within and toward the military. Within the military, racial tension had reached critical proportions. White House officials speculated that the Newark and Detroit riots of 1967 had created a confrontational attitude that spilled over into the military arena. African Americans were no doubt also affected by a revolution of rising expectations: there were no black Marines in 1943, 60 black Marine officers in 1965, and 294 black Marine officers in 1970. But the improvement curve only sensitized African Americans to their overall minority position: only 1.1 percent of all Marine officers were black.[92] Whatever the cause of black discontent, it was an inescapable part of military life. The Army dealt with Joe Miles of the Fort Jackson Eight by sending him to a remote posting in Alaska, but it was too late to prevent the issue of free speech within the Army from becoming a cause célèbre in 1969–1970. Pete Seeger, Norman Mailer, Dr. Benjamin Spock, and even the English philosopher Bertrand Russell rallied to the cause of the Eight.[93]

No branch of the armed forces was immune to the corrosive effects of racial discontent. Lieutenant Commander William S. Norman, a combat warfare officer in a carrier division, complained of "institutional racism" in the Navy: when he decided to quit, his commanding officer noted that "Vietnam was secondary to [Norman's] feelings of what was happening to blacks who were part of the war."[94] In February 1970, the former Marine officer and intelligence specialist William R. Corson addressed a protest meeting in Washington that included a number of congressmen. With white soldiers routinely referring to the Vietnamese as "gooks, slopes, and dinks," he declared, America had lost its moral authority to fight the war. Black soldiers were shooting at white soldiers in battle, and back at base, white officers were being murdered in fragging incidents. Corson said to a White House staffer, Dave Miller, that "many units are inoperable unless the blacks give tacit consent."[95] Even allowing for some exaggeration, episodes of the type that Corson described were bad for military morale. Perhaps just as worrying from the viewpoint of certain members of the public, was the specter of a war-crazed, racially embittered G.I. with an expert finger on the trigger of an M16 automatic rifle and heroin in his veins being let loose on the streets of America. Stories about erratic, violent ex-G.I.s gave a very misleading impression of the average black veteran but were still alarming.[96]

Black resistance to the draft complemented the trouble within the armed forces. Publicity on the matter had ensured that almost everyone knew that if you were white and went to Harvard, your chances of being killed in Vietnam were small, but if you were black and lived in Mississippi, with its all-white draft boards, it was a different story. Furthermore, when draft board decisions were appealed to the Supreme Court, white supplicants tended to succeed, black ones not; of the three African Americans who triumphed against the odds to take their cases that far, two failed. In 1970, in the campaign of the Southern Conference Educational Fund on behalf of Walter Collins, such points were made forcefully. A civil rights worker in the early sixties, Collins had started to organize black opposition to the war in New Orleans. A gerrymandered all-white draft board gave him a I-A (fit to serve) classification in 1966, and he received a five-year prison sentence when he refused to enter the Army. In the 1970 campaign against his conviction, several other African American protesters were cited who had been similarly convicted.[97]

The administration offered a brighter picture of blacks in the war, contending that there had been certain statistical ameliorations. Secretary of Defense Melvin Laird wrote to the presidential special assistant Leonard Garment about this in April 1971. Laird noted the decline in the number of "blacks killed in action" expressed as a percentage of all battle mortalities. The figure had declined from 17.8, the average for 1961–1967, to 10.1, the percentage for 1970.[98] An optimist could believe that the old anomalies were disappearing. Certainly, the American armed forces were more democratic and racially integrated than their British counterparts, where all senior officers remained white and upper class until the end of the century. Recently, it has been estimated that over the course of the war, black casualty rates and the percentage of African Americans drafted to Vietnam were only slightly disproportionate in relation to their share in the civilian population.[99]

These final figures should not be allowed to obscure two vital points. First, the post-1968 changes in battlefield mortalities came too late to prevent black hostility to the Army and the war. Figures obtained by the National Association of Black Students as late as 1969 still showed a markedly disproportionate casualty rate, and the issue burned deeply into black consciousness. Second, overall racial proportionality, such as it was, came about because of a shrinkage in the number of black soldiers in the second half of the war. That shrinkage highlights the earlier racial discrepancies and can be taken as evidence more of a continuing revolt against the war than of a sudden access of liberalism in the White House.[100]

African Americans did not waver in their opposition to the war, and, in spite of their difficulties with the Democrats, they continued to distrust the Republicans. According to Roy Wilkins's estimate, only a handful among the one million African American "leaders" who thought about politics were potentially Republican voters (around seven million African Americans usually voted in presidential elections).[101] This degree of hostility among the now enfranchised African Americans constituted a potential problem. The winning over of "redneck" support through the Southern strategy could have been expected to outweigh marginal losses among the black electorate, but Nixon, a thoroughly professional politician, valued support from any quarter and realized that he could ill afford to alienate moderate white opinion by seeming to be indifferent to the African American vote.

In 1971 the rebellion of the Congressional Black Caucus underlined the seriousness of the matter. Even though white politicians used many ploys to disempower black people, the African American representation in the Congress increased from five in 1965 to eighteen in 1975. Given the logrolling in the legislative process, that is a significant number, even if it still badly underrepresented the share of blacks in the population. For the first time in a hundred years, black Americans were in a position to legitimize their demands by using the legislative process. The ten African American representatives, who formed their own caucus in 1969-1970, contained, in individuals like William Clay (Dem., Mo.), Chisholm, and Louis Stokes (Dem., Ohio), battle-hardened veterans of the years of civil rights struggle.[102] And they had discovered the principle of strength in unity. According to Rob Singh, an authority on the Black Caucus: "There is a powerful difference between an individual black politician . . . criticizing the president for his neglect of black America, and his censuring the chief executive on behalf of an organization perceived . . . to represent all blacks."[103]

Convinced that Nixon was unsympathetic to African Americans, the Black Caucus asked for a meeting with the president in February 1971. Nixon refused to see them, as he had done throughout the preceding year—contributing, according to the *Philadelphia Inquirer*, to his reputation for not caring about black people. But by now the Black Caucus had planned its riposte. Its members embarrassed the president by boycotting his State of the

Union address. Attempting to repair the damage, the president at last agreed to meet the Black Caucus on March 25. Amid a fanfare of publicity, the caucus handed Nixon a list of sixty demands. Most of them had to do with the rectification of injustices to black people at home. But the primary foreign-policy recommendation was for withdrawal from the Vietnam War by the end of the year. The caucus cited a "significant" increase in black discontent with the war in the past two years, attacked the education system that equipped young African Americans for nothing better than the infantry, and referred to the frustration felt by black soldiers about racial inequities. In a television interview in May, Congressman Diggs said in his capacity as Caucus chair that the financial squeeze caused by the war "is a priority point." With more than a hint of menace, he added, "We are in the process of looking toward the 1972 elections."[104]

In the wake of the meeting with Nixon, members of the caucus formed themselves into a kind of shadow cabinet, each having a sphere of responsibility and prepared to "comment in depth" on a particular specialty. In the realm of foreign policy, Diggs, his anti–Vietnam War credentials already secure, was assigned to Africa. The mantle of war critic fell partly on the capable shoulders of Shirley Chisholm. In the black shadow cabinet, she specialized in the African American G.I. and on veterans' affairs.[105]

A former Marine, Ronald V. Dellums (Dem., Calif.), had the Southeast Asia brief. In 1967, Dellums had attracted attention as a war critic and in 1968 he had backed the black students involved in a radical confrontation with S. I. Hayakawa, the conservative president of his alma mater, San Francisco State College. In California's Seventh District, which included both rebellious Berkeley and the black ghettoes of Oakland, birthplace of the Panthers, he then defeated the labor-backed incumbent for the Democratic nomination—perhaps helped by his father, C. L. Dellums, having been a leader of the first black U.S. union, the Brotherhood of Sleeping Car Porters. In 1970, Ronald Dellums was elected to the Congress by what one historian has described as a "coalition of hippies, white radicals, and black militants." A *Los Angeles*

Times journalist dismissed him as a "dressed-up dude who plays to the New Left the way the late Sen. Joe McCarthy played to the far right."[106]

But to his admirers, the spokesman for "Bezerkeley" was a patriotic and articulate opponent of the war.[107] He was one of several antiwar candidates sent to the Hill that year, and his arrival in Washington with the others legitimized the protest movement in a way that the law and order sloganeers found difficult to counter. A month after Nixon met with the Black Caucus, Dellums embarrassed the administration by importing the Bertrand Russell hearings on American war crimes. Owing to pressure from the U.S. government, those holding the hearings had been hounded from one country to another, seemingly proof that the alleged perpetrators of atrocities are seldom arraigned when they are protected by the powerful. But ever since November 1969, when details of the My Lai massacre had emerged, there had been a campaign to investigate alleged U.S. atrocities more fully. On March 16, 1968, an American infantry company on a routine search-and-destroy mission had entered the hamlet of My Lai in Quang Ngai province and, though encountering no resistance, destroyed property, raped several women, and killed between 175 and 400 men, women, and children. In March 1971, Lieutenant William L. Calley, Jr., the commanding officer at My Lai, was convicted by court-martial of premeditated murder. Dellums now held unofficial hearings over a period of four days. They were controversial. According to one critic, some of the witnesses "sounded as if they had memorized North Vietnamese propaganda." But among the eleven House members who attended the opening session, some—for example, Ed Koch, Bella Abzug and Patsy Mink—would be standard-bearers in the congressional campaign to stop the war.[108]

It could be argued that none of this should have worried Nixon, that he had no incentive to listen to black opinion on the war. Between 1935 and 1991 every African American in the House of Representatives was a Democrat. African Americans were not going to vote for Nixon anyway, so he might as well concentrate on winning the unreconstructed white vote.[109] But Nixon did not think that way. In 1968 he had calculated that he would need only 2 percent of the black vote to win but aimed to gain 12 percent to help him govern effectively. Accordingly, he kept a precious trophy at his side during much of that campaign: Edward Brooke, who was not just the only black man in the Senate but also a Republican.

To understand the intensity of Nixon's political concern with African Americans as he began to contemplate the challenge of reelection, it is necessary to divest oneself of historical hindsight. The Republican election victory of 1968 had been close and owed much to a three-way fight. It would have required a crystal ball to foretell that Wallace would run again in the Democratic primaries, that he would be immobilized by an assassin's bullet in May 1972, and that the election result would nevertheless be a Nixon landslide. With an eye to future tactics, the president therefore studied the midterm elections carefully. In July 1970, just in time for the midterm elections, a group of leading blacks across the nation met to form the National Black Silent Majority Committee. They aimed to show that the majority of African Americans did not riot, held patriotic views, hated communism, and opposed busing as a way to end segregation in schools. Nixon wrote an encouraging letter to Clay Claiborne, the former civil rights journalist who directed the group. About the same time, the National Republican Congressional Committee issued a pamphlet, *Black Leadership in the Nixon Administration*, with photographic portraits of African Americans, twenty men and five women, associated with the Nixon administration; one of them, a city council member in the District of Columbia, Henry S. Robinson, was a reminder that Nixon supported home rule for the African American–dominated national capital.[110]

During the midterm election campaigns, the president's attention was particularly drawn to New York. In a successful bid to be elected to the Senate, the conservative hawk James Buckley devised a strategy that appealed to Nixon and would provide a model for his own plan for dealing with minorities. Though by no means a notable promoter of African American welfare, Buckley had appealed to "the majority of black New Yorkers who repudiate the fanatic hatreds preached by the militant few," repeating the message for the three other high-profile social groups—students, labor, and women—and praising the young men who recognized "the blessings of American citizenship" and did not "shirk" their responsibilities in Vietnam.[111] The idea was to appeal to "majorities" within the "minorities" in the knowledge that, in practice, it would be necessary to win over only a small percentage in order to win.

Nixon's chances of winning over a higher proportion of the black vote were impaired by his footdragging on desegregation, his obstruction of busing initiatives, and the failure of the Black Capitalism program that he had launched in 1969 to encourage small African American businesses. But even before the Black Caucus started its activities, he and his supporters took steps to damp down black opposition to the war.

Leonard Garment played an important role in Nixon's management of minorities. The son of hard-working central European Jewish immigrants, Garment was educated at Brooklyn College and played the clarinet in various jazz bands, including Woody Herman's. He was originally a liberal Democrat, but he worked as a junior in the Nixon law firm and in 1966 helped the future president present a case to the Supreme Court. In May 1969 he joined the White House staff as special consultant to the president on civil rights and human rights.

The *Washington Post* greeted Garment's appointment with the headline "President's Idea Man: Outsider with Inside Ties." Conscious of the critical gaze of his liberal friends, Garment explained his motivation as the desire for "continued competition in the assimilation sweepstakes." He had a wide-ranging brief without portfolio that he described as that of an "ombudsman for the door-pounding outside world." His role in Nixon's first term resembled that of Cliff Alexander in the Johnson administration, but by bearing the sixties experience in mind and by knowing what Nixon wanted, he was able to dissect American society in a more thorough and professional manner. Nixon allowed him to handle students, women, and labor, as well as African Americans.[112]

Following the 1970 midterm elections, Garment detailed possible strategies for dealing with minorities, especially African Americans. There was to be a publicity campaign explaining the administration's effort to help black and poor people and presidential contacts and meetings with black congressmen, ministers, journalists, and other opinionmakers. Aware of the hill to be climbed, Garment counseled caution; black mayors, for example, should be met individually, not collectively. There was to be a presidential guerrilla campaign to pick off and win over important African Americans one by one.[113]

The government in the meantime pushed forward in the areas of affirmative action and military reform in a manner designed to take some of the sting out of black criticism of the war. The Veterans Administration increased its percentage of black employees. Nixon expanded the affirmative action provisions of the Johnson administration to cover construction contracts of over $50,000 nationwide (LBJ had had a pilot plan for contracts in Philadelphia). Secretary of Labor George Shultz promised more "effective implementation of existing law" in the area of civil rights and related programs. Staff numbers at the Equal Employment Opportunity Commission rose from 359 to 1,640 between 1969 and 1972. Leading from the top, Nixon doubled the number of African Americans in senior government jobs. The administration also commissioned a study by the NAACP into the question of disproportionate punishments being meted out to black soldiers.[114]

With this record, Nixon could hope to keep Senator Brooke of Massachusetts on board. Brooke had criticized King in the wake of the Riverside speech but denied that he himself had abandoned the "doves" for the "hawks." No, he insisted, he remained an "owl."[115] Then, in 1970, he began to display distinctly "peacenik" tendencies. On May 1 he condemned the U.S. bombing of North Vietnamese sanctuaries in Cambodia. On August 27 he announced his support for the Hatfield-McGovern "end the war" amendment calling for the withdrawal of American troops from Vietnam. He declared himself opposed to the draft and in favor of an "all-volunteer armed force."[116]

Charles ("Chuck") Colson was given the job of becoming "close friends" with Brooke.[117] Colson had entered the administration as a special counsel to the president in 1969. After a while, Nixon entrusted him with delicate missions, culminating in those undertaken by the "Plumbers," the Special Investigations Unit established in July 1971 to prevent leaks of sensitive information and ultimately involved in the Watergate break-in. But Colson's original and main job was to devise means of recruiting minority support, especially from African Americans and labor, and this was the reason for his cultivation of Senator Brooke.

In March 1971, Colson recommended a leak to the effect that "the President offered Ed Brooke a position in the Cabinet." This ploy would boost Brooke and show that Nixon was "concerned with the Blacks." It would have the further advantage that the post would not actually have to be given away, because it had already been ascertained that Brooke wanted to remain in the Senate "because he is the only Black there." When Senators Clifford P. Case (Rep., N.J.) and Charles McC. Mathias, Jr. (Rep., Md.) pressed for a Vietnam withdrawal deadline, an apparently compliant Brooke now told Colson that he would "not join in their colloquy." In the Senate, Brooke opposed a congressionally imposed deadline for withdrawal, arguing that the president should be allowed to set the timetable, evidence in Colson's view that he was "trying to deflect" the Case-Mathias assault. On April 14, Brooke met with National Security Adviser Henry Kissinger and with Colson and promised not to engage in criticism of the administration's Southeast Asia policy for thirty days and not to join the "Dump Nixon" movement associated with the antiwar Republicans Pete McCloskey (Calif.) and Charles E. Goodell (N.Y.).[118]

Brooke nevertheless remained unhappy with Nixon's Vietnam policy. The senator's own state, Massachusetts, was a hotbed of antiwar feeling, and he, like the president, was up for reelection in 1972. His unhappiness is evident in his otherwise resounding endorsement of Nixon's reelection in mid-May 1972. In an address to students at the University of Massachusetts, he criticized the president for not setting a withdrawal deadline, for continued U.S. bombing, and for giving military support to the Vietnamese. The White House aide Howard Cohen told Colson, "If you want to use EWB outside Massachusetts for RN, you had better be sure that it is limited and controlled." Colson apparently agreed, although one of his colleagues scribbled disrespectfully on a memo, "What does Colson want? Egg in his beer? This is a hell of good defense before the most hostile possible audience."[119]

Brooke's behavior epitomized the African American dilemma over the Vietnam War. On the one hand, he detested the war. On the other, he was a minority leader who perceived that by conforming to foreign policy norms he might enhance his own and his people's chances of breaking through America's glass ceilings and achieving higher social and political status. He contrived to sit on the political fence in a manner that invited concessions to black Americans as a means of keeping him loyal. As a result, the White House courted him; perhaps the silent majority ploy did not monopolize Nixonian strategy.

The Democratic presidential candidate George McGovern, in his campaign against the war, had strong grounds on which to appeal for the African American vote. Brooke could hardly condemn his demand for withdrawal; the Black Caucus strongly endorsed it. McGovern's support staff compiled statistics to show that black veterans of the war had a higher unemployment rate than their white counterparts and that the disparity was increasing. Black veterans had also endured an exceptional number of "less than honorable discharges," which meant that the affected individuals did not qualify for various veterans' benefits, such as educational and employment assistance. The Democratic candidate told a Los Angeles meeting of Asian Americans for McGovern that he saw "racial prejudice as one of the most offensive aspects of the Administration's policy in Vietnam" and that "the Vietnamization program constitutes a statement by the Nixon Administration that Asian lives are less valuable than American lives."[120]

McGovern's heavy defeat in the 1972 election (Massachusetts was the only state he carried) was by no means a prowar verdict. Individual antiwar candidates—for example, King's former assistant Andrew Young running for an Atlanta congressional district—succeeded in the same round of voting, and Nixon had given his own campaign an antiwar cast by announcing that peace was at hand. Nevertheless, the result was a triumph for the incumbent's reelection strategies—not the least important of which concerned the black voter and the war issue.

In deciding between options, Nixon took into account their congeniality to African Americans. Vietnamization was a response to new strategic thinking and to public opinion at large, but it had the additional advantage of assuaging the black disproportionate-casualty grievance and of being easier to implement than some other approaches to discrimination. Similarly, whereas withdrawal from the war was part of a complex international diplomatic fix known as "linkage," withdrawal can also be seen as an option with the attraction of being cheaper than putting an end to discrimination to help make Vietnam a just war. At the same time, through affirmative action Nixon did do enough, just enough, to persuade nonliberal white voters that they could vote Republican without being labeled out-and-out racists. Here, the neutralization of Brooke was a prerequisite.

Do these Nixonian political successes indicate that African American opponents of the Vietnam War were no match for the "tricky" operator in the White House? Certainly, their opposition was flawed even before Nixon's wily aides set to work on it. Major black figures had rounded on King after his Riverside speech, sowing seeds of doubt in the minds of would-be protesters. King's assassination deprived African Americans of an astute leader. Other factors, too, weakened black protest. The white backlash leading to Nixon's election in 1968 was partially a verdict on Riverside, even if it drew on other, more important sources. Nor could African Americans cooperate effectively with Fulbright, a hero to so many white protesters, because his opposition to the war rested heavily on his belief that it was "abhorrent that white men should have to spill their blood to safeguard the freedom and independence of yellow men."[121]

These weaknesses notwithstanding, African American opposition did sap the war effort in Vietnam. At home, black soldiers had initially strengthened that effort. Their high volunteer rates and vulnerability to front-line assignments had at first promised a liberal, multiracial, democratic, high-morale war effort. But morale in Vietnam slumped. Racial resentments contributed to fragging, camp riots, and other breaches of discipline and finally threatened a manpower shortage. Although cause and effect should not be too simply delineated, it is not entirely coincidental that the conflict in Vietnam was both the first foreign war in which African Americans had a full combat role and the first such war that America lost. That is a comment not on the valor of the black soldier, which no sane person would question, but on the racial politics of America.

Little wonder that Hanoi radio crowed about the "black uprising" that was part of "the American people's resolute struggle against the U.S. war escalation."[122] Black protest affected morale not just in America and Vietnam but also in other countries. International opinion was already skeptical about the American cause, and the injection of a racial element into the debate was especially injurious to the United States in the Third World, ensuring that Washington would be isolated, condemned to minority status in the world opinion forum by the activities and discontents of a minority within its own borders. It was hard to counter the question posed by the Indian commentator Kumar Das: "As the number of American lives lost in the war has declined, it seems the U.S. Government has turned more destructive of lives and property in Vietnam. . . . With guns borrowed from the developed world, how long should poor Asians kill each other?"[123]

According to the journalist Thomas B. Morgan, who toured the world and wrote a book on anti-Americanism in 1967, "Our race crisis and the war in Vietnam," together with "our postwar interventionism," were prime causes of U.S. unpopularity abroad. He was thinking of liberal-left opinion, but more conservative analysts, too, gave the Johnson administration cause for concern. Among the newspapers that portrayed mass protest as a liability to the war effort were Britain's *Daily Telegraph*, France's *Figaro*, West Germany's *Stuttgarter Zeitung*, and Iran's *Ettela'at*.[124] Clippings gathered by the McGovern campaign team in 1972 suggested that

Vietnam had become a serious political issue in Britain, Canada and Australia, countries usually staunchly loyal to the United States. The *Manchester Guardian*, for one, asked: "How long can the Americans go on killing innocents and destroying a culture and still retain the position of moral superiority which is the only thing that entitles them to be in South-east Asia at all?"[125] The Vietnam War was no light matter for countries like Australia and Sweden where the issue influenced the outcome of elections.[126] Some Americans, cherishing isolationist myths, may have given little thought to foreign opinion. It could be argued, however, that America had won past wars partly because it carried world opinion. It did not in the case of Vietnam, and lost.

The challenge that African Americans mounted to the moral basis of the war affected opinion at home. When that challenge helped to produce a reform of the draft system, the government found itself confronted with the prospect of middle-class anger—specifically, from the white families whose young men would now be affected—making Vietnamization a political necessity. But the story of the African American impact on the nation did not end there, for by now there were enough black representatives in the Congress to establish the Black Caucus and to present a collective demand for an end to the war. Along with the agile, fence-sitting Senator Brooke, the representatives in the caucus contributed to the legitimization of the antiwar movement. They added to the pressure on President Nixon to run as a peace candidate in 1972 and to end the war early in the following year.

The role of African Americans in bringing Southeast Asian hostilities to a close needs to be kept in perspective. Other social groups, like students and women, also had roles to play. Black opposition to the war had inherent weaknesses, such as the diversity of motives outlined by the historian Mullen. A weakness not of their own making was that African Americans provoked a powerful and restrictive backlash against the protest movement. Thus, black opposition peaked in 1967 but was weaker at other times. In summary, it is evident that African Americans had a triple accelerator effect on U.S. policy toward Vietnam. In the early years of the conflict, they bolstered the war. In the middle stages, they hastened the peace. But in the final stages, African Americans played an involuntary part in the politics of backlash that delayed U.S. withdrawal from the war. That delay might have been longer still, but for the continuance of the black demand for peace.

5 Women

WOMEN WERE EFFECTIVE OPPONENTS OF the Vietnam War. They supplied the antiwar movement with literary luminaries like Mary McCarthy, stars like Jane Fonda, and publicity-capturing organizations like Women Strike for Peace (WSP). They were especially important in helping to legitimize the antiwar movement from 1970 on, with Congresswoman Bella Abzug to the fore in cutting off the funds that sustained the U.S. military effort in Indochina. Whereas students started the antiwar campaign and African Americans took up the standard two years later, it fell to women to make the final charge.

The pronounced affinity of women with the legitimization movement arose from their minority mentality and their ambitions for political breakthrough. Here, however, some serious qualifications must be borne in mind. Women were a majority of the population. Some women deeply resented being labeled members of a minority group, and a few, prominent in voluntary organizations and drawn from the upper classes, thought of themselves as insiders having an influence on policy by indirect means.[1]

Against this may be set evidence indicating that women had long played the outsider's role in politics. The sociologist Gunnar Myrdal had in 1944 identified "striking similarities" between the predicament of women and that of African Americans.[2] There can be few more graphic illustrations of the power of the outsider concept than the following extract from Shirley Chisholm's campaign book, *Unbought and Unbossed* (1970). Chisholm was the first African American congresswoman. "Women," she wrote, "are a majority of the population, but they are treated like a minority group. . . . Of my two 'handicaps,' being female put many more obstacles in my path than being black."[3]

Yet, and this is an important qualification, it was precisely because women felt they were excluded from full participation in the American democratic process that it was tempting for them to try to improve their acceptability by supporting the Vietnam War. Antimilitarism was all very well in peacetime, but not in wartime. A character in Mary McCarthy's novel *The Group* (1963) noted the distinction, declaring that "in *peacetime* . . . she was a pacifist."[4] Some women thought that they would have to become politically indistinguishable from their more belligerent menfolk before they could break through to a position of full equality. One did not have to be a feminist to think this way. Many women abhorred the stridency of feminism but wanted political equality. According to this line of reasoning, the new woman, to shed her minority status and to capitalize on her demographic advantage, would have to be an Amazon in foreign policy.[5]

This point of view prevailed among women in the early stages of the war. But after a while, they turned against it, becoming, in effect, wartime pacifists. They resolved the conflict between the desire to protest and the desire to win political legitimacy by inventing a tactical synthesis: they legitimized protest. Their preference for political and legislative means of opposing the war went hand in hand with legitimization of women in politics.

In accomplishing the dual goals of protest and progress, women had an advantage over African Americans and students: they were able to turn against the war without incurring a major backlash. Women had suffered from backlash in the past and suffered from it again in the future.[6] One reason for their escape in the sixties may have been that students and African Americans took the heat. Another reason for the underdeveloped backlash was the slow pace of sixties feminism. There was no great reaction against women in the sixties because they did not achieve a great deal in that decade and did not discomfit the male world. Women even went backward in some respects. For example, they started the decade with twenty members in the Congress and ended it with eleven. Between 1957 and 1970 the number of women in the U.S. Foreign Service declined from 8.9 to 4.8 percent of the total; women made up three-fourths of State Department personnel but supplied less than 4 percent of its senior officials. According to India Edwards, director of the women's division of the Democratic National Committee, women were a "at a lower ebb in the political life of this country" in 1969 than they had been at any point in her long career. There had been a particular deterioration under Presidents Kennedy and Johnson.[7]

On the one hand, women faced a power deficit. On the other, given their slow and even negative record, the foreign policy establishment was taken unawares when women rebelled against the war. The establishment had neglected to build the apparatus of backlash. They had no law and order issue or Southern strategy to launch against women. This lack of response encouraged women to proceed with their protest and allowed them to do so without effective political retribution.

At first, women were behind the war. As ever, support for a war was one way an outsider group could climb the greasy pole of status advancement. There were other reasons, too. Prowar female newspaper reporters and women in politics were, of course, influenced by the same arguments as men were, but in the early stages of the war an additional element in the standard anticommunist arguments appealed especially to women: the apparent link between totalitarianism—with its accomplishment of objectives through coercion—and physically based male misrule of women. Democracy was inherently attractive to women. The lack of democracy in the U.S. ally, South Vietnam, was upsetting, but the promise of reform there and the argument that the fight in the Mekong delta was the essential element in the fight to contain the spread of international communism did resonate with women. They saw a gender-specific ideological reason for supporting any war against communism, and Vietnam seemed to fit the case.

Prowar feeling among women retained its strength throughout the peak years of student and black protest. Women serving in Vietnam in the military, for example, voiced few significant political protests until the end of the sixties. One reason may have been that they were barred from combat and failed to experience the full horror of war at first hand.[8] Another was their small number: between 1962 and 1973, only 7,500 women served on active military duty in Vietnam. The highest estimate for the total number of military and civilian women serving in Vietnam is 55,000, an eleven-year aggregate figure that includes nurses, air traffic controllers, photographers, cartographers, clerks and secretaries, intelligence specialists, missionaries, teachers, journalists, and flight attendants.[9]

Nurses made up 80 percent of American women serving in

Vietnam. They were true disciples of Florence Nightingale in that they rarely questioned the reasons for the casualties under their care.[10] If they did think, they were prone to do so in Cold War stereotypes. Lily Adams of the Army Nurse Corps recalled an incident at the Twelfth Evacuation Hospital at Cy Chi: "Another guy, I remember, lay there and told me he was dying for nothing. I was just about to talk about the domino theory and try to make him feel better, but someone told me, 'He doesn't want to listen to that shit.'"[11] Although some nurses were traumatized by the horrific battle injuries that they had to treat and by the sight of so much human suffering, others remembered their Vietnam days as a vivid and comradely period. Georgia Dullea, a veteran nurse and counselor, caught herself wishing she could go back: "Life over there was so real and in some ways so much easier."[12] Nurses who enjoyed themselves in Vietnam boosted military morale and contributed to the military cause.

According to the historian Virginia Elwood-Akers, a "large" number of women reported on the war in Vietnam, and two of them were killed. She observed that these reporters were not conspicuous for their feminism and were neither more nor less supportive of the war than their male colleagues.[13] Marguerite Higgins, it is true, was famously prowar. An old Asia hand by virtue of having been born in Hong Kong, Higgins had won a Pulitzer Prize for her coverage of the Korean War. In July 1963, making her seventh visit to Vietnam on behalf of the *New York Herald Tribune*, she found herself opposed to the anti-Saigon clique of eminent male liberal reporters: David Halberstam of the *New York Times*, Neil Sheehan of United Press International, and Charles Mohr of *Time*. Returning for a tenth visit in 1965 to report for *Newsday*, she argued strenuously for escalation of the war. Her book *Our Vietnam Nightmare*, published that year, urged Americans to show more willpower than the French, who had used their 1954 defeat at Dien Bien Phu as an excuse for capitulation to the Communists. She criticized the Kennedy administration, which had withdrawn support from the regime of President Ngo Dinh Diem (the Kennedy administration lost faith in Diem because he failed to democratize; the South Vietnamese leader was assassinated in November 1963, and a period of political instability followed). Higgins insisted that "Vietnam's rights as a sovereign state clearly entitle it to install a measure of authoritarian rule and curb civil liberties." When she died in January 1966, she received a hero's burial at Arlington National Cemetery.[14]

Madame Nhu appealed to Marguerite Higgins to support her campaign for women's rights in Vietnam. The widow of Ngo Dinh Nhu, South Vietnam's security chief and younger brother of the deceased prime minister and president Ngo Dinh Diem, Madame Nhu was a headstrong figure. President Kennedy had even suspected her of conspiring with a potential presidential challenger, the strongly pro-Saigon Senator Barry Goldwater.[15] Higgins did not respond to Madame Nhu's brand of militant Catholic feminism (no contraceptives, no dancing) and distanced herself from that leader who, she noted, had incurred the "venomous" hatred of the Vietnamese intelligentsia.[16] Clare Boothe Luce, another American with media prominence, was similarly cautious. A former playwright who had married the influential publisher of *Time* and *Fortune* and served as a determinedly anticommunist U.S. ambassador in Italy in the 1950s, Luce thought the strategic interests of the United States demanded the defense of South Vietnam. Like Higgins, she was sympathetic to Madame Nhu, whose husband had been assassinated along with Diem—but she supported her only in personal matters, not in politics. Madame Nhu's arrogance, as well as the socially conservative views of prominent female American hawks, helped to ensure that, women's aversion to autocracy notwithstanding, there would be no feminist dimension to women's support for the Vietnam war.[17]

It could be argued that this was not a weakness in the sixties prowar movement, for most women preferred not to be involved in feminism or other radical causes. Indeed, Jeannette Rankin, who had been the first U.S. congresswoman and was now a leader in the antiwar movement, had a low opinion of women on the home front: "They've been worms. They let their sons go off to war because they're afraid their husbands will lose their jobs in industry if they protest."[18] In January 1968 a group of her supporters tried to shake "traditional" American women out of their torpor, claiming that their apathy had led too many to "hanky-wave boys off to war with admonitions to save the American Mom and Apple Pie."[19] Their admonitions acknowledged the conservatism of sixties women even as they tried to shake it.

The deliberations of the League of Women Voters (LWV) further illustrate the initial reluctance of women—in this case, a powerful group of women—to agitate against the war. The LWV was a nonpartisan educational and pressure organization. It was in decline, its membership having halved since the twenties; women were increasingly interested in paid jobs at the expense of voluntary work, and many feminists were put off by the culture of an organization whose members were known to be "ladies" and who still tended to label themselves with their husbands' first names—for example, the congressional secretary of the LWV identified herself as Mrs. Francis P. Douglas. But the LWV's upper-middle-class composition preserved for it an influence out of keeping with the decline in its numbers. It was a breeding ground for political women, it performed a prominent role in stimulating national debate, and it had a long-term interest in foreign policy.[20]

In August 1965, Mrs. Douglas explained to a member that there was "a wide divergence of opinion" on the Vietnam War in the LWV Council. The LWV president, Mrs. Robert J. Stuart, had been exchanging friendly letters with President Johnson about U.S. policy in Vietnam. But the question now arose: Should the LWV's long-standing commitment to the resolution of international conflicts through the United Nations prompt a recommendation to the administration that it put more faith in that channel?[21]

The LWV did, in 1965–1966, encourage President Johnson to proceed through the United Nations. Doing so was a way of defusing internal opposition, and other organizations also promoted that course—the Young Women's Christian Association (YWCA), for example. In 1966 the national student council of the YWCA passed a resolution urging an end to the war through negotiations with South Vietnam's revolutionary National Liberation Front. In response, the YWCA national board called instead for the United States to seek free elections through the United Nations.[22]

The quiescence of such tactics is apparent. The LWV stressed the importance of acting in an undemanding manner. Its foreign policy secretary Mrs. Donald C. Mills devised a standard letter of advice for replying to communications from concerned women: "It is important to select carefully the times and circumstances for communicating to the President in this matter." In 1967 the LWV program secretary, Anona Teska, explained that the league would take no position on the peace terms suggested by U.N. Secretary-General U Thant, for to do so would be an implied judgment on Johnson's policy position. The league had not studied the problem enough to arrive at such a judgment, and there was no significant pressure from the rank and file for such a study to be undertaken. The LWV never moved from this determinedly nonpartisan position. In 1971 a despairing member learned that the LWV council was still split on the issue. In 1972, Vietnam was allowed onto the LWV convention floor, but only as in an expression of members' personal views, and not in a motion having binding effect on league policy. The Vietnam War had presented an opportunity for debate—the war was undeclared and hence did not demand automatic allegiance to the flag—but the ladies of the league rejected the politics of confrontation in favor of institutional unity and the preservation of influence.[23]

Similar elements of conformity are to be found among the women of the Ninetieth Congress (1967–1969).[24] To be sure, congresswomen had the potential for troublesome rebellion. Although only twelve women had seats in the ninetieth Congress, a gross underrepresentation of their sex, their representation was greater numerically than that of African Americans (seven) and students (none). Two of the congresswomen were strategically placed. Frances Page Bolton (Ohio) had been the ranking Republican member of the House Foreign Affairs Committee since 1960, and Margaret Chase Smith (Rep., Maine) was the minority leader on the Senate Armed Services Committee. At least three of the congresswomen were distinctly unhappy with the American role in Southeast Asia: Julia Butler Hansen (Dem., Wash.) had urged President Johnson to accept U.N. mediation on Vietnam; Patsy Takemoto Mink (Dem., Hawaii), the first Asian woman elected to the Congress, was an early opponent of the war, as was Edith Green (Dem., Ore.).

Serious trouble did not materialize until later. Although most women in the Congress took an interest in Vietnam, they tended to concentrate on veterans' affairs and on support for nurses. One reason for their restraint may have been their concern with women's rights. In this sense, their predicament paralleled that of African Americans, for whom the Great Society program seemed to promise improvements. Martha Wright Griffiths (Dem., Mich.), the first woman on the powerful House Ways and Means Committee, helped to frame the sex discrimination amendment to Title VII of the 1964 Civil Rights Act and campaigned for its enforcement once enacted. In 1967 she attacked high defense spending, but every congresswoman must have been aware that a challenge to the Johnson administration over the Vietnam War might place women's gains in jeopardy.[25]

With these factors inhibiting opposition to the war, the role of its supporters was easier. Republican backing was particularly valuable to President Johnson, as it had been to Presidents Wilson and Roosevelt in earlier wars, and at every stage the Johnson administration received bipartisan support for its war policy from congressional women. In the House, Charlotte Thomson Reid (Rep., Ill.) was notable for her defense of Johnson's Asia policy—in 1968, for example, she supported a measure that denied loans to students who had participated in antiwar demonstrations. In the Senate, the administration had a formidable supporter in Margaret Chase Smith.

Smith's quiet style belied her record as the most powerful and successful elected woman politician in American history. She was known for her determined advocacy of greater equality for women in the armed forces and had won widespread respect for her courageous denunciation of Senator Joe McCarthy in the early 1950s. From the outset, Smith was against American involvement in the Vietnam War. But she was a firm anti-Communist, and once the war had started, she considered her role to be that of "loyal opposition." Thus, she hounded Secretary of Defense McNamara to fight the war more effectively and to give America's fighting men better support. She opposed bombing halts. Although she defended the right to dissent, she thought that war protesters were giving succor to Ho Chi Minh, and deplored their activity. Smith's long-deceased husband had been a labor reformer in the 1920s, and she greatly admired President Johnson's legislative ambitions; they held each other in mutually high regard and affection, a bond that their bipartisan stand on the Vietnam War reinforced. Smith regretted Johnson's decision not to run again in 1968, but she defended the Vietnam policy of Nixon, her fellow Republican, with equal conviction, if less personal warmth.[26]

Strong though their loyalty may have been, the women who supported the war lacked a gender-specific reason for supporting the hostilities in Vietnam as distinct from other wars in other places at other times. In contrast, women who opposed the war had both general and gender-specific reasons for doing so.

Debate is heated over the gender difference on the war-and-peace issue. Some feminists are incensed by the hypothesis that women oppose war because of their nurturing instincts. They object to the idea that they are innately or essentially different from men and to its corollary that they will in perpetuity be lumbered with caregiving activities of the type that carry a menial status. Other discussion focuses on the notion that it is men, not women, whose beliefs and behavior differ from the rational, peaceful norm; women simply have the advantage of being free from male conditioning. Still another theory holds that women should oppose war because war perpetuates patriarchy. This argument helped to give a special edge to women's critique of the Vietnam War, for the new feminism of the sixties looked beyond women's-rights issues and offered a more fundamental critique of male-dominated society.

In general, though not always by a wide margin, American women have been more antiwar than American men have. Depending on their viewpoint, they have advanced various reasons for their distinctively peaceful stance: their maternal instinct, their objection to war-induced inflation, their conviction that war is an artifact of male domination. In relation to the Vietnam War, women's opposition to price escalation was probably the weakest of these factors. By the 1960s, changing expenditure patterns within the family meant that women were no longer the unpaid guardians of the American pocketbook, as they had been in the 1920s. But consumerism may still have been a residual factor—in 1967, Denver housewives protested against war-induced price rises.[27]

The sharpness of women's critique of the Vietnam War derived from the nature and impact of that conflict in the sixties. Women had long argued that war demeaned them, being a men's game, and the declining status of women in public life in the sixties seemed to underline the point. The very fact of the war, it could be argued, was a symptom of women's loss of power in the United States, and its effect was the reinforcement of male hegemony. Gender aspects of the war played into the hands of its American opponents, especially in light of the contrast with the Vietnamese Communists. In Vietnam, Confucianism and polygamy had subordinated women for centuries. But the communist leader Ho Chi Minh emphasized the principle of gender equality. In June 1969 the South Vietnamese Provisional Revolutionary Government appointed a woman, Madame Nguyen Thi Binh, as foreign minister.

The Communist-nationalists thus appeared to be fighting for women as well as against Saigon and the Americans. Vietnamese women rallied to the cause and, depending on geographic area, could compose up to one-third of the fighting force of the Viet Cong. In contrast, the American and South Vietnamese governments restricted women to ancillary roles. Prostitution further reinforced the sexist image of the American cause. Prostitution was, in fact, rife in Hanoi as well as Saigon, but it had a higher profile in South Vietnam, plus official encouragement, and offended American women because the prostitutes served American men. Finally, the racial overtones of the war were conspicuous, not least because of the publicity that arose from the antiwar activities of African Americans. The women's rights movement had been allied to the fight against racial discrimination ever since the antislavery crusade. All these factors meant that the campaign against the Vietnam War had, potentially, a special appeal for American women.[28]

But the nascent female opposition to the war had certain weaknesses. No critique of the war attained the status of a universal article of faith among American women. Consciousness of gendered aspects of the war affected minorities of women in different ways and reached a lower plane in the sixties than in the seventies. Another weakness was the problem of male chauvinism in the antiwar movement. Women activists complained widely that men in the movement excluded them from decisionmaking and allocated them to menial tasks like food preparation—women at Berkeley cooked until 1968—typing, and the provision of sex. Bob Dylan's lyrics had a disturbingly misogynist strain. Tom Hayden apologetically admitted the male domination of the early SDS, and recent accounts gleefully relate how he had failed to reform even by the late sixties, when he still reflexively handed his laundry to the nearest woman and at one point found himself expelled from a Berkeley commune, accused of manipulative chauvinism.[29]

Men defended their dominance, especially in the antidraft movement, by stating that it was their lives that were at risk and therefore their prerogative to dictate tactics.[30] But their attitude was more deep-seated than that. The New Man—sensitive, diaper-changing, egalitarian—had not yet arrived in 1964–1965, when the antiwar campaign began in earnest. Radicals can be stubborn, too; the very backbone that makes them effective protesters can make them autocratic—the outcomes of the revolutions of 1789 and 1917 are prime, if extreme, examples. Finally, young men who refused to serve their country were accused of cowardice and so, against their better judgment, may have suffered from a loss of self-esteem. Ordering women about and flaunting the availability of sex in those envied sixties orgies was a way of restoring a sense of virility.

Male chauvinism in the peace movement alienated women and caused division in their ranks. But chauvinism and its consequences must be kept in perspective. Male chauvinism was hardly peculiar to the peace movement. It was to be found in the civil rights and, notably, the Black Power movements. And it was especially a feature of the war machine, from officers' clubs in Vietnam to the White House. President Johnson observed of a male dove in his administration: "Hell, he has to squat to piss!"[31] His attitude appealed to men who despised peaceniks and looked down on women. Norman Mailer—although he had once stabbed his own wife—drew attention to the actions of "working class" soldiers in breaking up the 1967 Pentagon demonstration: they singled out women to beat and humiliate. The predominantly middle-class feminists took note.[32]

Also, there is another side to the charge that male-chauvinist antiwar leaders engaged in sexual exploitation. Women connived at, if they did not invent, the effective antidraft slogan Girls Say Yes to Boys Who Say No. When, in 1967, the singer Joan Baez posed with two other women for a resistance poster bearing that caption, she did so of her own volition, even if her act did provoke a storm from "women's libbers."[33] The reputation of the peace movement for chauvinism arose in part from heightened expectation; a male antiwar protester was expected to be revolutionary in every respect, and his failure to be a New Man was commensurably disappointing. Distorted expectations could mask the change that was taking place. Years later, Hayden claimed that although only a few movement men had read Simone de Beauvoir in 1963, Betty Friedan's book was on their reading list as soon as it appeared that year. If the New Man had not quite arrived, he was about to.[34]

Male chauvinism impaired the peace movement in some ways. Yet it was less extreme than might be supposed, and it did stimulate feminist debate. Far from preventing the construction of the platform from which women launched their effective post-sixties protest, chauvinism in the antiwar movement may even have contributed some planks. Most important, it paled into insignificance compared with the gender chauvinism of war supporters. It was the chauvinism of the hawks that goaded the peace feminists into action.

Women's protest against the war was extensive and came in many varieties. It ranged from the activities of communist partisans like Anna Louise Strong, Bettina Aptheker, and Angela Davis to more conservative protests like the "Fuck the Army" rebellion by some military women at the end of the sixties. Tactically, it embraced individual acts, like the self-immolation of a solitary Quaker mother in Detroit, and great collective enterprises, like the production of antiwar newsletters with circulations running into tens of thousands.[35] Yet the volume and variety of protest is no more than one might expect in a country that prides itself on individualism and libertarianism and contains a large population of women. To appreciate more fully the way that sixties women built a platform for successful resistance to the war, it is helpful to review their contributions systematically in terms of organizations, personalities, and dramatic episodes.

According to one strain of New Left reasoning, anti-oppression organizations are incapable of effecting significant social change, because being structured destines them to become part of the opposing power elite. It has further been observed that women's antiwar organizations were not always capable of commanding attention in the media, the prerequisite for political impact. But the sixties threw up new women's organizations that were too immature to be incorporated into any power structure. The most important of them, WSP, contributed to major media-grabbing demonstrations, repeatedly commanded attention in its own right, and supplied a new generation of women with political training.[36]

The children's book illustrator Dagmar Wilson and three of her suburban neighbors in Washington, D.C., established WSP in 1961. The name of the organization, Women Strike for Peace, derived from the housewives' "strike" and accompanying marches organized for November 1, 1961. They progressed to other types of demonstration, backing the campaign for an atmospheric nuclear test ban treaty so effectively that they won tacit recognition from President Kennedy, who made strong appeals to mothers and grandmothers in whipping up support for enactment of the treaty in 1963. They built up a network of contacts through two existing organizations. The Women's International League for Peace and Freedom (WILPF), established in 1919, had been formidable in the

1920s and 1930s and agitated against the Vietnam War in its own right. It was a source of contacts, even if early WSP supporters regarded it as bureaucratically constipated. The National Committee for a Sane Nuclear Policy (SANE) was another resource, even if it was dominated by men and had made enemies by purging itself of left-wingers. The WSP itself was post-McCarthy and could even be regarded as precociously post–Cold War. Although it contained a contingent of "red diaper" women—the progeny of an earlier generation of radicals—its members were typically respectable, suburban, middle-class mothers worried about their children's prospects in a nuclear world. Wilson was an Englishwoman with an upper-class accent; attempts by congressional red-baiters to label her a puppet of Lower East Side radicals fell flat.[37] Amy Swerdlow, the WSP press officer and in later years a historian, argues that WSP "helped to legitimize a radical critique of the Cold War and U.S. militarism."[38]

WSP expressed concern about Vietnam from its earliest days and in 1965 made the war the main focus of its protest activities. In the spring of that year, after the United States began to bomb North Vietnam, Mary Clarke and Lorraine Gordon of WSP visited Hanoi, the first representatives of the U.S. peace movement to do so.

At home, the WSP contributed to the mass demonstrations against the war, giving a gendered twist to the doves' dialogue. In a manner consistent with the "nurturant motherhood" outlook of its early days, it drew attention to the fate of children in the war. In 1966, WSP members protested the indiscriminate American use of defoliants that had resulted in horrifying injuries to Vietnamese children by trying to block the napalm shipments of the Dow Chemical Company from San Jose, California. These "housewife terrorists" and "napalm ladies"—so dubbed in the newspapers—were arrested and convicted. In January of the next year 2,500 angry WSP marchers hammered on the locked doors of the Pentagon. This, too, was worth publicity, and women began to rival students as image makers. They proved adept at coining memorable slogans. Their paper daisies heralded "flower power." They delivered to the office of General Hershey, head of the selective service, a coffin inscribed with the words "Not Our Sons, Not Your Sons, Not Their Sons."[39]

An organism more than an organization, the early WSP was spontaneous and chaotic. Reliable estimates of its numerical strength and support are well-nigh impossible to obtain. Fifty thousand women were reported to have taken part in the original housewives' strike in 1961, but a more carefully researched estimate by Amy Swerdlow suggests that they numbered twelve thousand at most.[40] Women-only demonstrations were imaginative and colorful and attracted publicity once the antiwar movement gathered momentum, but direct-action episodes did not draw large numbers of participants. There appears, however, to have been a wider residual sympathy for the WSP and its goals. On December 10, 1965, President Johnson received 100,000 cards with this appeal: "For the sake of our sons . . . for the sake of our children . . . give us peace in Vietnam."[41] That many cards did not mean that many activists, but it did mean dedicated women with widespread support. In May 1966 a WSP delegation from New York turned up in Washington to present one of Senator Javits's staff with a petition. It consisted of four yellow sheets of paper with 112 signatures and some remarks. One of the remarks, by Rose Hochman of Bayside, New York, gives an impression of WSP's cumulative outreach: "In several one hour periods on weekends I have been getting 40–50 signatures on WSP peace pledges. The people have no confidence in this war and will not support those in the Congress who do not work to stop the war."[42]

The message also indicated that a change was taking place in WSP. Members were taking an interest in the legislative process. Their interest was a prelude to the legitimization of the women's campaign against the war. It also signaled the arrival of a new feminism. The woman who personified these processes was Bella Abzug.

A distinguished civil rights lawyer, Abzug had been involved in the WSP since the beginning and was its political action coordinator. She was determined to give the organization more legislative power and to link that goal to the achievement of feminist objectives—"I wanted an end to nuclear testing for *women*, for us ourselves, not just for our kids."[43] By the mid-sixties, Abzug's most important political objective was the ending of the war in Vietnam. At the outset, few WSP women had been either feminist or politically minded, but their involvement in the peace movement gradually made significant numbers of them more conscious of women's rights and congressional politics. From 1965 on, WSP women, numbered in their "thousands" according to Swerdlow, worked in the Democratic Party to promote peace candidates and to work for the Dump Johnson movement. They later provided the core of support for Abzug's 1970 congressional bid, in aid of which 235 WSP volunteers worked at her campaign headquarters.[44]

In the meantime, the formation of Another Mother for Peace (AMP) in March 1967 had ensured that pure and simple motherists would never be without a home in the antiwar movement. AMP was the creation of Barbara Avedon and fourteen other women associated with the Hollywood film industry. Run from Beverly Hills, it was nonpartisan and endorsed no candidates. It demanded an end to the war and the establishment of a cabinet-level secretary for peace. It appealed to the idea of nurturant motherhood, arguing that women were by nature more peaceful than men because they were responsible for the seeds of life. AMP had a gift for coining images and slogans. Lorraine Schneider designed its best-known logo: a message, "War is not healthy for children and other living things," arranged around a flower. Madison Avenue could only struggle to match this and another of its slogans: "All the flowers of all the tomorrows are in the seeds of today."[45]

One of AMP's first actions was to print a thousand Mother's Day cards for sympathizers to send to their respective members of Congress. The cards contained a poem demanding, in the name of motherhood, peace, not "candy or flowers." The verse was execrable by AMP's literary standards, but it was a huge success and had to be reprinted over and over again until 200,000 cards had been sent in all. AMP now started producing peace Christmas cards, and the combined total printed and sent was half a million by the end of the year. By 1968, AMP was thought to have a membership of around 100,000, about the same as WSP, although that did not mean a combined total of 200,000, because there was some overlap. By 1971 the AMP newsletter reached an estimated 240,000, and by the following year a further 10,000 had been added to its mailing list.[46]

The ability of AMP to reach substantial numbers of women through its slogans and literature was important, but its main propaganda value lay in its recruitment of female celebrities. Donna Reed served as one of AMP's three co-chairs. Her endorsement of the peace cause was a stunning event. She had won an Oscar for her role in the film *From Here to Eternity* (1953). She was the star of the family-based *Donna Reed Show* on television, a registered Republican, and the mother of four sons. She seemed an unlikely radical. But one of those sons reached draft age and became eligible to fight in Vietnam. Despairing of the war, Reed went beyond the apolitical stance of AMP and campaigned in the 1968 Democratic primaries for the peace candidate Eugene McCarthy. Her support for AMP was a firm reassertion of the universality of the peace movement. Anyone, not just black malcontents or beatnik campus lefties, could join.[47]

Another consequence of Reed's involvement was that the personality-addicted American media would publicize AMP. Other celebrities who backed AMP were Debbie Reynolds, Patty Duke, Mercedes McCambridge, Joanne Woodward, Felicia Bernstein, Shelly Winters, Elaine May, and Julie Harris. Woodward's actor-husband, Paul Newman, also helped to promote the AMP cause. In the 1950s, Senator Joe McCarthy, with local help from the president of the Film Actors Guild, Ronald Reagan, had all but suppressed free speech in Hollywood. By the late 1960s, however, the genie had escaped from the lamp, and the celebrities who helped to define Americanism in the popular eye were no longer implicit authenticators of U.S. foreign policy. Instead, it had become fashionable to be associated with the peace movement.[48]

The stars of AMP were not the only ones associated with the cause. In 1967 the antiwar movement's very own Joan Baez went to prison for helping young men resist draft induction. Baez had been a comfortable icon for the middle-class protester. Although she admired the down-and-out incantations of Leadbelly, she had started her career in the Radcliffe-Bennington milieu made available to her by her father, an MIT professor and Quaker. Even her prison, the Santa Fe Rehabilitation Center, was, according to Baez, "the equivalent of a girls' summer camp." Her sympathies and social class as well as her talent and commitment strengthened Baez's appeal within the protest movement. She complemented the Hollywood stars. Nor did she lack star companions back east. One of Broadway's most vibrant celebrities, Barbra Streisand, joined forces with Leonard Bernstein (husband of Felicia) to produce *Broadway for Peace '68* to raise funds for antiwar congressional candidates.[49]

Literary women added an intellectual stamp to the campaign being waged by their sisters of the screen and stage. In February 1966, Frances Fitzgerald started a one-year sojourn in Vietnam. Her family background no doubt stimulated both her confidence and her rebellious approach to reporting on Vietnam. Her mother, Marietta Tree, had been U.S. representative to the U.N. Trusteeship Council, and her father, Desmond Fitzgerald, had been in charge of CIA covert operations in the Far East until 1965, when he became the deputy director of the agency in overall charge of clandestine affairs.[50] ("Frankie") Fitzgerald found herself, like Higgins before her, at odds with the majority of journalists in Saigon. She wanted to study the people and their politics, not just battles. Her real fame as a critic of the war lay in the future, but in the sixties she was already sowing the seeds of dissent, a task in which she was prominently assisted by two novelists turned political advocates, Mary McCarthy and Susan Sontag.

Already an antiwar activist when she visited South Vietnam in 1967, Mary McCarthy found much to criticize in that country. She was, in contrast, impressed on her visit to the North Vietnam capital in March 1968. Like Sontag, who made a visit two months later and was equally affected by Hanoi, she was disturbed by the ubiquitous portraits of Stalin. She nevertheless perceived, or chose to perceive, a clean city with no prostitution and no ragged children. Following the trail blazed by WSP emissaries,

McCarthy tried to speak for and to all women, North Vietnamese and South Vietnamese, Asian and American. In her book *Hanoi* (one of several she wrote on Vietnam), she noted that "the theme of separation plays a great part in the war literature of the North," especially in letters written by women.[51]

In January 1968 two events occurred that illustrate the strengths and weaknesses of the women's movement against the war. The first concerned the Jeannette Rankin Brigade (JRB), a new ginger group thought up by Dagmar Wilson and a few of her friends when they were incarcerated with a few hundred others in a single room after the Pentagon demonstration in fall 1967. The JRB took its name from a Montana Republican, Jeannette Rankin, the first U.S. congresswoman, who had voted against both world wars—in 1941 the only national legislator to do so. The Vietnam War rekindled her antimilitary ideals. She opposed Johnson in the 1964 election because he was a warmonger and later declared that she "wanted to go back to Congress to vote against a third war."[52] Ill health frustrated this ambition, but the JRB proceeded to gather support in the peace movement and from the stars Joanne Woodward and Diahann Carroll. On January 15, 1968, the opening day of Congress, the eighty-seven-year-old Rankin led five thousand black-clad members of the brigade in a march on the Capitol to press the peace cause. The demonstration was not allowed within the Capitol grounds, and Vice President Hubert Humphrey at first kept the women waiting in the snow, where folk singer Judy Collins led them in a rendering of "We Shall Overcome." Humphrey relented, allowing Rankin, Coretta Scott King (King's widow), and a few companions inside.[53]

The JRB appealed against its exclusion from the Capitol precincts, and the Supreme Court later ruled in favor of demonstrations there. But another development was of greater importance at the time. A splinter group of younger persons known as the "New York women" crossed the Potomac River and buried "Traditional Motherhood" at Arlington cemetery. The stirrings of the new feminism had been evident in the antiwar movement for some time. Tired of male domination, a group of women at the

SDS conference in December 1967 had formed a workshop and called for the "re-assertion of the personal" among women. A rebellion was gathering momentum against the separate-spheres, nurturant-motherhood stereotyping of women. Betty Friedan said publicly: "I don't think the fact that milk once flowed within my breast is the reason I am against the war."[54] At the Arlington ceremony, Kathie Amatnick reminded her listeners of Friedan's critique of the "feminine mystique." The sympathies of those gathered there were distinctly in favor of direct action and distrustful of male-dominated congressional politics. Peggy Dobbins's "Liturgy for the Burial of Traditional Womanhood" lamented the sins of women who thrilled to the sound of "martial trumpets" and gloried in "lusty men."[55] The Arlington ceremony dramatized the arrival of women's liberation on the protest scene, and some in the antiwar movement feared that the new development would be a distraction. In the end, it revitalized debate, diversifying the appeal of the antiwar movement.

Close on the heels of the Rankin march came another dramatic episode, the Kitt affair. Eartha Kitt's confrontation with the president and his wife on a White House social occasion on January 18, 1968, provoked strong reactions, exhibiting as it did outright skepticism of the administration's good intentions toward black people and the war. One conservative newspaper offered the headline "Country Rallies with Rage as Kitt Blast Backfires."[56] The Texan politicians George Bush and Bob Casey denounced her. Edna Kelly of New York contacted the White House the next morning to offer to make a supportive speech in the House, where she was a member of the Committee on Foreign Affairs.[57] Hostile journalists hinted that Kitt was mentally unbalanced, that she was trying to boost her career by seeking publicity, that she was a political naïf manipulated by Stokely Carmichael, that her tough life had embittered her and made her incapable of sound judgment, that she was rude and strident. Nightclub owners canceled some of Kitt's engagements, and at least one radio show banned her music. Letters arrived at the White House supporting Mrs. Johnson and denouncing Kitt. Isabelle Shelton of the *Washington Sunday Star* speculated that Kitt's outburst would only publicize the First Lady's fight against crime, which was fast developing into "the biggest domestic issue in the up-coming campaign."[58]

The backlash against Kitt might seem to suggest that women suffered after all from instant and powerful reactions if they dared to criticize the war. But the critics did not dwell on her gender. One woman from a military family telephoned the White House to say that "my heart and I'm sure that the hearts of millions of other *white* women in America go out to Mrs. Johnson to think that she had to invite people like Eartha Kitt to her home and then to be treated like that."[59] One columnist could not contain himself. Listing black singers who behaved well, he denounced Kitt as a "gutter snipe," condemned the black celebrity Sammy Davis, Jr., for defending her "Tobacco Road exhibition," and warned that "baseless accusations do no more than backfire."[60] Perhaps it was an old story. A black person had acted "out of character" and was being pilloried for it.

Kitt was not short of supporters, however. The show business magazine *Variety* referred, in fact, to "split reviews all round."[61] Kitt's widely reported criticism attracted endorsements from Dr. Martin Luther King, Jr., and congressional doves and inspired pro-Kitt demonstrations outside the White House by members of WSP.[62] Although the singer's perspective was partly that of a black American, she undoubtedly struck a chord with many white women. By this time it was evident, on the basis of several polls, that women were more hostile to the war than men. According to Gallup polls, for example, the percentage of white women supporting the war sank from 48 in 1965 (men: 58) to 40 in 1968 (men: 48) and 30 in 1970 (men: 41).[63] A theme of the sixties, as revealed in later fiction and oral history, was the efforts of women to stop their menfolk from going to Vietnam. In the words of the journalist and interviewer Myra MacPherson, "There is no 'typical' woman of the Vietnam Generation who did not go to war or did not have a brother, lover, husband, or father in Vietnam." Mass revulsion combined with the emergence of prominent women opponents of the war—who, according to one historian, took "center stage by the end of the sixties"—meant that Kitt could be confident of widespread female backing.[64] She and other women who took part in dramatic episodes simply added to the impact of organized rebellion by women and endorsements of the antiwar cause by stars.

LBJ's response to women's protests against the war was sluggish and unsympathetic, a product of the Stygian gloom of a self-incarcerated mind. He did not entirely ignore the need to cultivate women's support for the war. He did, for example, encourage the creation of better opportunities for women in the armed services. One argument for this reform was that if more women were recruited to noncombative roles, fewer men would have to be drafted, meaning that fewer men would be worrying about transfer to Vietnam, and there would be less discontent about the war. At the 1967 signing ceremony for a bill easing barriers to women's promotion, the president further claimed that he was striking "another blow for women's rights," and on that occasion he underlined his commitment to women serving in Southeast Asia by presenting medals to two Vietnam nurses.[65]

Yet the president's efforts to keep women on board were slight and desultory. India Edwards of the Democratic National Committee said that "Lyndon Johnson doesn't understand national politics." This was partly a comment on the egocentrism of male leadership: "Every man has his own organization." But it was also a grouse that Johnson did not pay serious heed to the women's division of the committee, failing to realize that women, in contrast to Texan oilmen or Detroit autoworkers, were not concentrated in a particular state or interest group; rather, they constituted a national lobby.[66] The historian Paul Conkin notes that Johnson "*verbally* embraced the cause of women's equality" and "*dutifully* appointed a few women as ambassadors."[67] In nominating Patricia Roberts Harris American ambassador to Luxembourg, Johnson perhaps thought he had offered two tokens for the price of one: she was the only woman and the only African American to head a U.S. diplomatic mission in Europe. But there were limits to the loyalty that he could expect in exchange for such a gesture. "After the resumption of bombing in 1966," Harris recalled, "I ceased to have questions-and-answers on this [bombing] because it was too difficult to define and justify."[68] Generally, the president's lukewarm approach to women's rights appears to have encouraged reciprocal equivocation in some of his appointees.

The Johnson White House was exceptionally unsympathetic to female peace campaigners. A comparison might here be made between Johnson and his mentor Franklin D. Roosevelt. FDR had also been uncomfortable in the presence of such people, but at least he had agreed to meet them. In contrast, LBJ delegated the chore to subordinates.[69] In May 1965, Chester L. Cooper met a WSP delegation. Cooper was a member of the National Security Council and was sufficiently respected in the White House to be entrusted with (fruitless) negotiations with Hanoi, but he was not a topflight member of the administration. He was fully capable, however, of articulating the administration's hostility to the WSP. He told a WSP member from Roslyn Heights, New York, that of all the peace groups he had met, WSP was the most difficult. After a three-hour meeting, its delegation had told him that it was pointless to listen to the administration, for its "officials produced lies and propaganda." When WSP pressed for a meeting with Johnson, Cooper decided to say that the president was unavailable, but wondered whether he should not offer to see them once again. National Security Adviser McGeorge Bundy consulted Jack Valenti, a White House staffer who was close to the president. Valenti replied: "In my judgment, if anyone sees this group they should be well down the totem pole."[70]

The White House response to the Kitt affair in January 1968 was even more unsympathetic. It took stock of its support and then discredited its new critic. It dropped Kitt from its projected youth advisory panel and called up security files on her. Since 1956, in spite of the singer's erstwhile political inactivity, no fewer than five U.S. intelligence agencies had collected information on her. In the CIA dossier, the profane and philandering President Johnson could learn of assertions that Kitt had a "vile tongue" and had displayed "loose morals" in Paris.[71] These reactions point to the persistence of a fortress mentality. Until the Tet assault on January 31, the While House still clung to the belief that its Vietnam policy was not a disaster. The Johnson administration had made some minor adjustments to its military policy in order to satisfy women but saw no reason to make any significant concessions.

President Nixon was more adroit in handling the women's peace movement. He had to be, because the movement was gathering momentum. In his first administration, female stars and personalities concentrated their fire as never before on a foreign war. The women's antiwar campaign moved toward legitimization and benefited from a decisive breakthrough by women into the political arena. All this culminated in considerable pressure for withdrawal by the presidential election year of 1972.

A few illustrations will indicate the force and pervasiveness of women's discontent with the war by the early 1970s. Even nurses, traditionally invisible in political terms, started at this stage to doubt American policy.[72] In 1971, Frankie Fitzgerald made another trip to Vietnam that reinforced her view that America should stop shooting people whose culture it did not begin to understand. She campaigned for the presidential peace candidate George McGovern and, in mid-1972, published her book on Vietnam, *Fire in the Lake*, to the accompaniment of ecstatic reviews. The book "catapulted her to fame," making her the intellectual star of the antiwar movement.[73]

In 1972 two other prominent women undertook exhausting tours to campaign against the war. Jeannette Rankin visited Vietnam several times.[74] The film actor Jane Fonda had been against the war since 1969, but in February 1972 she began her love affair with Tom Hayden, whom she eventually married. The affair transformed each individual. Hayden reentered the political mainstream and threw his energy into the Indochina Peace Campaign (IPC).[75] In July, Fonda visited North Vietnam, where she posed provocatively for a photograph on a communist tank and made several radio broadcasts to American pilots. Her goals were to show Americans that the war continued in spite of President Nixon's claims to the contrary and to dissuade pilots from flying bombing missions. In September, Fonda and Hayden made a pro-McGovern IPC speaking tour of the industrial Northeast of the

United States, reaching ninety-five cities. They appealed to reason, not emotion, and stressed their patriotic intent—an approach that, according to Hayden, won a favorable reception.[76]

But the women's campaign against the war was not always plain sailing. The Fonda protest, for example, infuriated some war veterans and gave hawks and conservatives the opportunity to observe that she was a rich and privileged traitor (Fonda was a Vassar dropout, and the screen fame of her father, Henry, had given a flying start to her acting career). The venomous anti-Fonda tirade developed momentum; indeed, she had to be banned as a topic of discussion in a Vietnam veterans' Internet discussion group in the 1990s.[77] The reaction to Jane Fonda heralded the serious anti-women's liberation backlash that followed political breakthrough of the early 1970s.

The full backlash did not develop in time to cripple the women's antiwar movement. Still, fear of reprisals of other types did inhibit some women in their opposition to the war. Some Jewish women, for example, worried about an anti-Semitic backlash if they pushed their case too hard. Other factors bled the antiwar movement of some of its vitality or served as a distraction from the cause. A number of Jewish women—to pursue that theme—were less concerned about Vietnam than about the fate of Soviet Jewry. In any case, the gender distinctiveness of the Jewish women's antiwar stance remains a question. Jewish men, as represented by the male-dominated American Jewish Congress, had been critical of the war since 1969. When, in May 1972, the president of the National Council of Jewish Women (NCJW), called on the U.S. Congress to "reassert its constitutional authority" and end the war, she used her married name, Mrs. Earl Marvin, in defiance of the new feminist conventions and in contrast to the prime minister of Israel, Mrs. Golda Meir, who used her own first name. Yet, cavil as one may about distractions and distinctiveness, the NCJW had 100,000 members across the nation and did declare against the war.[78]

Furthermore, the evidence points overall to a greater opposition among women than among men. Data collected by the Harris poll organization in 1971 presents a complex picture but does confirm women's relatively greater disposition to oppose. In 1970, of the women polled, 63 percent thought that antiwar pickets did more harm than good, but they also tended to think that troop withdrawals from Vietnam were progressing too slowly. In 1972, Harris conducted several polls aimed at women. Compared with men, these women were, if anything, unconcerned at the inflationary and other economic costs of the war. But they favored an end to the war more strongly than men did; withdrawal from Vietnam was the top political priority for 49 percent of female respondents, compared with 44 percent of the males. Sixty percent of both men and women thought that President Nixon was doing an excellent or pretty good job of "working for peace in the world." But both sexes thought that "when it comes to getting us out of Vietnam . . . women in public office could do a better job than men . . . or just as good a job as men."[79]

Women's letters to their congressional representatives seem to confirm that women wanted peace in Vietnam and trusted members of their own gender to achieve it. Such correspondence is irregular and cannot be neatly quantified. Nevertheless, members of Congress received spates of letters on Vietnam from time to time, and some deductions can be made from them. Senator McGovern, for example, received one such rush of letters after an antiwar speech he made in 1967. On that occasion, 35 percent of the "dove" letters sympathetic to his position came from women (who supplied only 29 percent of the "hawk" letters). This compares with a batch of antiwar postcards sent by men and women from New York's Lower East Side to Congresswoman Abzug in 1971: this time, 65 percent were from women. Other data, tabulated below, shed light on the question, How many of a legislator's correspondents on either side of the Vietnam debate were women?

Senator Javits (Rep., N.Y.)	1965	0%
Senator McGovern (Dem., S.Dak.)	1967	32%
Senator Javits (Rep., N.Y.)	1968	40%
Senator Smith (Rep., Maine)	1970	42%
Congresswoman Abzug (Dem., N.Y.)	1971	65%

The interpretation of this evidence is full of pitfalls, and the evidence itself is for only four legislators, but in the absence of countervailing quantification, it would be perverse to ignore its implications. Political correspondence confirms the opinion polls' indication of a distinctively strong antiwar tendency in women. Additionally, it would appear that women increasingly opposed the war or preferred to write to female legislators like Smith and Abzug on the matter, or both. It would seem that they especially valued Bella Abzug, the feminist champion of the antiwar campaign.[80]

The midterm elections of 1970 increased the salience of women in the politics of peace. There was a swing against the Republicans and against the war. Ronald Reagan and Nelson Rockefeller, both Republicans, won the gubernatorial contests in California and New York, respectively, but the Democrats picked up eleven governorships and did well in congressional contests. According to one historian's calculation, only five peace candidates for the House lost, whereas twenty-four won, giving the Hill a more liberal and antiwar cast.[81] And, according to a postelection analysis conducted by the pollster George Gallup, the women's vote had been decisive in many states in securing victory for the Democrats.[82]

In the election campaigns, women hit their stride as a confident new political and pro-peace force. The New York senatorial race confirms this. Keenly observed and informally backed by the White House, James Buckley was running as a hawk on an independent Conservative ticket. Local press reports hint in diverse ways at the rising influence of women. A Middletown, New York, newspaperwoman warned: "Electing a man is like marrying him—don't expect to reform him once you get him." The *New York News* ran a story on "two middle-aged men" who approached Equal Rights Amendment pickets outside the gubernatorial campaign headquarters of the Conservative Party. Buckley, they announced, "loves women." The *News* reporter deduced from the pickets' scathing response that feminists would "reject all suitors." The news from upstate was different. In the Albany metropolitan area, women came out "from under their frizzies and dryers long enough" to tell a pair of investigators from the *Schenectady Union-Star* that Buckley would win. Even in this more conservative area, however, beauticians reported strong antiwar views among their customers, and one woman "in the pre-setting stage" said, "Women are the ones who elect the candidates, you know. They tell their husbands how to vote."[83]

Bella Abzug of New York City was one of the peace-ticket victors in the 1970 elections, and she was very much a women's candidate. Swerdlow recalls that WSP volunteers worked hard for male candidates, too, "but never with the same pride and conviction." Abzug's arrival in the Congress was stage-managed as a triumph for peace; there was a second, unofficial swearing-in ceremony on the Capitol steps at which five hundred WSP supporters chanted, "Two, four, six, eight—tell 'em Bella set the date." True to her promise, Abzug introduced H.R. 54 on her first day in office, a "Resolution to Set the Date" for American withdrawal from the Vietnam War. The nominated day, July 4, symbolized the patriotism and legitimacy of the reinvigorated peace campaign.[84]

The resurgence of political feminism helped to make women for peace a force to be reckoned with. In 1966 the establishment of the National Organization for Women (NOW) heralded a campaign to reform marriage and to democratize the professions, including politics. The National Women's Political Caucus, formed in 1971, had the specific aim of building a women's power bloc within both the Republican and the Democratic Parties. Looking back at the growing power of women in the 1970s, Abzug recalled that between 1968 and 1972 the number of women delegates to the Democratic convention tripled to 40 percent while Republican women delegates doubled to 35 percent.[85] Women began to achieve more in the Congress, with 1972 a "watershed year" for emancipating legislation, according to Abzug.[86]

Betty Friedan, the first president of NOW, was antiwar. So were other prominent feminists, like Robin Morgan and Bernadine Dohrn. In campaigning against the war, Abzug was assured of strong support from women—although here it should be remembered that the Lower East Side, her constituency in New York, had a strong tradition of male radicalism, too. Abzug emphasized the importance of public support for the work of peace advocates in the Congress. In February 1971 she led a nationwide "Barnstorming Tour" by twenty-seven members of Congress, who spoke on the theme "Peace and Priorities." Republican and Democratic male representatives supported her in this campaign, in which the colorful WSP leader mesmerized the media.[87] In opposing the war in the Congress, Abzug valued the support of three Democratic women: Ella Grasso of Connecticut, Patsy Mink of Hawaii, and Shirley Chisholm of New York.[88] Chisholm, like Abzug, was an uncompromising public foe of the war. "This is a war the United States cannot win," she said on the ABC *Issues and Answers* program in June 1972. At the time, there was an effort to delay American withdrawal until the North Vietnamese returned all prisoners of war (POWs), and, to stave off peace without "honor" and to stir up opinion at home, the administration was reclassifying as POWs personnel who had gone missing in action (MIA) and were in fact dead. In defiance of this psychological ploy, Chisholm urged American withdrawal regardless of the release of real or apocryphal prisoners of war.[89] Her determination is another sign of the powerful challenge to the war that women mounted both outside and inside the Congress in the early 1970s.

The Nixon administration failed to dam the tide of female resentment at the Vietnam War. This was not because the new president was blind to the potential problem with women. He noted in April 1969 that his appearance at a LWV reception had been a "real disaster" because "we didn't control it."[90] Some of the officials within his circle were also attuned to the political threat implicit in the new feminism. Daniel P. Moynihan, an antiwar Democrat who had joined the Nixon administration as director of the new Urban Affairs Council, warned the president in August 1969 that "female equality" would be a major political consideration in the 1970s.[91]

Someone who articulated the feminist viewpoint in a way that offered possible political guidelines to Nixon's senior advisers was Rita Hauser, a conservative New York lawyer appointed by Nixon to the U.S. delegation at the United Nations. In May 1969 she urged that more senior positions be given to women within the administration. In March 1970 she sent Nixon's speech writer William Safire a memorandum on the worldwide "feminine revolution." American women—a "social minority" even though a majority of the population—demanded parity of treatment with other minorities. Hauser cited campus and media attention to the issue and predicted that this would lead to "increasing feminine militancy in the 1970s."[92] In April 1971, claiming to have spoken to "hundreds of thousands of women" over the past year, she detected an "emergent responsible feminism" and warned Nixon that his team was "missing the boat for 1972" in not paying enough attention to women.[93] Hauser was just one official and had a junior status, but she contributed to a collective voice that was not ignored. A year later, at the start of the presidential election campaign, the White House commissioned special polls of women on gender-difference issues.[94]

Aware though the White House was of a woman problem, it lacked the opportunity and the image to neutralize it. The "Angry White Men" had not yet materialized, and there was no significant antifeminist backlash to exploit. The Nixon administration was further hampered in its handling of the woman question by its reputation for male chauvinism. Writing in the aftermath of the Republicans' rebuff at the 1970 polls, the newspaper columnist Jack Anderson attributed "Nixon's women trouble" to the perception that "crewcut H. R. Haldeman, the guardian of the president's door, is anti-women."[95] If women were a "waste of time" to Chief of Staff Haldeman, they were just a "hobby" to National Security Adviser Henry Kissinger, for whom, according to the White House social secretary Lucy Winchester, the "cleavage factor" was an obsession.[96] In a 1970 fund-raising function, Vice President Spiro Agnew appealed to Maryland Republicans to give generously in order "to keep Bella Abzug from showing up in Congress in hot pants." In the same election campaign, President Nixon declared, "I want a woman to be a woman," a remark translated by "millions of women" (according to Jack Anderson) as "a woman's place is in the home."[97] Such remarks may have been no more chauvinist than those made by previous generations of male politicians, but when reported in the new climate of the early seventies, they invited trouble.

But indiscretions do not amount to policy. Nixon was attempting to undermine the Democratic coalition established in the New Deal and to replace it with a new Republican majority.[98] To this end, he did try to cultivate women's votes. In February 1969 the president assured a California supporter that he favored the idea of a women's advisory council. With support from the White House staffers Moynihan and John D. Ehrlichman, who thought the proposal was "politically . . . a golden opportunity" to "champion female equality," the idea resulted in the establishment, on October 1, 1969, of the Presidential Task Force on Women's Rights and Responsibilities.[99] In 1970, Nixon set up the Presidential Commission in Celebration of Fifty Years of Woman Suffrage. Over the next two years, Nixon repeatedly and personally pushed the need to recruit more support from women, as well as the notion of giving women a special voice in the White House. He requested Kissinger "to be more discreet regarding his glamorous young women."[100] By early 1971 the administration was claiming to have hired more female employees than the Kennedy or Johnson administrations. In December of that year, Nixon used his executive powers to extend the provisions of the "Philadelphia" plan, originally conceived as a way of securing fair employment opportunities for African Americans. It was now to cover women, thus establishing the principle of gender equality in federal hiring practices. Similarly, the Equal Employment Opportunity Act signed by Nixon in 1972 applied to women as well as to nonwhite ethnic groups. Joan Hoff argues that these achievements belie Nixon's chauvinistic historical image, whereas her fellow historian Hugh Graham sees evidence of a "Second Reconstruction" affecting both race and gender.[101]

The Nixon administration tried to increase its appeal to women when it exploited the POW-MIA issue. Here, the Stockdale affair supplied an opportunity. Vice Admiral James B. Stockdale was shot down on his two hundredth mission over North Vietnam on September 9, 1965. He survived nearly eight years of torture and solitary confinement at the hands of his communist captors. In June 1969, Stockdale's wife, Sybil, formed the National League of Families of American Prisoners in Southeast Asia. President Nixon and Defense Secretary Laird met with and personally encouraged Sybil Stockdale. With financial and other help from the government and the Republican National Committee, the league became a long-term pressure group on the politically potent, if apocryphal, POW-MIA issue. In the shorter term, the POW-MIA issue was part of the political armory of the Nixon administration as it tried to fend off women's attacks on the Vietnam War with rhetoric about loyalty and family values.[102]

But Nixon saw little political advantage in encouraging women to be active. In April 1971 he scribbled the following on a memorandum from White House counselor Robert H. Finch recommending that more women be recruited: "This is an excellent job. . . . However I seriously doubt if jobs in govt for women make many votes from women."[103] The president had even less faith in women's political abilities. After the LWV had criticized his foreign trade policy in 1971, he exclaimed to Haldeman: "My God! Can't they stay out of subjects they know *nothing* about."[104]

The truth is that Nixon was neither equipped nor inclined to come to terms with a new political role for women. In the absence of alternative tactics, the answer was capitulation to the cumulative forces of which women had become such a robust component. To win the election in 1972, it became necessary to ensure that peace was in the air. American and Vietnamese representatives negotiated in Paris. Finally, on October 26, just two weeks before polling day, Secretary of State Kissinger announced that "peace is at hand."[105] Little matter that it was not and that the "Christmas bombings" of North Vietnam by B-52s occurred before the Paris peace accord of the following year. Electoral damage had been done to the Democrats, for their candidate, George McGovern, had focused heavily on the peace issue and could not hope to recoup his losses in other spheres. President Nixon successfully presented himself as the statesmen who would bring peace, cutting the ground from under Senator McGovern's feet.

McGovern's political weaknesses contributed to Nixon's success. On the face of it, McGovern was ideally qualified as a peace candidate. Nobody could accuse him of shirking his duty to his country. A B-24 pilot in the Army in World War II, he had flown thirty-five combat missions over Germany, Austria, and Italy, winning the Distinguished Flying Cross and Air Medal with three clusters. Because of his liberal inclinations, however, this record was to no avail. His problem with conservatives was not limited to the Republican Party. Even within his own Democratic Party, he later recalled, opponents leveled against him "the groundless 'three A's' charge (that I favored acid, amnesty, and abortion)."[106] To compensate, McGovern needed to appeal successfully to those social groups who might support his antiwar case.

McGovern tried to cultivate women. He put Jean Westwood, the first woman to chair the Democratic Party, in charge of his election campaign. He took the time to respond to a WILPF questionnaire on "foreign, military policy," stating (in spite of his later denial) that "I support amnesty for those young men who on grounds of conscience have refused to participate in the Vietnam war."[107] According to his campaign memoir, the topic on which he spoke most frequently in the course of the election was the Vietnam War—"the issue which made my candidacy possible"—but he also delivered "major addresses" on women's rights.[108]

McGovern's appeal to women was not necessarily a hopeless one. The hitherto nonpartisan WSP officially endorsed McGovern's candidacy. At the 1972 party conventions, a far greater number (and proportion) of women were committed to McGovern than to any other candidate, Democratic or Republican. Largely motivated by opposition to the Vietnam War, these women were newcomers to politics and relatively inexperienced, yet they represented what could have been a salutary breath of fresh air.[109] They did in some cases make a difference in elections. One of their main political victims in 1972 was herself a woman, Margaret Chase Smith. Hitherto noted for her vote-winning capability and support for the war, Smith lost her Senate seat to a peace candidate drawing on the support of Maine's disillusioned, antiwar women.[110]

McGovern's appeal to women nonetheless misfired. To nullify the impression that he was wedded to special interest groups, the Democratic candidate toned down his promises to deliver reforms beneficial to women. Complaints that Jean Westwood was mismanaging the campaign introduced a sour note into the New Feminist Age. There seemed to be a shortage of New Men in the McGovern ranks. Women had resented staffers' use of the phrase "Nylon Revolution" in the primary campaigns, and, those won, McGovern's female helpers protested that they were not allowed to influence campaign policy to a degree commensurate with their numbers. Gloria Steinem and Shirley MacLaine complained that the campaign had been stripped of its feminist appeal. In the language of one study, women "watched the reasons for their commitment to politics evaporate."[111]

Like President Herbert Hoover in his doomed reelection campaign of 1932, McGovern tried to turn the tide at the last moment with an appeal to women voters. But, to an even greater extent than Hoover, he hit the wrong note.[112] His television address of November 3, 1972, focused on Vietnam and accused Nixon of lying about the imminence of peace and about the inflationary effects of the war: "Ask a housewife is the cost of living under control." On November 5, two days before polling, he again focused on the war: "A housewife may look at the ballot and think of last week's grocery bill."[113] If his speech had been delivered in the 1920s, when women spent well over 90 percent of the family budget, it might have had a greater appeal. But by typifying women as housewives distinctly responsible for domestic chores, the Democratic candidate revealed himself to be out of touch with consumer economics and on a different planet from some of the more militant women who might have been expected to support him. In the election, McGovern and his women failed to raise the tempo of the campaign or improve Democratic turnout. Nixon received only 1 percent fewer votes from women than from men.[114]

Although the inadequacies of the McGovern campaign were

real enough, women failed to support him only because they had succeeded in another respect. Adding their very considerable impetus to that of students and African Americans, they had brought the peace movement to its legitimate and successful fruition, forcing a change of heart in Nixon and making the election of a peace candidate unnecessary. In fact, the strength of the antiwar campaign in its final stages was such that a new question has to be asked: Why did withdrawal take so long?

6 Labor

MOST MAINSTREAM UNION LEADERS SUPPORTED the Vietnam War. The Johnson and Nixon administrations found their support comforting because the labor leaders could claim to speak for the common, working person, which would help to undermine the antiwar campaigners' claim to be the champions of the exploited masses. Labor's patriotic support for the war had tangible results: it encouraged and enabled the White House to hold out for military solutions instead of accepting peace terms early.

The virulent opposition faction that developed within the labor movement must also be considered in any appraisal of the workers' role in the Vietnam War. President Johnson knew that the sons and brothers of laborers were fighting and dying in the war, and he also worried about the economic impact of the war on working people. Labor protest encouraged President Nixon to take special measures to preempt criticism and to recruit blue-collar support. But even these measures could only stave off, not prevent, opposition, and labor discontent helped Nixon toward the conclusion that he would have to settle for a negotiated peace, however slowly it came.

AFL-CIO president George Meany was a political mainstay of the Vietnam War. In 1974 he admitted to having been wrong all along, but that admission was much too late to have an effect on the politics of the war.[1] Earlier, Meany had summed up his attitude during the initial stages of the war: "We had some vocal opposition at the local level, but at the top level we had no opposition at all."[2] In the course of the conflict, Meany gave the White House conspicuous and almost obsessive support. He could be fiercely outspoken in defense of labor's prerogatives at home, but another side of him came to the fore in connection with foreign policy, that test of patriotism and national identity. A man of humble Irish American origins, he had been a plumber, then risen to his AFL-CIO position, earning $90,000 a year. He personified the American Dream come true, and he wanted labor collectively to make the kind of foreign policy commitment that would enhance its status at the national bargaining table.

Meany believed in the political abilities of Lyndon Johnson, which encouraged him to treat the president as a political lifeline for organized labor and to deliver the strongest possible support on foreign policy.[3] According to his biographer Joseph Goulden, "No nonofficial American clung closer to Johnson than did Meany. Meany spoke more on Vietnam than on perhaps any single issue during 1965–68."[4] When labor problems in Vietnam threatened to slow down the unloading and distribution of supplies in the port of Saigon and in the Cam Ranh Bay supply base, Meany, with the help of the president of the International Longshoremen's Association (ILA), Thomas W. Gleason, helped to unravel those problems. At home the AFL-CIO president dealt firmly with any potential dissent within the labor movement. In 1965, for example, he quashed incipient protests voiced by the secretary-treasurer of the United Automobile Workers (UAW), Emil Mazey.

He did so with the assistance of the UAW president, Walter Reuther. In the 1930s the charismatic Reuther had been a socialist, demonstrating his sympathies by working in the Gorky Auto Works in the Soviet Union. But the leader once dubbed "the most dangerous man in Detroit" had developed into a cautious pragmatist. He would not contemplate taking a risky political position that would jeopardize the gains promised to his members by LBJ's Great Society program.[5] Though uneasy about the war, Reuther defended the Vietnam policy in the period of escalation, 1965–1966, both in international labor conferences and within his own union.[6]

John Kenneth Galbraith, economist and chair of Americans for Democratic Action (ADA), told Walter Reuther that the failure of the UAW to align itself with the peace movement robbed the antiwar campaign of the kind of organizational stability it needed.[7] However, in reality, labor leaders like Reuther only reflected the sentiments of their followers. Across the nation, there was heavy rank-and-file support for the war. This had been evident from the beginning and became conspicuous once the students' peace campaign started. In 1965, Joseph Curran's National Maritime Union sponsored a prowar parade along Fifth Avenue in New York City. Curran insisted that agents from Moscow and Beijing were behind the antiwar movement. Again in May 1967, in the wake of Martin Luther King, Jr.'s Riverside antiwar speech, longshoremen, sailors, carpenters, and other workers marched down Fifth Avenue in a seven-hour parade, this time led by the ILA president, Gleason. Their banners proclaimed, "My country right or wrong," some of the marchers chanted, "Burn Hanoi, not our flag," and a few marchers, in the words of an evidently delighted Gleason, "beat up young war protesters and draft card burners."[8]

A poll of union members in January 1967 found that the "vast majority" supported President Johnson's policy in Vietnam. A poll of delegates at thirteen state labor conventions in the fall of 1967 had found, similarly, that only 276 out of 3,542 favored U.S. withdrawal.[9] Meany believed, as he informed the AFL-CIO convention in 1967, that prowar labor "spoke for the vast, silent majority in the nation."[10] This imagery was soon taken up by another high-profile group, Citizens Committee for Peace with Freedom in Vietnam. Formed at the prompting of the White House, the committee had about a hundred members, including such luminaries as former president Truman and former vice president Nixon, as well as Meany. At the launch in November 1967 the committee declared itself the "Voice from the Silent Center." Labor thus furnished the basis for a significant political strategy: an appeal to the mythical jingoism of the inarticulate.[11]

Why did labor support the war even as it escalated during the Johnson administration? Here, certain long-term factors came into play. One was the desire of labor leaders to play an influential role in American society. Labor leaders were almost without exception self-made men. Meany is one example, Jay Lovestone another. The influential head of the AFL-CIO's rigidly anticommunist International Affairs division, Lovestone had climbed from humble origins as a Lithuanian immigrant. Labor leaders accepted American foreign policy in order to convince themselves, as well as others, that they were part of the elite. Perhaps, too, there was an element of trade-off: give me something for my union, and I'll support your foreign policy.

The anticommunism of the labor leaders was not invented for the contingencies of the 1960s. It had its roots not just in breakthrough aspirations but also in other long-term considerations. Meany's and Lovestone's antipathy to the left sprang from a number of sources. Lovestone, for example, was a former Communist who now attacked his former comrades with the zeal of the convert. American organized labor had, moreover, adopted the philosophy that what's good for business is good for labor—and communism was by definition bad for business. Yet another factor that prompted the anticommunism of the AFL-CIO was the dread of domestic radicalism felt by its established leaders. Radicalism might lead to the rise of a rival, left-led labor movement and of "dual" (parallel) unions that would steal the thunder, members, and funds of the existing, more conservative organizations. Finally, labor's red-baiting abroad was a useful device for outfacing those who were still inclined to red-bait the organized labor movement at home.

Labor's involvement in the military-industrial complex was another historically rooted reason for its support of the Vietnam War. Although only a minority of businesses were involved in defense contracts, the military-industrial lobby had always managed to be effective, and at least a portion of organized labor, like some research universities, stood to benefit from its political successes. Of particular note, in the case of the Vietnam War, is the dependence of "fortress California" on the defense industry. California had become a major industrial component of the "arsenal of democracy" in World War II but had had little industry before the war. This meant that reconversion could not take place at war's end, because there was nothing to reconvert to. California had become addicted to U.S. military expenditures, and the federal government continued to subsidize the state economy. Taxpayers' money went into defense projects, space research, and the strategically important shipbuilding industry. Federal money helped to industrialize and enrich California, and the Vietnam War promised to extend the boom. Major corporations tied in workers' loyalty with bonus schemes. The Vietnam Run, the war-stimulated trade route from the West Coast to the far rim of the Pacific, stimulated the ports, warehouse businesses, and industries of California. Its importance to the maritime economy of the state and to everyone's prosperity seemed self-evident. California, which was on the brink of becoming the key state in national elections, seemed particularly vulnerable to the consequences of a de-escalation in Vietnam.[12]

The Vietnam Run was one of the more important short-term stimuli to hawkish working-class sentiment. Another stimulus was the conspicuous involvement of middle-class students in the protest movement and the apparent condescension behind their criticism of organized labor's support for the war. Students seemed to be engaging in an arrogant "revolt against the masses." The masses staged a counterrevolt. Opinion polls suggest that even those blue-collar workers who were themselves critical of the war had a low level of tolerance for long-haired protesting students and for what they regarded as the snobbery and self-indulgent arrogance of the student "counterculture." The style of student protest, distorted as it was by the media and by politicians seeking their own goals, prompted a moral contempt in the workplace. This contempt inspired proud displays of the Stars and Stripes on the porches of American homes and a spirited defense of the working-class men fighting in Vietnam.[13]

Other short-term factors generated prowar sentiment with racial undertones. The factors were black militancy and the political exploitation of that militancy. By the mid-1960s, African Americans had accomplished a major civil-rights breakthrough, and it was white labor, not the prosperity-cushioned middle classes, that contemplated making the potentially painful adjustments and sacrifices inherent in conferring equality on people of color. Then, just when tolerance was required, the urban race riots of the mid-sixties gave equality a frightening dimension. It was at this point that Martin Luther King, Jr., attacked the war, making it doubly easy for populist labor spokesmen to fan white working-class resentment while seeming to remain racially tolerant. The *AFL-CIO News* and other labor sources took care not to attack Dr. King directly; instead, they publicized attacks on King by other prominent black leaders, like Senator Edward Brooke and NAACP director Roy Wilkins. Hostility to black radicalism could also be dressed up as a tactical critique. The leader of the needle trades union, William Ross, declared, "You cannot go against the policy of your country and expect to aid civil rights!" Patriotic support for the war against Asians had become a subliminal code for the reassertion of white racial supremacy at home.[14]

A final short-term factor prompting labor's support for the Vietnam War was the Democratic control of the White House between 1961 and 1969. Labor had supported the Democrats since the mid-1930s and could expect more support from Kennedy and Johnson than from a Republican incumbent. It suited the labor leaders to sustain a Democratic administration.

In summary, labor offered extensive support for the war. The strength of that support is evident not just statistically but also in terms of the reasons for that support.

Labor opposition to the war in Vietnam developed a significant momentum, nonetheless. It was strong enough both to inspire a political response from President Nixon and to suggest that Nixon's preemptive actions were perhaps no more than delaying tactics. There was ample reason for labor's discontent. The political commentator Michael Barone recalled: "The strategists of the Kennedy and Johnson administrations made a war in Vietnam that they did not ask their own sons to fight."[15] Vietnam was indeed a working-class war; the sons of the less affluent fell in disproportionate numbers.[16] Project 100,000 targeted the social classes from which blue-collar workers derived, and, according to a study commissioned by the Veterans' Administration in 1978, at least two-thirds of those who served in Vietnam were working-class or low-income.[17] It was all too clear to blue-collar workers that Vietnam was a poor man's graveyard and that the war ran contrary to the principles of social justice. To make things worse, the riches created in the early stages of the war were unevenly spread, and by the end of the war, there was increasing evidence of "stagflation," inflation combined with unemployment and economic stagnation. All this spelled trouble for U.S. policy in Vietnam.

Labor opposition to the Vietnam War was both early and late. Some of the earliest criticism came from old bastions of the left, much attenuated by the 1960s, but strategically placed with a view to making trouble for the Vietnam Run. Then, in the years 1964–

1969, labor protesters took a back seat while students and African Americans staged their rebellions. Nevertheless, rank-and-file union opinion was beginning to change even in this middle period. A Gallup poll indicated that by the end of 1967, union families shared national misgivings about the war, even if they still showed above-average overall support for President Johnson. When AFL-CIO leaders claimed that their private polls showed that the rank and file were even more hawkish than the union bosses, the *New York Times* concluded that "labor leaders are not always good barometers of the thinking of their members."[18] By this time, union voices had made themselves heard in the Dump Johnson campaign, and by the approach of the 1968 election, peace agitation by labor was quite powerfully under way. Then, when Nixon was president, the antiwarriors among laborers showed that they were no longer confined to the left and could rattle Meany's power base. They threatened not the strategic periphery of American industry, the ailing maritime sector, but its strategic center, the automobile industry.

Some of the very earliest criticism of American involvement in the Vietnam War came from Harry Bridges and the International Longshoremen's and Warehousemen's Union (ILWU). Bridges was a tough Australian immigrant who had defied several attempts at deportation. He had married an Asian-American woman, was imbued with a Pacific vision, and had an enduring conviction that labor had a right to shape foreign policy. He had already caused trouble for one Democratic administration, having defied President Roosevelt by instigating the San Francisco general strike of 1934. As befitted one of the great mavericks of the labor movement, Bridges's political affiliation in the 1960s was a matter for speculation. He may have been a Communist or at least a communist sympathizer in his earlier career, although he later denied it, and claimed to have registered as a Republican as long ago as the 1940s.

Certainly, Bridges did not toe the Democratic Party line. Rather, he paid heed to his own beliefs and to the needs and convictions of his union members. The union that he headed, ILWU, was a powerful organization with a high strategic war or antiwar potential deriving from the nature of its members' work: loading ships on the West Coast, the eastern end of the Vietnam Run. Its jurisdiction on the coast and in Hawaii meant that its members benefited from war-induced prosperity. Yet the ILWU consistently opposed the war, and from an early date. In May 1962, Bridges criticized President Kennedy for shipping U.S. ground troops to Thailand and South Vietnam. His criticism was a matter of principle, as was that of the students who followed in his wake. But he also seemed to be offering a partisan political issue to the Republicans. He observed, in the union journal *The Dispatcher*, that the presidential candidate Wendell Willkie had declared for Asian self-determination in 1942 and that another Republican, President Eisenhower, had "refused direct U.S. intervention" in Indochina.[19] Thus Bridges opened a significant, if idiosyncratic, chink in labor's support for American Southeast Asian policy.

Using time-honored labor union tactics, *The Dispatcher* publicized the activities of approved legislators and singled out those Pacific politicians who could be relied upon to oppose the war. Between 1963 and 1965, peace-crusading Senator George S. McGovern received lavish encomiums both in the magazine and at the ILWU biennial convention. In 1964, *The Dispatcher* praised the antiwar stands of Senators Wayne Morse (Ore.), Ernest Gruening and Bob Bartlett (Alaska), and Hiram Fong (Hawaii) and, in 1965, conferred a similar accolade upon five California representatives: Congressman George E. Brown, Jr., state Senator Alan Short, and Assemblymen John Burton, Willie Brown, and William Stanton. Foreshadowing an argument taken up in the Nixon administration, the journal predicted that ending the war would not be economically disastrous. On the contrary, it would lead to better and lucrative relations with communist nations. The China trade in particular would "end West Coast unemployment."[20]

With the escalation of the war in 1965, the ILWU consolidated its antimilitarist position. At the biennial convention, the chair of the Resolution Committee, Charles Duarte, nominated Louis Goldblatt for the secretary-treasurership: "He is an oasis of men, a Red Sea of progressive thinking in a barren desert of American trade union leaders." Duarte proposed the antiwar resolution of that year, and it was passed then, as at successive future conventions. The ILWU was motivated by left-wing principles, by the conviction that prosperity depended on peace on the Pacific Rim, and by racial liberalism. The last factor was especially important in the case of Hawaii, which carried weight in union deliberations because Local 142 (Honolulu) had ten times as many members as the next largest local (Local 6, San Francisco). The longshoremen's opposition to the war was formidable because it derived from the national leadership and had the solid backing of Local 142. The practical implications of this rank-and-file involvement spread beyond the union: Hawaii elected, in addition to Senator Hiram Fong, the equally antiwar congresswoman, Patsy Mink.[21]

Even in the ILWU, opposition had its limits. Bridges was a pragmatist as well as a radical. Shortly after ILWU families in Honolulu celebrated Labor Day 1965 with picnics and a parade and speeches in favor of "Peace and Pork Chops," Bridges cautioned against any attempt to use the union's strategic position to stop the war through strike action. He recalled how in the 1930s the union had so naïvely and ineffectively "tried to halt the shipment of scrap iron to Japan." Noting the criticism directed by students, intellectuals, and liberals toward the ILWU's willingness to benefit from war-induced trade in the 1960s, he nevertheless rejected the call for an arms-shipment boycott on the ground that it would fail in the absence of any promise of nationwide labor solidarity.[22]

A West Coast waterfront arms boycott would have created difficulties for the U.S. war machine. If the ILWU had joined forces with the Bay Area students in a concerted campaign, a near-revolutionary situation might have developed. It would have been limited to one locality, to be sure, but the locality could not have been more vital in terms of the war. But Bridges was unwilling to accept the cost: the probable destruction of his union and the replacement of its members by longshoremen from the rival, prowar ILA union. Bridges's caution enabled the Johnson administration to escape what would have been a major crisis.

But the White House was still faced with an old left critique of the war offered by a group of unions formerly associated with the Communists. The United Electrical Workers joined the ILWU in calling for an immediate end to the war. So did the International Union of Mine, Mill, and Smelter Workers. Mine, Mill was depleted in numbers but had radical antecedents, for its leaders proudly wore the mantle of an early twentieth-century antiwar union, the Industrial Workers of the World. Other unionists joined in, and in the fall of 1965 a small radical convention in New York formed an organization called Trade Unionists for Peace. The other unions were not so strategically placed as the ILWU, however, and represented only a modest minority within the labor movement.[23]

More ominous for President Johnson than the possibility of leftist trouble was the rumbling of discontent in the UAW, for the autoworkers were at the vital center of the American economy, and their union had hitherto been a bastion of liberalism and the Democratic Party. At the AFL-CIO convention in San Francisco in 1965, when Meany crushed the antiwar resolution offered by Emil Mazey of the UAW, the gallery had erupted with protest from Berkeley and San Francisco State students, who chanted, "Debate! Debate! Debate!"[24] Gradually, the feeling grew among some union activists that Meany, Reuther, and AFL-CIO officialdom were suppressing dissent and did not represent the true feelings of the rank and file.

Although there was no systematic national polling of union membership or blue-collar workers (or the "working class," however defined) on the subject of the war, there was healthy cause for suspecting that the masses did not quite fit the hawkish stereotype. After all, it was one thing to detest middle-class students who enjoyed draft deferments, quite another to support the war that killed one's own sons. Local opinion polls in Dearborn and San Francisco in 1966–1968 showed higher antiwar proclivities among the working class than among the middle class.[25] Opinion surveys of UAW members in Michigan showed that as early as June 1966, a majority favored a negotiated settlement in Vietnam. According to a spring 1967, survey, "UAW members are considerably more dovelike today than is the electorate as a whole."[26]

The sentiment was not confined to the rank and file. In spite of Walter Reuther's uneasy struggle to remain loyal to Johnson, a rift opened, and widened, between the leadership of the UAW and that of the AFL-CIO. Walter's brother, Victor, directed the International Affairs Department of the UAW and resented Meany's use of the AFL-CIO to back Johnson's policy in Vietnam. In May 1966, as the UAW convention in Long Beach, California, called for improved relations with communist China, Victor Reuther attacked Meany and Lovestone for having "permitted themselves to be used by the CIA as a cover for clandestine operations abroad."[27] The charge was true, as later revelations confirmed, but Meany denied it with a fury that signaled a sharp deterioration in Meany-UAW relations.

Walter Reuther found it hard to break with his belief that President Johnson was the anticipated standard-bearer for the kinds of social reform espoused by the UAW. In the fall of 1967, even as he delivered a speech calling for a halt to the bombing in Vietnam, he endorsed LBJ for reelection.[28] But shortly afterward, and to the distress of President Johnson, he took the UAW out of the AFL-CIO, just as his union was about to contribute $120,000 to the political fund that Meany's federation would have used to help with LBJ's reelection. Reuther was disenchanted both with AFL-CIO apathy regarding unorganized labor and the welfare state and with its support for the Vietnam War.[29]

By this time, there had been renewed efforts at interunion cooperation in opposition to the war. In January 1967 labor groups in the New York–New Jersey area, Chicago, and Los Angeles had formed branches of the new Trade Union Division of the National Committee for a Sane Nuclear Policy with the declared aim of opposing AFL-CIO–supported foreign policy and the Vietnam War. On the eve of the AFL-CIO convention in November, the same group organized the Labor Leadership Assembly for Peace, holding a Veterans Weekend convention attended by 523 labor leaders from thirty-eight states, most of them paying their own way.[30]

On the political front, elements associated with the labor movement were involved in the campaign to replace Johnson as the Democrats' presidential candidate in the 1968 election. In January 1967, ADA vice president, Allard Lowenstein, launched his

Dump Johnson movement because of the administration's Vietnam policy. He came under attack from Gus Tyler, assistant president of the International Ladies Garment Workers Union and chair of the Policy Committee for the 1967 ADA convention, who deplored the idea of tying the ADA to the single issue of peace in Vietnam.[31] In July, Joseph L. Rauh, Jr., proposed an alternative idea: the election of a peace caucus to the Democratic convention in 1968, with the object of forcing through an end-the-war plank intended to be binding on the next administration. Rauh, a former New Dealer who had also served as chair of the ADA, held out hopes of labor support. He acknowledged that "most" of the top leaders were committed to supporting the war in Vietnam: "However, many of the secondary leadership in the labor movement are troubled by labor's position on Vietnam and these constitute the bulk of labor delegates to any Democratic Convention. If anti-Johnson overtones can be avoided, there would be a possibility that many of these delegates, relieved of the pressure they would be under to support the President, would be in a position to help with the effort for a peace plank."[32]

Initially, then, Rauh opposed the Dump Johnson campaign. He feared that it would "fracture the liberal-labor-Negro coalition." Gus Tyler supported him with the observation that a fight against Johnson would place in jeopardy the careers of some notable doves in the Congress. With the approach of the 1968 elections, he cautioned, "American liberalism faces the most serious crisis of the century." Then, when Senator Eugene McCarthy entered the lists as a peace candidate, Rauh changed his mind. His endorsement of McCarthy in early December 1967 effectively placed him in the Dump Johnson camp.[33]

It is uncertain how much immediate impact the Lowenstein-Rauh moves had. In September 1967 even Emil Mazey was "not sure that getting a proper plank in the 1968 Democratic Party platform has any real meaning or will in any way affect the policies of President Johnson."[34] But Lowenstein and Rauh had at least succeeded in giving the impression that it might be possible to introduce a whiff of labor-backed practicality into the heady breeze of antiwar idealism. Labor unionists may have taken a back seat in the middle period of protest against the Vietnam War, but they still had something to offer the antiwar movement. Organized labor was notable for its institutional strength and its sense of continuity—concepts that were anathema to many students and yet, for that very reason, promised to be a useful complement to the campus peace campaign.

Antiwar protest within the labor movement undermined the AFL-CIO's ability to deliver an unsullied morale boost to the warmakers and presented the White House with a problem. President Johnson was aware of this. He responded by promising continuing prosperity and the delivery of his Great Society, by making it clear that he expected automatic loyalty to the Democratic coalition, and by cultivating top labor leaders.

From the beginning, President Johnson tried to propitiate Walter Reuther. In 1965 he personally reassured the UAW leader of his peaceful intentions in Vietnam, and Reuther was appointed as a "senior adviser" to the American delegation to the United Nations.[35] The same guiding principle is evident two years later, in LBJ's address to the AFL-CIO conference at Bal Harbour, Florida, on December 13, 1967. The president came equipped with a list of favors that he had conferred or might in future confer on Walter Reuther. In his speech he issued a reminder of the gains to labor that had resulted from its association with the Democratic Party: "Already," because of the recent Medicare legislation, "four million Americans have had their hospital bills paid." Johnson warned of the impending backlash against minorities and called on labor to stand firm. Then, in his peroration, he thanked the convention for the resolution that it had once again passed in support of "freedom's cause" in Vietnam: "I know that many of labor's sons have left their homes to risk their lives in Vietnam. I know that is torture for you, as it is for me. I know that you regret every dollar spent on war—dollars that should be spent on the works of peace. But you and I know that we must persevere."[36]

Although Johnson was anxious to keep labor on board, he would not do so at any price. One of his goals was to establish a new Department of Transportation to deal with such matters as road safety, but in 1966 the Congress objected to including the Maritime Administration in the proposed department.[37] Johnson was furious at its exclusion and refused to support its independent status. The upshot was a running feud with the business executives and union leaders in the industry and with the politicians who supported them. The Sailors' Union of the Pacific warned that "ninety-eight per cent of . . . supplies and sixty-six per cent of our military personnel are sent to Vietnam on ships."[38] Senator Thomas H. Kuchel, a Republican of California, lamented that "since 1960, our fleet has declined by one quarter while the Russians have doubled theirs and have passed us in the number of ships afloat."[39] William S. Mailliard, a Republican representing the areas adjoining each end of the Golden Gate Bridge (the Sixth District of California), supported the war and worried about the sealift capability of the declining U.S. merchant marine. He believed the time was ripe for a reinforcement of the mercantilist shipping laws of 1915 and 1936, designed in part to protect the jobs and working conditions of American sailors.[40]

In spite of this evidence of the dawning Republican consciousness of the possibility of poaching the labor vote, Johnson made no concessions. Even though the Seafarers' International Union (SIU) and the seven-million-strong AFL-CIO Maritime Trades Department demanded that the Maritime Administration be given greater autonomy and more extensive powers, the president cut its budget early in 1968, leaving it in a subordinate position within the Commerce Department.[41]

But in the means used to rally labor support within the maritime industry, the White House did show signs of improved sensitivity. When a White House staffer drafted a friendly presidential reply to Harry Bridges's good wishes on achieving peace in late 1963, LBJ's aide George Reedy had, in a panic reaction to any perceived association with a former Communist, scribbled on the note, "NO! NO! NO! EMPHATICALLY NO! DON'T SEND! JUST FILE!" A few years later, in November 1968, Johnson "deeply appreciated" a telegram in which Bridges commended the president for announcing a bombing halt.[42]

President Johnson needed a similar political sensitivity in

dealing with the economic effects of the war on labor. In July 1965 the chair of the Council of Economic Advisers, Gardner Ackley, told Johnson that "on a coldly objective analysis" the war "was likely to be favorable to our prosperity."[43] Johnson soon developed private doubts on this point but publicly continued to insist that the nation could afford both the war and the Great Society. He may have been aware that reconversion, far from delivering immediate peace dividends, would impose some painful readjustments on the American workforce. As early as July 1966 the economist Walter Heller alerted him to the need to prepare an economic strategy for peacetime. It would be useful as propaganda, enabling the president to argue that he had plans for peace that were being wrecked by the warmongering Vietnamese Communists. A peace plan would also help to preempt any slump in business confidence caused by prospects of military withdrawal and by worries about an accompanying decline in demand. Johnson asked his Coordinating Committee on Economic Planning for the End of Vietnam Hostilities to respond to Heller's suggestion, and his advisers drafted a statement praising the cooperation of business and labor with the war effort, claiming that the war could still be fought without harmful economic consequences, and issuing instructions for the planning of economic reconversion.[44]

Deliberations on the economic consequences of peace continued. In November 1967 the director of the Bureau of the Budget, Charles L. Schultze, assured the president that "Great Society programs have not been greatly reduced as the result of Vietnam." Research available to his office indicated that the war chest had been filled more from reapportioned space program funds than from resources diverted from the Great Society. Subsequently, reconversion plans focused on the revitalization of the space industry. For example, a federally sponsored study of California arms businesses concluded in 1968 that some defense jobs could easily be converted into space jobs. Civilian-contract wage rates would, however, be 5 percent lower than those for equivalent jobs in the defense industry.[45]

In the short term, the ending of the war would carry economic and therefore political penalties. With an election looming in 1968, the administration refused to take a longer-term view that carried short-term risks and stuck with the war, which seemed to confer prosperity on workers and to have the support of the AFL-CIO hierarchy. It relied on diplomatic rapport with that hierarchy, combined with patriotic propaganda and promises that the Great Society programs would continue unimpaired.

In selecting the presidential candidate of the Democratic Party, the labor leadership therefore remained influential. After Johnson had declared that he would not run, Meany endorsed Hubert Humphrey. The vice president could hardly disclaim the policies that he had loyally supported hitherto; he had to stick with the war, so he was open to criticism as a stand-pat candidate. Yet Meany did not even bother to consult the AFL-CIO council before delivering his support to Humphrey. Additionally, the AFL-CIO president did his best to undermine the peace candidates. He perceived that Gene McCarthy's "pretense at political divinity" and his belief that the educated knew best would annoy working people in the union movement. He also put pressure on local labor organizations to withhold their support from Senator Robert F. Kennedy's campaign for the Democratic nomination.[46]

Meany might very possibly have been unable to deliver labor's organizational machine without the fortuitous and mind-concentrating intervention in the presidential campaign by the American Independent Party candidate, George C. Wallace. The white-backlash candidate made serious inroads into the white labor vote, not just in the South but outside it, too. Psephologists have since argued that labor was particularly disenchanted with the Democratic Party between 1968 and 1972, and disenchanted workers were ready to listen to a fresh voice. What alarmed union leaders was that Alabama, the state of which Wallace had been governor, condoned low wages and employers' exploitation of local workers. The American labor bureaucracy rallied to Humphrey in an effort to minimize support for Wallace. The Democratic candidate played his part by at last promising maritime expansion and other measures desired by labor and by making a late declaration in favor of a halt to the bombing in Vietnam. Even Victor

Reuther, openly critical of the war by June 1968, came out in favor of Humphrey, even if he did constantly urge him to end the war.[47]

The result was a closer election result than might otherwise have been the case. Nixon, however, was able to play on the endurance of the war, on social disorder, and on the price rises that were —it seemed increasingly apparent—a consequence of wartime expenditures. He claimed to have a secret plan for peace but satisfied the hawks by stating his intention of continuing the war if necessary. On the stump in Union Station, Kansas City, on October 16, 1968, he declared: "The Administration has struck out on keeping the peace abroad, on keeping the peace at home, on providing prosperity without inflation." That message, with its hint at labor's economic self-interest, was good enough to win the election for a Republican candidate who, in reality, had no peace plan at all.[48]

President Nixon courted labor in a way designed to bolster domestic support for the Vietnam War and help his reelection prospects in 1972. An appeal to working men's patriotism and prejudices was a key element in his strategy to create a "new majority" for the Republican Party—and for himself as president. The inspiration for his campaign came partly from Senator James Buckley's New York senatorial campaign in the 1970 midterm elections. His tactics may also be understood against the background of an ominous groundswell of labor discontent about the war.[49]

Although Meany and the national labor leadership continued to support the war after the 1968 election, there was a perceptible erosion in enthusiasm after Nixon's arrival as president. One reason for the waning in support was the residual antagonism of labor against any Republican in the White House. Another was the cumulative impact of extra, war-induced spending on the economy. Even before Nixon's inauguration, economists had warned of the damaging effects of the Vietnam War. Foreseeing the dangers, Secretary of Defense Robert S. McNamara had tried to keep military expenditures under control. Nevertheless, in the final days of the Johnson administration, the Coordinating Committee on Economic Planning for the End of Vietnam Hostilities had concluded that the war was a general burden on the economy. Nixon's advisers—for example, John B. Connally, Jr., the renegade Democrat-appointed secretary of the treasury—similarly worried in December 1970 about the strain placed on the economy by defense expenditures. In May 1970, Nixon's old friend Bernard Lasker, chair of the New York Stock Exchange, reportedly told the president that the Vietnam War was causing distress on Wall Street.[50]

Perhaps it should not be too lightly assumed that the Vietnam War caused inflation, business stagnation, and unemployment and that this deterioration accounts for labor's disenchantment. Disenchantment had set in before the economic problems became apparent, indeed at time when the war seemed to be creating prosperity. Also, the direct military costs of the Vietnam War are a matter of some controversy amongst economists: they were substantially smaller ($140 billion) and more spread out (1965–1976) than those of World War II ($360 billion; 1941–1945) and were paid for out of an expanded and more prosperous economy.[51] Again, economic considerations were not always paramount. Although California's antiwar Democratic senator, Alan Cranston, noted in mid-1970 that "the rank and file of labor 'have had enough' because these are the people most adversely affected by the inflation, tight credit and unemployment caused by the war in Southeast Asia," he added: "However, I believe that their outrage against the war is not motivated by financial considerations. The American working man is deeply committed to current efforts to end the war. These people have seen the tragic casualty lists become too long and too filled with the names of their sons."[52] Even if the main aim of organized labor was the advancement of the economic well-being of union members, it did have other concerns. Nevertheless, at a time when conservatives complained about the inflationary effects of the Great Society (total expenditure, 1964–1972: $199 billion), labor could find both moral and economic reasons to object to combined military and indirect Vietnam War costs—estimated at $943 billion.[53]

In Nixon's first year in office, there were signs of labor's spreading disenchantment with the war. Unions whose members had been direct beneficiaries of the Vietnam Run now began to voice criticism. In August 1969, *West Coast Sailors* published its first article critical of the war. The author of the article, the veteran civil-rights campaigner Bayard Rustin, denounced campus disruption and called instead for ballot-box tactics to end the war. The Moratorium Day demonstrations on October 15 came within a whisker of being called a "general strike" and, unlike some earlier mass protests, attracted substantial labor support in cities like New York and Detroit. When the San Francisco Labor Council supported the Moratorium Day parades, it was evident that one of the main AFL-CIO bastions had fallen to the antiwar forces. The *San Francisco Chronicle* rubbed salt in the wound, reporting the claim of labor rebels that the AFL-CIO position on Vietnam symbolized "the great gulf between the labor bureaucracy and the membership."[54]

Given this perceived slippage in support by common people and wishing to convince Hanoi that the American people still stood firm, President Nixon delivered a notable speech on national television and radio on Monday, November 3. He explained his policy of Vietnamization and offered justifications for fighting on. And, famously, he appealed for the support of "the great silent majority" of his fellow Americans. Later, he said that he wrote the "silent majority" paragraph at four on the Saturday morning of the weekend before his speech, suggesting that the phrase came in a flash of political intuition, rather than as the result of analysis based on evidence.[55]

The president had not invented the concept. As long ago as 1919, Senator Lodge had assumed the support of "the great silent mass of the people" in opposing the Paris peace treaty; at the AFL-CIO convention of 1967, Meany had claimed that prowar labor "spoke for the vast, silent majority in the nation"; and LBJ's Citizens Committee for Peace with Freedom claimed to be the "voice from the silent center." But Nixon did elevate and give new prominence to the notion that a good leader ignored raucous minorities and heeded instead virtuous majority opinion. The conjectural incoherence of the invisible masses had suddenly become a conspicuous political asset.

Nixon's appeal provoked some debate. On the one hand, researchers like Andrew Greeley of the National Opinion Research Center at the University of Chicago contended that white "ethnics" supported the war. These descendants of the "peasant populations of Eastern and Southern Europe and Ireland" were virulently anticommunist, resented any criticism of the foreign policy of the United States, and detested protesting rich kids, African Americans, and feminists. In short, the white ethnics, by now heavily represented in the labor unions, were the backbone of the working-class silent majority. Greeley was not alone in this perception. The presidential speech writer William Safire argued later that Catholics and Jews, as well as labor, were significant components of Nixon's "new majority," a concept that clearly embraced the "silent" masses.[56] Not everyone agreed. The peace activist Sanford Gottlieb contended that "there is not yet any hard evidence that the ethnics are more hawkish than others in the same socio-economic brackets."[57] Pollsters found "silent majorities" against the war as well as against those who protested it. To complicate matters further, in 1970 a group of academic analysts used poll data to show that male white union members were strong hawks but that their wives were pronounced doves—"a sharp division to have under the same roof." These professors argued that the silent majority was little more than "a cleverly designed symbol," but they feared that it would become "more important for the reality it creates than the reality it describes."[58]

In a sampling not restricted to union members, Gallup polls in July and October 1969 indicated that manual workers and low-income people were more dovish than the rest of the population. How then, asked a writer in *Dissent*, did the misconception arise that blue-collar workers were hawks? Impishly, he suggested that it was because they had precisely those characteristics that conservatives attributed to the silent majority: they were more reticent than high-income voters and rarely demonstrated, so one could label them hawks with no evidence to the contrary and little fear of articulate contradiction.[59]

The president became convinced of the correctness of the silent majority doctrine. In his memoirs, he fondly recalled that after his speech he received eighty thousand letters and telegrams of support and achieved a 68 percent approval rating in the opinion polls. "Very few speeches actually influence the course of history," he wrote, but "the November 3 speech was one of them." The response to it indicted that "the Silent Majority had made itself heard."[60] That this was not strictly true did not really matter. If he could convince others to believe in the myth of the prowar silent majority, he could make the concept politically potent and even self-validating.

There now occurred an event that made the silent-majority ploy seem plausible, an event that served as the prelude to the crucial strategy that prolonged the war: the hard-hat demonstration of May 1970. It presented a political opportunity to a Republican president with a shaky record in labor affairs. Nixon needed a boost, for he could not hope to shake off the enmity of organized labor on domestic matters. In the final stages of the 1968 presidential campaign, he had been attacked as a supporter of the employers against the oppressed migrant agricultural workers of the West and as a blatant eater of "scab grapes" in defiance of the contemporary consumer boycott in support of workers' rights.[61] He talked of wage restraint as a solution to war-induced inflation, giving rank-and-file union protesters their widely displayed slogan No Vietnamese Ever Froze My Wages.[62] With the midterm elections approaching in the fall of 1970, he had a pressing need to improve his image. Safire recalls that Nixon, blocked on the domestic front, was anxious for an opportunity to win labor's support "on the matter that mattered most, foreign affairs." The opportunity, when it arrived, was golden, for it involved hard-hat construction workers, a group that by the 1970s had become—in the words of the historian Joshua Freedman—"the central symbol of American labor."[63]

At noon on May 8, about two hundred construction workers

wearing their hard, yellow safety hats descended on a group of students who had gathered in the financial district of New York City to protest the extension of the war to Cambodia. Clutching American flags and shouting "All the way, U.S.A.," the workers burst through police lines and beat up some of the protesters. Their number swollen to five hundred, the hard hats thereupon marched to the city hall, where a half-mast flag mourned the recent shootings at Kent State. The defiant workers sang "The Star-Spangled Banner" and dispersed, after assaulting a few more students.[64]

The next day, labor unionists across the nation joined counter-demonstrations to affirm their *dis*approval of the Cambodian incursion. But they could not match the novelty and news appeal of the New York hard-hat demonstration.[65] The hawks now seized their opportunity. Ten days after the original demonstration, the *New York Daily News* carried an advertisement in which the Building and Construction Trades Council of Greater New York announced an official rally at City Hall Park on Wednesday, May 20. The purpose of the rally was "to demonstrate that love of country and love and respect for our country's flag are not as old-fashioned and as out of date as the 'know-it-alls' would have us believe." The sponsors emphasized that they did not condone violence, and the demonstration was in fact peaceful, though still dramatic and colorful—some Native Americans (legendary in the steel erection industry for their fearlessness when working at great heights) turned up in tribal headdress.[66] Chuck Colson, special counsel to President Nixon, thought the rally was "an enormous success." He said that estimates of attendance ranged from 100,000 to 250,000 and that smaller, counterpart rallies had been organized in Buffalo, Pittsburgh, and San Diego. In his memorandum for the president, he reported on the provenance of the demonstration: "Peter Brennan, who is President of the New York Council, and Thomas Tobin, Secretary-Treasurer, were the prime movers in organizing the 'hard hats' parade two weeks ago and the rally last week. (Jay Lovestone and others were involved but this group required very little encouragement.) They had the active cooperation and involvement of the Longshoremen, Teddy Gleason's union."[67] Brennan, in particular, would soon play a key role in Colson's plans.

At a loss to explain why the silent majority had suddenly taken to the streets in noisy support of the war, some commentators took a cynical view. Ever since the days of Damon Runyon, workers in the New York building trades had had a reputation for being plug-uglies, with leaders prone to corruption and disposed to agree to sweetheart contracts, employers choosing to deal with favored labor leaders in exchange for no-strike deals. Therefore, there were dark suspicions concerning some of those who had organized the rallies: Sidney Glasser of the Glaziers' Union had been convicted of extortion; Biagio Lanza of the Plasterers, of bookmaking offenses; Thomas Gleason, of contempt of court in connection with discriminatory practices on the waterfront; and Brennan was accused of colluding with politicians in keeping the construction trades "lily-white." The suspicion was that—like the mobsters Al Capone, who claimed to hate communism, and James Hoffa, president of the Teamsters and a staunch supporter of the Vietnam War—the building trades leaders were fishing for public and political support.[68]

Economic theories were also brought forward to explain the hard-hat phenomenon. One was that building trades union leaders had cooperated with conservative, prowar employers in organizing the hard-hat demonstrations and that these employers had promised to pay workers (or even pay them bonuses) for time lost. After all, both events had occurred on workdays. This overcame the economic obstacle that had kept blue-collar workers out of peace demonstrations: the fear of losing pay or even their jobs.[69] Another economic theory held that the construction workers feared that peace would bring recession; student protesters were therefore a threat to their prosperity.[70]

But the hard-hat incidents also reflect disdain of protesting students and feelings of comradeship with the fighting men in Vietnam. With no new draftees being sent to Vietnam and efforts having been made to correct racial imbalances, the fighting was, to a greater degree than ever, being done by the sons and brothers of white working-class men. The situation was custom-made for expressions of fraternal solidarity. The hard-hat workers obliged and even made the pulse race—this in an era of workplace boredom and blue-collar blues. For those in search of social scapegoats, they offered a heady mix of all-round chauvinism. They were not just student-haters and racists but misogynists, too. Easy work in the building trades was "tit work." When three brawny workers turned on a young woman who tried to stop the pulverization of a student during the Manhattan demonstration, they smashed her glasses and punched her into the hospital, explaining that they were treating her "like an equal."[71] *Time* magazine reported on the demonstration thus: "Callused hands gripped tiny flags. Weathered faces shone with sweat. . . . New York's brawniest union marched and shouted . . . in a massive display of gleeful patriotism and muscular pride."[72] No matter that 53 percent of unionists disapproved the hard-hat action of May 8.[73] The image of a working-class war was compellingly vivid and was immensely useful to President Nixon.

In the aftermath of the hard-hat demonstrations, the president showed his awareness of the advantages of courting labor. While his silent-majority appeal had seemed to buffet the moratorium movement and promised to deliver political dividends, the Cambodian incursion proved controversial and was potentially damaging in political terms. Nixon, who anticipated that the support of labor for the Cambodian venture would be "vital," had obtained Meany's prior support for the incursion.[74] Now, heartened by the hard-hat phenomenon, he went for broader endorsement. On May 12 he gave the AFL-CIO executive council a special briefing on Cambodia. In a symbolic gesture of respect, he visited them instead of granting them an audience in the White House. Colson promised the president that White House staff would work with the AFL-CIO council to "start a major campaign among the AFL/CIO membership."[75]

In pursuit of this last aim, Nixon planned a further meeting with the twenty-three low-ranking union officials who had been responsible for the hard-hat parades. Colson briefed the president not to mention students and not to preach patriotism to the group, because its members were already "hard line."[76] Once the group had arrived and the photographer had finished his work, Michael Donovan of the Plumbers Union, a Gold Star Father by virtue of having lost a son in the war, told the president that he wished America had gone into Cambodia earlier. George Daly presented the president with his hard hat, which had "Nixon" emblazoned on it in bold letters. Other members of the group said that they had built America "with their own hands" and resented seeing it torn down by radicals. Enjoying all this, Nixon claimed that his father "had been a carpenter and bricklayer" and warned his listeners (eleven of whom bore Irish names and three Italian) that "hundreds of thousands of [Vietnamese] Catholics . . . would be slaughtered if we pulled out of Vietnam."[77] The following day, the official journal of the ILA published an open letter of appreciation from the president to Gleason, thanking him for his support over foreign policy. Clearly, the White House was reveling in its new rapport with labor.[78]

Early in June the Swedish prime minister, Olof Palme, visited the United States. A poster issued by the "rank and file" of the ILA denounced him for welcoming "American military deserters and traitors to Sweden" and called for a demonstration. When a number of longshoremen picketed one of his speeches, Palme claimed that he was told by State Department security men that the pickets had been paid a bottle of whisky and forty dollars each to cause him trouble. The longshoremen objected to the story, and the AFL-CIO complained to Colson, who thought the matter "should be clarified." But Colson's real interest was in egging on blue-collar demonstrators. He had already asked the "hard hats" to "run an ad in the New York papers" calling for a patriotic demonstration on July 4.[79] All this indicates that even before the Buckley campaign, the Nixon administration was working hard to develop an in with labor.

In the hard-hat demonstrations the Nixon administration had detected the germ of a winning strategy for the presidential reelection campaign of 1972. Meantime, the midterm elections were a rebuff for Republicans and hawks alike. In the campaign, however, the White House found its tactical mentor in James Buckley, the senatorial candidate of the Conservative Party of New York State. According to a *New York Times* survey, ending the war in Vietnam was the top political issue in New York. But Buckley defied the national trend against Republican hawks, and won. An important element in his strategy was his appeal to the labor vote.[80]

Buckley, a Catholic, shared the conservative views of his older brother, the television-show host and columnist William F. Buckley, Jr. In particular, James Buckley took a hawkish and fervently anticommunist view of foreign policy. In World War II he had fought the Japanese in the Pacific. He took an apocalyptic view of the latest Asian war. "If this country goes under," he warned at a Franklin County Women's Republican Club picnic, "the world goes under." Although he ran as the candidate of an independent party, Buckley was a registered Republican. He supported Nixon's conduct of the war and claimed that the president was "frustrated by a hostile Congress" in his attempts to end it.[81] In taking this stand, he differentiated himself from the Republican candidate, Charles Goodell, whom Governor Nelson Rockefeller had appointed to fill the seat vacated upon Robert Kennedy's assassination, for Goodell, though professing loyalty to President Nixon on other counts, had infuriated some of his erstwhile supporters by turning against the war.[82] Representative Richard L. Ottinger, the Democratic candidate, was also an opponent of the war. Like Goodell, he was considered a political liberal. Buckley thus had the advantage of a split liberal vote and of being, at the statewide level, the sole hope of conservative hawks. Governor Rockefeller was running for reelection as a Republican liberal, and the other Republican incumbent, Senator Jacob Javits (not due for reelection in 1970), was a leading sponsor of congressional initiatives to repeal the Tonkin Gulf Resolution and to terminate U.S. combat involvement in Cambodia.[83]

What gave added spice to the Buckley campaign was the offstage presence of two potent challengers for the 1972 Republican nomination: Governor Reagan of California, representing the party right, and Rockefeller, representing the party left. Although the circumstances of Buckley's candidacy were a little awkward—he was set to dislodge a Republican incumbent—they were also convenient, because his candidacy was an experiment with no strings attached. If Buckley went down, he would not be a drag on Nixon's fortunes; if he won, he would not be a threat to Nixon's own candidacy, for, unlike Reagan and Rockefeller, he was not running as a Republican.

In the event, the Buckley campaign succeeded in a way that seemed to offer some useful lessons for the Nixon reelection strategists. It came as no surprise that the Conservative Party candidate commanded the support of staid, upstate areas, because the region to the north of the Westchester County line was considered natural "Buckley country."[84] The candidate could also rely on what the political commentator Kevin Phillips later described as the Irish Catholic vote at the end of the New York City subway lines.[85] But the real point of interest lay in Buckley's appeal to labor, which became an electrifying electoral factor immediately after the hard-hat demonstration of May 20.

A few days after the demonstration, Buckley explained his reasons for running for the Senate. He argued that America was in a "state of siege" from a "radical fringe" that comprised a small minority of the protest movement yet contrived to "set the tone." If elected, he would fight the liberals and doves on Capitol Hill and would help President Nixon to lift the siege. In his opening salvo, he argued that majorities within supposedly disaffected groups—he mentioned women but placed his main emphasis on students, African Americans, and "the rank and file of American labor"—were part of the silent majority that supported law and order at home and recognized the country's duty to halt the march of communism in Vietnam: "We live in times which have made it necessary for 150,000 Americans last Wednesday, and for us here tonight, to make these public demonstration[s] of our faith in America and in our destiny as a free people."[86]

Buckley singled out issues of interest to labor as he campaigned around the state. Speaking in Nassau and Suffolk Counties, Long Island, where job losses were threatened, he stressed the need for continuing government investment in the local high-technology defense industry—essential alike to regional prosperity and to the security of the free world. Naturally, the Democrats struck back. Ottinger, the Democratic candidate, attacked Buckley for favoring anti-union legislation and opposing the minimum wage.[87] By the end of July, however, the conservative columnist John Chamberlain detected a prospective Buckley victory based on the labor vote. Like other conservatives, he took cheer from the endorsement of Buckley by the Irish-American Michael Maye, a leader in the hard-hat movement and the head of the 28,000-strong New York Firefighters' Association. Chamberlain warned that the AFL-CIO planned to spend $850,000 on Democratic candidates, which might help doves. But in deciding how to vote, workers could place material self-interest second, he said, "for Meany's foreign policy—and, by extension, the foreign policy stand of the AFL-CIO—is the Nixon Policy."[88]

In July and August respected journalists began to suspect that the Nixon administration was backing the Buckley campaign. The syndicated columnists Rowland Evans and Robert Novak said that Buckley was "blessed with the silent support of President Nixon's top political advisers in Washington," while Andrew Tully reported that Attorney General John Mitchell was discreetly raising money for Buckley, a sign of Nixonian support even if the president could not come out for him officially.[89] That these guesses were close to the mark is suggested by a memorandum from Colson to H. R. Haldeman dated September 21, 1970. The presidential chief of staff had asked if Brennan and the other New York hard-hat groups could be used to support Buckley. Colson replied: "Lovestone has been passing the word that Buckley is his candidate. I don't think that at this stage of the campaign, it would be helpful to have anything more overt although we might be able to arrange it later. Our friends are very cooperative in this effort."[90]

White House interest in the hard hats had undergone a smooth transition into informal support for the Buckley campaign. Lovestone was a source of intelligence—when Chicago labor leaders called for a National Rank-and-File Conference to denounce Nixon's "anti-labor, racist onslaught" and to condemn the Vietnam War, he assured the White House that their committee was a "communist sponsored organization."[91] But Lovestone also made a more direct contribution. Colson reported in late July that the veteran implementer of U.S. clandestine Cold War policy was "actively working to organize the labor movement behind Buckley." Colson supported Lovestone's thesis that "if the labor vote is divided and if a slight majority of the Republicans vote for Buckley that coalition is enough to elect him in a three way race."[92]

On September 8, Haldeman charged Colson with "responsibility for our battle plan of winning over the union leadership and the rank and file," a task accepted by Colson "with real delight." A few days later, Colson reported to an approving Haldeman on his progress in "romancing the union leadership." He was meeting with Lovestone every two weeks. The labor leadership was faltering in its loyalty to the Democrats though not yet crossing over to the Republicans, so it was important to cultivate the rank and file as well as the union leadership. His immediate strategy would be to concentrate on key unions. The maritime unions took pride of place. Here, Nixon had an advantage, because in the fall of 1969 he had proposed a $3.8 billion program to build thirty ships per annum for ten years. Colson would also target the construction trades, the Teamsters, the fire and police unions, the Republican-led Allied and Technical Workers, and UAW local leaders "who are strongly patriotic, anti-student and keenly aware of the race question (witness: . . . the Wallace hard core in the UAW)."[93] Although the plan was national, the influence of the hard-hat experience and the New York senate contest is evident, as is the tacit encouragement given by Haldeman and Colson to the Buckley campaign.

On November 3, Buckley received 39 percent of the votes cast, Ottinger 37 percent, and Goodell 24 percent. Colson had from an early stage believed that some of the unions regarded foreign policy as the "overriding issue" in the campaign, and a case can be made for the view that enough workers deserted the antiwar candidates to make a difference to the result.[94] During the campaign, the conservative journal *National Review* noted that Buckley had received a rousing reception from blue-collar workers in upstate industrial cities like Syracuse, Rochester, and Buffalo, especially when he mentioned the hard-hat demonstrations.[95] Back in New York City, the Taxi Drivers' Union came out for Buckley in the final days before the election, while construction workers greeted

Goodell at the World Trade Center with chants of "Go back to Cuba," "Where's your Viet Cong flag?" and "We want Buckley."[96]

It had been part of the Nixon plan to dissuade Meany from delivering his customary support to the Democrats in the 1970 midterms. Meany was courted via Colson and was invited as an honored guest to a special White House Labor Day dinner.[97] But in the last days of October the labor chief issued a "three-alarm" call for a campaign to defeat Buckley and to put the Democrat Ottinger in the Senate. He attacked Vice President Spiro Agnew for launching a "smear" campaign against labor and accused President Nixon of tacitly backing Buckley, "a reactionary who would take us back to the 1890s" in terms of antiworker legislation. The Conservative Party candidate favored right-to-work laws, an end to rent controls, and the abolition of tax-exempt status for unions if they undertook any political action. The president of the New York State AFL-CIO, Raymond Corbett, distributed twenty thousand anti–Conservative Party leaflets among construction workers and, he claimed, persuaded the Ironworkers to desert Buckley. Meany's intervention may have been too late to prevent a trend of damaging defections from the Democratic Party. Buckley later estimated that 900,000 labor union members voted for him.[98] But the AFL-CIO chief had dealt a blow to White House plans and showed that much remained to play for.

California reinforced the lesson that Nixon should keep an avenue open to labor. The political circumstances in California were different from those in New York in that Reagan had been a rival for the Republican nomination, might be again, and could not be endorsed too firmly. But that did not make the governor's tactics any less important as an object lesson in how to succeed. That the state possessed so many electoral college votes was enough to concentrate the mind of any serious politician, and the role of labor attracted attention accordingly.

The key contests in California in 1970 were the Tunney-Murphy senatorial race and the Reagan-Unruh gubernatorial race. The incumbent Republican Senator, George Murphy, faced an uphill battle against John V. Tunney. The son of Gene Tunney, vanquisher of Jack Dempsey in 1926 in the heavyweight boxing championship of the world, John V. was ancestrally advantaged. He was a representative of California's dovish left. He remarked of Murphy: "He has been hawkish on Vietnam, he has proved himself primarily an advocate for special, affluent interests." On the defensive, Murphy tried to show that he was capable of a constructive approach to peace. After a visit in October 1970 to the Lockheed Missiles and Space Company, Sunnyvale, where jobs had already been cut to 19,000 from the 1968 level of 31,000, Murphy demanded that the federal government "set up a jobs-for-peace agency to aid conversion of the defense-oriented scientific-industrial complex to peace-time activity."[99]

Throughout the 1970 reelection campaign, Murphy blended his customary conservative rhetoric with judicious statements showing an awareness of the labor vote. Referring to the 22,000 workers (out of a total workforce of 30,000) released from the North American Rockwell plant following the end of the Apollo spacecraft scheme, he averred: "They were not laid off because of the Nixon administration but because of the extreme liberals, of which my opponent [Tunney] is a member. The people in charge of the House and the Senate cut back on military and space expenditures too fast." Murphy went on in a familiar right-wing style to ascribe the problems of the United States to the Soviet Union and to attack Roosevelt for having encouraged the Russians. The *Sacramento Bee* interpreted all this as a bid for the senior citizen vote, but it is significant both that Murphy showed concern for full employment in the context of impending foreign-policy decisions and that, having accepted this agenda, he went down to resounding defeat.[100]

The Democratic gubernatorial candidate was Jesse Unruh, a former sheet metal worker at an aircraft plant in southern California. Victorious against the hawk Sam Yorty in the Democratic primaries, the man intent on ousting Reagan from the governor's mansion had declared himself a dove early on. Yorty had accused him of opportunism, of capitalizing on the change in opinion that now made it politic to be antiwar.[101] Certainly, the antiwar tide was running strongly in California. The Democratic senator, Alan Cranston (not up for reelection in 1970), was a noted dove. In

May 1970, when 451 union leaders from the Bay Area placed in the *San Francisco Chronicle* an advertisement critical of U.S. participation in the Indochina conflict, Cranston had the full text printed in the *Congressional Record.* He added his own comment: "This advertisement is a significant indication of how American working people feel about our tragic involvement in Cambodia and Vietnam. The rank and file of labor 'have had enough' because these are the people most adversely affected by the inflation, tight credit and unemployment caused by the war in Southeast Asia."[102] The *New York Times* agreed: The advertisement indicated "the shattering of labor support in this area for President Nixon's Indochina policies."[103]

Unruh deplored the 7 percent unemployment rate and accused Reagan of being responsible for it. The former metalworker said that Reagan was "a man without a plan" for reconversion in the defense and aerospace industries, adding: "California deserves better treatment than to be thrown out of work as the price of peace."[104] The *Sacramento Bee* agreed with Unruh that America needed "a jobs policy to encourage greater employment without feeding inflation."[105]

Reagan was less vulnerable than the unpopular Murphy. Yet even Reagan was forced to respond to the war-linked criticism of which his opponent Unruh was the most articulate exponent. In his Hollywood days, the governor had served as president of a labor union, the Screen Actors' Guild. But Reagan had abandoned the liberalism that had once made him a New Deal supporter. Unruh portrayed him as an enemy of organized labor and predicted right-to-work laws if he were elected. Reagan responded with a full-page advertisement in the *Sacramento Bee* entitled "Labor Supports Governor Ronald Reagan." The advertisement was more an expression of hope than a statement of fact, but it illustrates the importance that the Reagan camp attached to labor. In the event, Reagan won by a 53 to 45 percent plurality. His majority was halved, but his performance could still be compared with that of Buckley, who had the special advantage of a three-person race.[106]

The prominence of the labor issue in the 1970 elections impressed political observers. On the eve of the election, the journalist Joseph Kraft speculated on the basis of evidence from California, New York, and several other states that white ethnics, African Americans, and organized labor were deserting the Democratic fold. He did not think that their departure would save the day for the Republicans in 1970, he but did think that, "failing a very bad turn in the economy—or, more likely, the Vietnam war," the trend would probably ensure Nixon's reelection in 1972.[107] It was in the hope of exploiting these possibilities that the Nixon administration conducted a review of labor's potential political role in planning a strategy for the next presidential election.

The policy of upgrading the labor strategy did not go unchallenged in the White House. Meany's intervention on the side of the Democrats could not be ignored, and Haldeman ordered an investigation into the notion that the administration might have gone too far in its courtship of labor leaders. The White House staffer Charles Walker claimed that Nixon's overtures to labor were annoying old Republican loyalists without winning new friends; Walker also thought that the powers of the unions should be restricted as a means of controlling inflation.[108] Another staffer, Jim Keogh, similarly reported to Secretary of Labor George Shultz that it had been a mistake to woo the labor leadership before the elections, and now the unions were "on the wrong side of a very big issue—inflationary pressure." But, in contrast to Walker, Keogh thought the administration should continue with its appeal to rank and file labor.[109]

Colson defended the strategy for which he was responsible. In a memorandum for the president, he noted that "organized labor represents over 19 million Americans and their families." The hard-hat factor had been the key to Buckley's victory, similar trends could be perceived elsewhere, and "you have made an historic breakthrough in the old Roosevelt coalition of the 'have-nots,' labor, the poor, the minorities." Blue-collar support for Nixon was booming, and "labor's rank and file may represent our most promising opportunity." In a separate communication to Haldeman, Colson insisted that the proper handling of labor would be vital to success in the presidential election of 1972. Shultz agreed. He told Nixon it was silly to think that American labor had "out-powered" management and needed to be slapped down: "Let's not slam the door on these people just as they reach a point when they become prime prospects for Republican allegiance." The secretary of labor saw problems ahead in the construction industry, where there would be inflationary wage demands, but overall the picture was not gloomy, and Meany's support over Cambodia suggested that the administration should take an "issue-by-issue stance" in labor matters.[110]

From President Nixon's point of view, the prospect of a pre-electoral alliance with conservative elements in the labor movement was attractive. As his staffer Pat Buchanan complained, people on the right of the Republican Party thought he was selling out to liberalism. The alliance with labor would perhaps make it possible to take traditional liberal territory without alienating the right or—the specter that both Buchanan and Nixon feared—giving Governor Reagan the opportunity to mount a successful challenge for leadership.[111] Even Buckley, in other respects so congenial to the Nixon camp, had run for office with the intention of influencing the selection of future presidential candidates in a conservative direction.[112] Thus, overtures to conservative labor on the basis of a hard-line foreign policy were highly convenient. They stymied the right while not precluding a modest opening to the left that would help to win the popular vote in the next election.

With these considerations in mind, President Nixon adopted Shultz's issue-by-issue approach, meaning that he would romance labor on foreign policy but not on problematic domestic issues. In doing so, he showed an inclination to continue to cultivate the rank-and-file elements thrown into prominence by the hard-hat demonstrations. His wooing of the rank and file was not due to waning support from the union hierarchy. On the contrary, statements released by the AFL-CIO executive council in February 1971 made it clear that the labor hierarchy still backed the administration on Vietnam. The reasons for the rank-and-file tactic may have derived in part from the nonmalleability of higher officials on domestic economic matters and from the political dangers implicit in dealing too closely with powerful labor leaders at a time when the administration was under intense scrutiny by the right. So the president aimed low. His telephone log book shows him making personal calls to the hard-hat leader Peter Brennan in March (Colson regarded this junior official as a bridgehead to the unions, and, to the consternation of some AFL-CIO officials, Nixon later appointed Brennan secretary of labor).[113] Nixon's assessments were pragmatic. He told Colson that he had "no use for the UAW leadership" or the International Ladies Garment Workers Union, whose leaders were "hopeless pacifists," but the Teamsters and construction workers were "our friends," and he continued to think that Meany, though "an all out Democrat," was "a great patriot." He urged Colson to ensure that friendly contact was being maintained with conservative labor elements, and Colson assured him that it was.[114]

Nixon courted labor with personal blandishments based on the hard-hat–Vietnam formula while, at the same time, taking a tough line on domestic matters. On July 2 he had a forty-minute talk with Brennan, who raised various grievances about the building trades. Nixon deflected his complaints with reminiscences about the hard-hat demonstration. He impressed Brennan by saying that he wanted his support as a patriot, not as a political partisan, and concluded by ruminating about the powerful Teamsters union, whose leaders he again described as "our kind of people."[115] Even as Nixon made such appeals, his administration was trying to break down the unionized monopoly of hiring practices in the building trades. Then, in mid-August, Nixon went on television to confirm some of labor's worst fears. In a move that made him popular with the public at large but elicited immediate condemnation from Meany, he announced an attack on national inflationary problems through a ninety-day price and wages freeze.[116]

Ever the politician, Nixon now met with Bridges. The longshoremen were in the midst of a bitter, three-month strike on the West Coast that threatened both the administration's anti-inflation strategy and the flow of supplies to the Vietnam War theater. But in response to presidential flattery Bridges took a conciliatory line and, in a remarkable move for a declared opponent of the Vietnam War, exempted military cargoes from the strike action. In general, Nixon's domestic policies made the wooing of labor more difficult than this. On November 18, for example, he addressed the AFL-CIO convention in Bal Harbour, Florida, and offended Meany not just by defending the wage freeze but also by seeming to upstage him. Undaunted by his chilly reception in the Sunshine State, however, Nixon pressed on with his strategy, no doubt aware that he needed only to dent labor-Democrat solidarity, not win over the entire labor movement. There were some promising signs: just before Christmas 1971 he released the Teamsters' Jimmy Hoffa from jail, winning the endorsement of that 2.5 million-strong union.[117]

In the event, Nixon had fewer problems with labor than his Democratic opponent in 1972, George McGovern. The hard-hat demonstrations and the Buckley victory had given credibility to Nixon's claim that the silent majority supported the Vietnam War. It was becoming fashionable to believe that an unrepresentative, elitist minority ran the antiwar campaign. According to Aaron Wildavsky in his book *The Revolt Against the Masses* (1971), the "white élite" in charge of the protest movement simply wanted to replace the white elite that ran the country; if only they were less elitist, they would probably be able to win over the hard hats, but they were incapable of "accepting the basic worth of the mass of Americans."[118]

In a similar vein, a survey of America's rich and powerful by the Bureau of Applied Social Research at Columbia University in 1972 found a preponderance of dovish views on Vietnam.[119] But these classes were socially isolated and did not provide a bridge to ordinary people. McGovern came from a "prairie background" with concerns remote from those of urban America. For his doctorate in history he had studied the Coalfield, Colorado, labor strike of 1914. With the assistance of a shadow writer, he published a nonacademic version of his dissertation in 1972, no doubt intending it to be a kind of campaign document. It offered a heroic view of the American worker and attacked a Republican icon, John D. Rockefeller. But although campus liberals may have found it appealing, they were pro-McGovern anyway; the book failed to address the bigger-slice-of-the-capitalist-cake concerns of the leaders of organized labor. It was also insensitive. The first sentence, "The exploited have come and gone," was dramatic but unfortunate: it seemed to suggest that workers were no longer exploited in 1972.[120] McGovern faced an uphill struggle in courting labor and in creating the belief that the mass of wage earners could help to defeat the Republicans and end the war.

McGovern did make an attempt to win the support of wage earners. In April 1972 he outlined his views on labor and foreign policy at a Jefferson-Jackson Day dinner in Detroit, a city where he could hope to benefit from the hostility of the UAW membership to the Vietnam War: "The so-called free world is not free but a collection of self-seeking military dictators financed by hard-pressed American workers. . . . the establishment center has constructed a vast military colossus based on the paychecks of the American worker. My policy would be to cut the vast waste from our bloated military budget and invest the savings in job-creating enterprises based on a guaranteed job for every man and woman who wants to work."[121]

With the approach of a presidential election, McGovern saw signs of hope. A few days before his Detroit speech, for example, the Milwaukee local of the International Longshoremen's Association voted against the war, a turnaround from their previously hawkish stance.[122] Three senior labor officials now visited Hanoi: Harold Gibbons, a vice president of the Teamsters, David Livingston, secretary-treasurer of the Distributive Workers of America, and Clifton Caldwell, a vice president of the Amalgamated Meat Cutters. Inspired by the Hanoi visit, a group of antiwar labor leaders took a further step. In June 1972, Emil Mazey, Harold Gibbons, Frank Rosenblum, secretary-general of the Amalgamated Clothing Workers of America, Louis Goldblatt of the ILWU, and others met in St. Louis to organize an antiwar convention attended by nine hundred delegates from thirty five international unions and founded Labor for Peace.[123]

Labor for Peace would be a ginger group rather than a lobby, because so many unions were already officially committed to supporting particular candidates and therefore could not be persuaded to change their endorsements. But the magazine *The Nation* considered the St. Louis initiative to be "a matter of major importance" because the leaders concerned were "acting for and in the name of their respective unions, with a combined membership of some 4 million—a significant section of the American labor movement." *The Nation* contended that Felix Rodriguez, political editor of the Californian Labor News Service, expressed the "general objectives" of the new movement when he wrote in an open letter to Meany and other AFL-CIO leaders that the war and military spending were "to blame for the economic gaps, inflation, unemployment . . . and the most critical division within American society since the Civil War. . . . It is pointless for consumers to complain about high prices, for workers to complain about frozen wages, for property owners to complain about high taxes, while this nation continues to wage a war nobody wants."[124]

According to the *St. Louis Post-Dispatch*, Harry Bridges "stopped an attempt by some delegates to the Labor for Peace conference here to call a one-day national strike in protest of the Vietnam war." The ILWU leader's blocking of a strike against the war disappointed those who knew that the union had supported McGovern's peace campaign ever since 1963, and Bridges was labeled a "fake radical."[125] Other unionists pressed the peace cause in diverse ways. David Livingston had talks with Le Duc Tho in Paris, in the course of which the North Vietnamese negotiator managed to convince him that the Nixon administration was behaving intransigently at the peace talks. Senator William Fulbright noted this with approval. Collaboration and consensus in the peace cause were in the air.[126] Further encouragement for the antiwar crusade came when, at the end of July, *Business Week* estimated that three-fourths of the AFL-CIO membership favored Senator McGovern.[127]

Yet McGovern, although he was primarily a peace candidate and although he was the standard-bearer of the party long favored by the unions, sometimes seemed to lack the confidence to appeal to labor to join the antiwar crusade. Labor Day gave him a prime opportunity to do so, but in an address delivered in both Ohio and California, the only remark that even remotely touched on foreign policy was his recollection of his days as a bomber pilot in World War II.[128] The UAW nevertheless soldiered on in its support of McGovern and peace. A special insert in the September 18 issue of its weekly *Washington Report* declared the following as its first principle: "We need President George McGovern to get us out of Indochina 'lock, stock and barrel' and free our Prisoners of War in his first 90 days." But the candidate himself seemed resigned to losing both the election and the fight for early withdrawal from the war.

The devitalization of the McGovern campaign originated mainly from the hostility of Meany and his camp. On September 18, the same day as the UAW's special appeal, the AFL-CIO president delivered a stinging attack at the United Steelworkers of America convention in Las Vegas, Nevada, stating that McGovern had manipulated the Democratic nominating convention and given it a middle-class and antilabor tone.[129] Although Meany himself was responsible for much of the tension with McGovern, the Democratic candidate's inability to relate easily to working men also played a part in the rift. The contrast with Nixon is evident. In a diary entry at the end of September written after yet another meeting with New York labor leaders, Nixon noted how much he admired the "character and guts and . . . patriotism" of working men and despised the "whine and whimper" of the "American leader class." With the union leaders who had just left the White House, he had more in common "from a personal standpoint than does McGovern or the intellectuals generally. They like labor as a mass. I like them individually."[130] Nixon's self-assessment may have been adrenaline-driven, but his perception of McGovern was shrewd.

McGovern's trouble with Meany had been evident for some time. He simply could not find the right things to say to the crusty czar from the plumbers' union. He once concluded a greeting with words that were well meant and mildly funny in a middle-class way, but indicative of his true attitude to blue-collar workers: "I wish you a long and productive future and hope that as a result of this encomium you can help me to get my plumber to make house calls."[131] The White House was, of course, already well primed to take advantage of McGovern's difficulties with Meany. When McGovern urged Meany to admit that he had been wrong in his support of the Cold War as well as Vietnam, Pat Buchanan thought the request was "adequate to very nearly drive a permanent wedge between McGovern and Meany's support." Nixon's reelection team should "elevate" the quotation, he said, and play on Meany's pride.[132]

In June, Jay Lovestone telephoned Colson to complain that "the high command in the Nixon crowd is boasting that they have a man close to Meany." This was Lovestone himself, and he wanted the rumor quashed because "it will do damage."[133] Evidence of the close link mounted as the campaign wore on. In July, Meany persuaded the AFL-CIO executive council not to deliver its customary endorsement of the Democratic candidate but to declare its neutrality instead. Even if many rank-and-file unionists remained loyal to McGovern, this lack of political endorsement was extremely damaging. James T. Housewright—who as president of the 650,000-strong Retail Clerks International Association urged his membership to support the Democratic candidate—telegrammed Meany to protest that the AFL-CIO "failure to endorse McGovern is tantamount to giving the election to Nixon."[134]

Meany's failure to support McGovern stemmed only partly from the Democrat's political persona. The real difficulty lay in McGovern's being a peace candidate when the AFL-CIO president remained a strong enthusiast for Nixon's Vietnam policy. Late in August the presidential assistant John Ehrlichman reported to Nixon on Shultz's recent "very good talk with George Meany." Meany emphasized labor's interest in foreign policy and defense and said "the President is perfect on foreign policy."[135] So strongly did Meany feel on these matters that, just before the election, he abandoned every pretense at neutrality. In a statement secretly prepared for him by a jubilant Colson in consultation with Lovestone, he dwelled on Vietnam, accused McGovern of being an apologist for the communist world, and urged working people to vote against the Democratic candidate for president.[136]

In the sixties, the New Left had feared that labor was finished as a radical force, was now a part of the military-industrial complex, and could not be relied on to take the lead in opposing the Vietnam War. The conduct of leaders like Meany and Lovestone amply justified these fears. Their support for the war was less important during the Johnson administration, when most people took it for granted and did not consider it to be a variable political factor requiring special attention. During the Nixon administration, however, labor's continuing support of the war and eventually of Nixon's reelection was a significant factor in unexpected ways.

The United States and North Vietnam had reached a military stalemate by 1969. The Communists realized that they could not defeat American armed forces in the field. They decided to sit it out, in the knowledge that although public opinion in their own, totalitarian country did not count, time was on the side of the protesters in the United States. Nixon and Kissinger, for their part, engaged in the diplomacy of détente with the Soviet Union and China, hoping for the ancillary effect of distracting the American electorate, making them forget about the Vietnam War.

But Nixon needed more than distraction to succeed electorally. He came up with an answer that allowed him to fight on in Vietnam while surviving and even thriving politically. In the words of the policy analysts Leslie Gelb and Richard Betts, "The system worked." Gelb and Betts argue that both Johnson and Nixon coped with opposition by steering a middle course between hawks and doves, by surreptitiously adopting the policy recommendations of some of their critics, and by blending the critics of the war into an "omelet," enabling them to attack a simplified entity, the "Left," in a manner likely to draw support from more conservative Americans.[137] But Nixon proved to have a further political skill. He unscrambled the omelet: he analyzed it, isolated a promising ingredient, and made his opening to labor. In this way, he won support that, added to the customary Republican loyalists, solidified his position both as a foreign policy maker and as a candidate for reelection in 1972.

James Housewright's claim that Meany handed the 1972 election to Nixon is an oversimplification. Nixon was already heading for victory and had already made inroads in the rank-and-file vote. But if the claim is broadened to include the New York hardhat element and their allies in the Teamsters union and elsewhere, one could argue that the labor movement strengthened Nixon and his position on Vietnam just when protest by other social groups, most recently emergent political women, was beginning to have a cumulative effect.

Diplomatic negotiations between the United States and North Vietnam since 1969 had mirrored the military stalemate, with both sides in the Paris peace negotiations taking an intransigent line. The United States held out for a stronger military presence on the ground in South Vietnam, only to give it up in the final settlement of 1973. The United States might well have achieved peace on the same basis in 1969 but for two factors. The first was the obduracy of Xuan Thuy, the chief North Vietnamese negotiator in Paris between 1968 and 1970; his successor, Le Duc Tho was tough, too, if more pragmatic.[138] The second factor was continuing domestic support for a tougher line. Labor's top leadership and a small, unrepresentative but heavily mythologized group of blue-collar workers helped the administration to hold out at a cost of many more dead on both sides of the Asian conflict.

The burgeoning rebellion within the ranks of labor did, however, induce some restraint and did inhibit Meany's open support for Nixon. Bolstered by protest in other sectors of society, the rebellion gave Nixon notice that what could be achieved through his opening to labor was limited. Without dissent in labor and elsewhere, Nixon might not have bothered to promise and finally deliver peace. The war might have dragged on even longer or might have ended by more drastic means. Yet none of the protests detracted from the impact of mainstream labor support for the war. If the military victory in Vietnam went to Hanoi, the political victory in America went to Meany and to Nixon. The result of that political victory was a prolongation of the war, if for a finite period.

7

Minority Mentalities and the Vietnam War

THE SOCIAL GROUPS CONSIDERED IN this book—students, African Americans, women, and labor—formed an important part of the consensus behind the Vietnam War. But significant numbers in those groups lost faith and, once disenchanted, mounted a formidable challenge to the grip exerted on foreign policy making by white, old, rich men.

One reason for the success of the antiwar campaign lies in the shock engendered by the sudden and virulent protest of these social groups, which left the White House unprepared. Another stems from what might otherwise seem to be the weakness of the protest movement: its qualities of variety, disunity, and disorganization. This state of near anarchy both appealed to youth and confused the government. Additionally, the specter of disorder was a form of unconscious social blackmail and helped legitimize opposition to the war. Direct action on the streets and campuses of the country ran counter to notions of political legitimacy. Showing what might happen with violent revolt contributed to the credibility and appeal of "legitimate" opposition within the orthodox political process.

The anarchy, it should be added, was often more apparent than real. Images of disorder were sometimes contrived, and intelligent calculation lay behind much of the protest. Disunity, too, had its limits. There may have been no repetition of the nineteenth-century alliance between women, labor, and African Americans, but intergroup cooperation did exist, if on an informal and ever-changing basis, a circumstance that permitted antiwar protest to escalate.

A final reason for the effectiveness of the protest movement was its serial nature, with the student rebellion peaking early, followed by the African American revolt and then by the women's campaign. The protests had a cumulative effect that sapped the resistance power of the policymakers. These various circumstances help to explain why the impact of the social groups was among the more significant causes of American withdrawal from the Vietnam War.

A summary of the impact of the four social groups should encompass not just their dovelike tendencies but also their nature and the effects of their support for the war. The groups left their imprint on the how as well as the whether of warmaking. Their initial hawkish disposition meant that the government sought a quick-fix, conventional military solution, instead of relying on long-term, low-cost counterinsurgency. Yet, from an early stage, the military solution had certain constraints. Fighting based on a conscript Army caused anxiety among the citizenry, and their anxiety encouraged the government to use bombing in order to limit U.S. casualties. When ground fighting increased nonetheless, and more soldiers were sent to Vietnam, Americans' horror at the sight of body bags rose in proportion. It soon became apparent that the principle of an egalitarian and democratic war had been abandoned. Against the communist threat of an ascendant proletariat, the government decided to fight a working-class war. The middle classes in the United States were to be immune from the discomfitures of battle. This outlook was unacceptable to the less privileged even if they did support the war. It led to campaigns against the draft and to changes in the composition of the Army. Because the comfortable classes persisted in their refusal to fight the Communists even as they insisted that the Communists had to be defeated, the war was finally de-Americanized, or Vietnamized.

The policy of de-Americanization was a prelude to withdrawal. But American disengagement was slow, and here, too, a social group played a vital role. Labor's continuing support for the war fulfilled the gloomiest prophesies of the early sixties New Left; it was exploited by the Nixon White House, and it helped the hawks to pursue their war for two more years. Thus, the four social groups did contribute to American withdrawal from the war, but historians should resist the temptation to romanticize the peacemaking role of those who tried to shape foreign policy from below.

All these circumstances invite speculation about the broader social bases of U.S. foreign policy. Generalizations extrapolated from case studies are risky and cannot be definitive, but they do have the merit of firm foundation, so the risk is worth taking. One generalization confirmed in this book about four social groups over a short period was suggested by my earlier study of a single group over a longer period, *Changing Differences: Women and the*

Shaping of American Foreign Policy, 1917–1994 (1995). The generalization is this: that certain social groups manifest a breakthrough syndrome that leads them to cooperate with foreign policy goals of which they might otherwise disapprove in the hope of collectively climbing the greasy pole of social advancement. This syndrome has been a long-term factor in American politics and foreign policy affecting individuals as well as groups. It shows little sign of disappearing. Ronald Reagan, for example, broke through to become the first former labor leader to be elected president and once in the White House acted out the most conformist role available to him, that of a Cold Warrior.

As a concept, the breakthrough syndrome does have its limits, and social groups have a long record of fighting for their own goals, regardless of the inducements to abandon their heartfelt opinions. For three of the four social groups discussed here, labor being the exception, the story of their involvement in the Vietnam War is that of the *collapse* of their breakthrough mentality and the pursuit of a foreign policy more consistent with the intrinsic aspirations of their members.

The experience of all four social groups in the Vietnam War suggests some other notions of general applicability. The framers of foreign policy do listen to the American people, despite their reluctance to admit it, and the more thoughtful of them "parse" American society, for the purpose of understanding what the people think, breaking it down into salient social groups each of which can be understood in its own special terms.

The jury is still out on whether, as the founding fathers claimed, American republicanism is inherently peaceful. If, in kingdoms, war is the sport of royalty, is it, in democratic America, the plaything of the ruling white, old, rich men? The answer is a study in the interplay of myth and reality. Given the early enthusiasm of American society for the Vietnam War, the claim that the war was a conspiracy of the rich seems doubtful. But the poor paid for the war with their lives and came to realize it. This realization entered American mythology precisely at the moment when the government was trying to democratize the battlefield through reforms of the military draft. Because the myth that war is the toy of white, old, rich men did help shape the peace discourse of the lower orders, the myth is significant. The line running from eighteenth-century republican antimilitarism to the era of the Vietnam War appears to be intact, at least ideologically.

The conclusions reached in this book confirm the need to reverse the inquisitorial thrust of the war and society equation. The Vietnam War influenced society, yes, but the reverse is also true. In a democracy, society is not passive. American society—parsed into the four social groups of labor, African Americans, women, and students—impacted on the Vietnam War. This does not suggest an iron rule of behavior; the force of the groups' impact in inducing the government to reconsider its policies was exceptional. But that impact was by no means unique. Social groups can influence policy, and in peace as well as in war. The end of the Cold War may well accentuate that process as internal groups gain in relative importance with the removal of such external constraints on foreign policy as the existence of an armed-to-the-teeth Soviet Union.

By looking at the Vietnam War in terms of the four social groups, it is possible to see that localities are important to the shaping of foreign policy. Students of domestic politics have for decades acknowledged that what happens at the state level can be important. But they have a disposition to believe that foreign affairs are too complex and remote from the concerns of Middletown, U.S.A., to be affected by local obsessions. There is some truth in this. Still, local studies can help the historian of foreign policy. Localities complicate the diplomatic process just as foreign governments and armies do, and the challenge to the historian is even greater, because the social composition and political weight of various localities change over time. Notably, in the twentieth century Massachusetts gave way to New York and California as the pacemaker of foreign policy.

A similar point of general interest might be made about the changing identity of those social groups that had an impact on foreign policy. Farmers were much less salient by the 1960s than they had been in earlier times, whereas students made a meteoric appearance on the scene, then an equally abrupt departure.

The position has never been static and will probably continue to change. The decline of the WASPs, noted by Digby Baltzell in the sixties, seems destined to be followed by the reduction to minority status of all Caucasians by the middle of the twenty-first century. Such changes do affect foreign policy.

Finally, there is room for speculation about the impact of minority mentalities on foreign policy. A "minority mentality" may be defined as an insurgent, hard-done-by mindset. Archetypally, it is articulated by ethnic or racial minorities, yet this mode of thought is not confined to them and is quite pervasive. It is, in fact, a distinctive feature of pluralistic America and assumes diverse forms and is subject to various interpretations. The militancy of organized labor might be taken, not as a chip-on-the-shoulder manifestation of minority mentality, but as a substitute for European-style class-consciousness and as an implicit acceptance of American capitalism. Similarly, the race riot could be regarded, not as the ultimate statement of minority resentment, but as an impotent form of protest displacement. In spite of this diversity and a controversial subject matter, the mentality of minorities did have impact, as did its components—breakthrough syndrome and conformity to the norm—and not just in the case of climbing the ethnic ladder but with regard to several social groups.

In the Vietnam War, minority mentalities were not confined to social groups; they affected Lyndon Baines Johnson and Richard Nixon. These presidents were post-WASPs; they did not come from the East Coast Establishment and were conscious of that fact. In spite of their actual power, they imagined themselves to have an affinity with outsiders. Sharing in the outsider mentality, they were appreciative of the acceptance-seeking, loyalist social groups but were also fearful of rebuffs, as anyone is fearful of rejection by one's own. Not surprisingly, White House comments on the politics of the Vietnam War were replete with references to minorities and minorities within minorities.

This kind of minority thinking culminated in a converse doctrine, the notion of the silent majority. In one way, Nixon's appeal to the silent majority was a simple appeal to a conjectured majority for support against the protesting minorities and to supportive majorities within minority groups for support against *their* internal minorities. Here, by definition, the presidential adoption of the silent majority gave credence to the political significance of its obverse inspiration, the minorities.

But there is room for two more comments on the majority-minority relationship. First, Nixon expected the silent majority to be topped up by a coalition of defectors from potentially defiant minority groups. His hoped-for friends were the workers who put pork chops above peace, the African Americans who craved status, not justice, the women who valued high society over social goals, the students ever in search of the glittering prize. These were the people, breaking through and clutching at the American Dream, as individuals or collectively, who would make up his majority.

Second, the silent majority was inarticulate—again by definition. The mentalities of the inarticulate, be they French peasants or American slaves, have sparked some inventive thinking among historians. President Nixon and his team likewise read between the lines and guessed at the true feelings of what they deemed to be the great majority of American people. Because they were professional politicians, they speculated opportunistically and clung to the hope that the majority would be malleable and could be persuaded to believe that their unexpressed thoughts were precisely those which the administration said they were. Nixon and his men got it right. I have tried to show that Nixon, Garment, and Colson understood the four social groups, especially labor, sufficiently well to blunt (though not extinguish) the minorities' challenges on the Vietnam War and to win the election of 1972.

Minority mentalities are particularly important to an understanding of both support for and opposition to the Vietnam War. They help to explain U.S. involvement in the war, its military tactics, Vietnamization, the decision to withdraw, the delay in implementing that decision, and the pre-Watergate durability of the final architect of the war, Richard Nixon.

Notes

ABBREVIATIONS

Locations

HI	Hoover Institution Library, Stanford, California
LBJ	Lyndon Baines Johnson Library, Austin, Texas
LC	Library of Congress Manuscript Division, Washington, D.C.
MCSL	Margaret Chase Smith Library, Skowhegan, Maine
MHS	Massachusetts Historical Society, Boston, Massachusetts
NACP	National Archives at College Park, Maryland ("Archives II")
PSC	Pacific Studies Center, East Palo Alto, California
RBMC	Rare Book and Manuscript Library, Columbia University, New York, New York
SB	Special Collections Department, Frank Melville, Jr., Memorial Library, State University of New York at Stony Brook, Stony Brook, New York

SGM	Seeley G. Mudd Library, Princeton University, Princeton, New Jersey
StJU	Special Collections, St. John's University Libraries, Jamaica, New York

Collections

ACBL	Papers of Ann Clare Boothe Luce, LC
BSA	Papers of Bella S. Abzug, RBMC
CC	Charles Colson files, SMOF
CH	Papers of Cordell Hull, LC
ECSF	Elizabeth Carpenter's Subject Files, LBJ
EMK	Egil M. Krogh materials, SF
EWB	Edward W. Brooke Papers, LC
HCL	Henry Cabot Lodge papers, MHS
JAC	John Applegarth Collection, HI
JCG	James C. Gaither files, OFWHA
JKJ	Jacob K. Javits Collection, SB
JLB	James Lane Buckley Papers, StJU
JLR	Joseph L. Rauh, Jr., Papers, LC
LG	Leonard Garment materials, SMOF
LGP	Leonard Garment Papers, LC
LWV	Records of the National League of Women Voters, LC
McG	George McGovern Papers, SGM
McK	William McKinley Papers, LC
MCS	Margaret Chase Smith Papers, MCSL
NAACP	Papers of the National Association for the Advancement of Colored People, LC
NCJW	Papers of the National Council of Jewish Women, LC
NLC	New Left Collection, HI
NPM	Nixon Presidential Materials, NACP
NSF	National Security Files, WHCF
NUL	Records of the National Urban League, LC
OFWHA	Office Files of the White House Aides, LBJ
POF	President's Office Files, WHCF, NPM
PPF	President's Personal File, WHCF, NPM
RFD	Research files (domestic), PSC
RRGC	Ronald Reagan Gubernatorial Collection, HI
SF	Special Files, WHCF, NPM

SMOF Staff Members and Office Files, WHCF, NPM
WHCF White House Central Files, LBJ and NPM

CHAPTER ONE Introduction

1. From Eartha Kitt's comments as recorded in the official transcript, "Remarks at First Lady's Luncheon for Women Doers," Jan. 18, 1968, p. 30, Box 45, ECSF.

2. The Kitt episode produced a great deal of emotion and anger, resulting in conflicting reports of the sequence of events. According to the Scripps-Howard staff writer Wauhillau La Hay, from whose report the "bad guy" quotation comes, Johnson appeared after the main Kitt outburst: *Washington Daily News*, Jan. 19, 1968. But this contradicts other accounts and the official White House transcript of the proceedings, the source of the "mini-mommy" quotation: "Remarks at First Lady's Luncheon," 6, 30, 32. For a reconstruction of events from a viewpoint hostile to Eartha Kitt, see Janet Mezzack, "'Without Manners You Are Nothing': Lady Bird Johnson, Eartha Kitt, and the Woman Doers' Luncheon of January 18, 1968," *Presidential Studies Quarterly*, 20 (Fall 1990), 745–760.

3. Guenter Lewy, a historian noted for his criticism of critics of the war, thinks that the opposition was effective but cautions against the view that America would necessarily have prevailed had there been a greater degree of national unity: Lewy, *America in Vietnam* (Oxford: Oxford University Press, 1978), 434, 436. Melvin Small, whose sympathies are with the protesters, offers a balanced appraisal of the ways their activities may have been effective or counterproductive, concluding (like Lewy) that protests can be surprisingly successful: Small, *Johnson, Nixon, and the Doves* (New Brunswick, N.J.: Rutgers University Press, 1988), 225–234. Terry Anderson is an antiwar sympathizer who takes a less than sanguine view of "movement" effectiveness: it "raised questions" about the war, but American withdrawal owed much to the fact that by the 1970s to support the peace process seemed patriotic: Terry H. Anderson, *The Movement and the Sixties: Protest in America from Greensboro to Wounded Knee* (New York: Oxford University Press, 1995), 237, 379. For reviews of the literature, see Gary R. Hess, "The Unending Debate: Historians and the Vietnam War," *Diplomatic History*, 18 (Spring 1994), 239–264; and Adam Garfinkle, *Telltale Hearts: The Origins and Impact of the Antiwar Movement* (New York: St. Martin's Press, 1995), 9–13.

4. Consulted in 1993, the electronic catalogue at the Robarts library, University of Toronto, yielded 2,700 book titles containing the word *Vietnam.* There were 3,550 books and articles, published mainly in the period 1980–1991, listed in Lester H. Brune and Richard D. Burns, comps., *America and the Indochina Wars, 1945–1990* (Claremont, Calif.: Regina Books, 1992), and the torrent of publication continues.

5. The reference here is to the domestic dimensions of the quest for peace. There is an abundance of scholarship on the international diplomacy. Examples of different approaches are Robert D. Schulzinger, *Henry Kissinger: Doctor of Diplomacy* (New York: Columbia University Press, 1990); and Gabriel Kolko, *Anatomy of War: Vietnam, the United States, and the Modern Historical Experience* (New York: New Press, 1994), part 5. Adam Garfinkle argues that the peace movement as a whole was counterproductive and observes that few historians have faced up to this problem: Garfinkle, *Telltale Hearts*, 1, 303*n*1.

6. Meany quoted in Joseph C. Goulden, *Meany: The Unchallenged Strong Man of American Labor* (New York: Atheneum, 1972), 358.

7. Richard M. Nixon, *Memoirs*, 2 vols. (New York: Warner, 1979), I, 506–507.

8. "If politics are supposed to stop at the water's edge for critics of foreign policies, presidents are not supposed to be concerned with their own political fortunes as they construct and implement those policies. Of course, things do not really operate that way": Melvin Small, "The Domestic Side of Foreign Policy," *Organization of American Historians Magazine of History*, 8 (Spring 1994), 15.

9. At the head of the memo Johnson wrote, "Put all these ideas in practice but keep ball out of my court as much as possible": Robert E. Kintner to the President, June 14, 1966, Special Files, 1927–1973: Handwriting File, folder "Handwriting—President Johnson, June, 1966," 2 of 5, Box 15, LBJ.

10. Nixon to Randy J. Dicks of Georgetown University, text issued as press release on Oct. 13, 1969, folder "Vietnam," WHCF, SMOF, LG, Box 40, NPM.

11. Memo of conversation, President and Dr. Walter H. Judd, Oct. 16, 1967, folder "Vietnam 7E (1) b 9/67–10/67 Public Relations Activities," Box 99, NSF Country File, Vietnam, LBJ. The unofficial head of the China Lobby and now a radio broadcaster, Judd had in 1963 lost his long-held congressional seat to the antiwar Minnesotan Donald M. Fraser.

12. Jeffrey Kimball, "How Wars End: The Vietnam War," *Peace and Change*, 20 (April 1995), 193, 200*nn*16–17.

13. Jacob K. Javits, "Non-Violent Change in Our Society," *Dartmouth Alumni Magazine*, July 1968, p. 21.

14. E. Digby Baltzell coined the term WASP to depict a *passing* American elite: Baltzell, *The Protestant Establishment: Aristocracy and Caste in America* (New York: Random House, 1964), 314. The acronym nevertheless passed into popular usage. For the sixties radicals who complained that white, old, rich men were in control, WORM might have been a more useful invention as a propaganda acronym.

15. See, for example, the attention given by Congressman Harold D. Donohue of Massachusetts to a Clark University poll of opinion in Worcester, Mass., on Vietnam withdrawal and the Cambodian incursion: *Congressional Record*, June 11, 1970, E5487. For an overview of polls in four different states, see Harlan Hahn, "Dove Sentiments Among Blue-Collar Workers," *Comments and Opinions*, n.d., 202–205. Both are in "1970 Issues: Vietnam 3 of 3," folder "U.S. Public Dissent," McG.

16. On Smith see Rhodri Jeffreys-Jones, *Changing Differences: Women and the Shaping of American Foreign Policy, 1917–1994* (New Brunswick, N.J.: Rutgers University Press, 1995), 122. On the relationship between Buckley and the Department of Defense see Secretary of Defense Howard H. ("Bo") Callaway to Buckley, June 26, 1975, file "Callaway, Howard H.," Box 1, JLB.

17. Law Students Against the War, Inc., nine-page untitled typewritten breakdown, by state and by city, of congressional candidates, May 25, 1970, and further six-page analysis dated June 26, 1970, folder "Vietnam 1979–71," Box 408, NCJW.

18. Nixon quoted in syndicated column by Marianne Means, dated Oct. 12, 1967, text in WHCF, Name File, Unruh H-K, Box 28, LBJ.

19. Historians wanting to take a fresh look at national domestic problems have often begun with a close examination of local politics. See, for example, David P. Thelen's analysis of Wisconsin in his influential article "Social Tensions and the Origins of Progressivism," *Journal of American History*, 56 (September 1969), 323–341. Massachusetts has attracted some of the few studies to have been completed linking local and international politics, possibly because of its scholastic prominence and opportunities and certainly because of its electoral importance until recent times; see William C. Widenor, *Henry Cabot Lodge and the Search for an American Foreign Policy* (Berkeley: University of California Press, 1980); Rhodri Jeffreys-Jones, "Massachusetts Labor, Henry Cabot Lodge, and the Abortion of Empire," in Serge Ricard and Hélène Christol, eds., *Anglo-Saxonism in U.S. Foreign Policy: The Diplomacy of Imperialism, 1899–1919*

(Aix: Publications de l'Université de Provence, 1991), 25–47; and Jeffreys-Jones, "Massachusetts Labour and the League of Nations Controversy," *Irish Historical Studies*, 19 (September 1975), 90–106. The impact of local politics on the Vietnam War is only lightly touched on in such studies as W. J. Rorabaugh, *Berkeley at War: The 1960s* (New York: Oxford University Press, 1989); and William C. Berman, *William Fulbright and the Vietnam War: The Dissent of a Political Realist* (Kent, Ohio: Kent State University Press, 1988).

20. The following figures for the four most populous states show why election watchers considered New York and California so important in a nationwide contest. In the 1960 presidential election, New York (which went Democratic) had 45 out of a total of 537 electoral college votes, California (Rep.) 32, Pennsylvania (Dem.) 32, and Ohio (Rep.) 25. In 1968, New York (Dem.) had 43, California (Rep.) 40, Pennsylvania (Dem.) 29, and Ohio (Rep.) 26 out of a total of 538.

21. According to the 1968 edition of *The Encyclopedia Americana* (New York: Americana Corporation), XX, 76, Negroes made up an estimated 11 percent of the population in 1960. On AFL-CIO membership (and it should be noted that some unions, like the Teamsters, were not affiliated in the 1960s), see Goulden, *Meany*, 324. Terry Anderson argues that "the sixties generation could be defined to include anyone who turned eighteen during the era from 1960 to 1972" and offers the figure of 42 million: Anderson, *Movement*, 89–90. That would be 22 percent of the 1970 census figure of 202,235,298 for the U.S. population, though only by the end of the "decade," by which time (1972) the oldest members of the cohort were thirty years old and thinking of mortgages. The higher education enrollment was 3.75 million in the school year 1956–1957 (*Encyclopedia Americana*, IX, 644), against a U.S. population of 179,323,175 in 1960. The resulting percentage of 2.1 is on the low side as a characterization of the whole of the sixties, because educational opportunities expanded more quickly than the general population in that decade. By any definition, however, students enrolled in higher education remained a small minority of Americans throughout the Vietnam War.

22. Women made up 50.7 percent of the population in 1960 and 51.3 percent in 1970: figures extracted from U.S. Bureau of the Census reports in Mary Beth Norton, David M. Katzman, Paul D. Escott, Howard P. Chudacoff, Thomas G. Paterson, and William M. Tuttle, Jr., *A People and a Nation: A History of the United States*, 4th ed. (Boston: Houghton Mifflin, 1994), A-22.

23. *Webster's Ninth New Collegiate Dictionary* (Springfield, Mass.: Merriam-Webster, 1988), 757.

24. Myrdal made a notable comparison between the status of women and that of African Americans in an appendix to his study *An American Dilemma: The Negro Problem and Modern Democracy*, 2 vols. (New York: Harper, 1944), vol. II, Appendix 5: "A Parallel to the Negro Problem," 1073–1078. Myra Macpherson linked women with "blacks and other minorities" in her *Long Time Passing: Vietnam and the Haunted Generation* (New York: Doubleday, 1984), xi.

25. Memo, "The Feminine Revolution," Hauser for Safire, Mar. 2, 1970, WHCF, Subject Files, Human Rights, folder "[Ex] HU2-5 Women. Beginning—12/31/69," Box 2, NPM.

26. Reflecting the predominant 1960s usage of the word *minority*, a "Bibliography of Sources Dealing with Minority Issues [connected with the Vietnam War]" appeared in 1989 and dealt exclusively with black, Latino, Native American, and Asian American soldiers and veterans: *Vietnam Generation*, 1 (Spring 1989), 151–159.

27. Henry Pelling, *American Labor* (Chicago: University of Chicago Press, 1960), 220. The final chapter in Pelling's book is called "The Permanent Minority." John R. Commons, the mentor of the Wisconsin school of labor history, introduced the notion into academic discourse in an article in the *American Journal of Sociology* in 1908, reprinted as "Class Conflict: Is It Growing in America, and Is it Inevitable?" in Commons, *Labor and Administration* (New York: Augustus Kelley, 1964 [1913]), 71–72. Andrew Levison challenged the view that blue-collar workers were a minority of the population while acknowledging the myth of the working-class minority: Levison, *The Working Class Majority* (New York: Coward, McCann, and Geoghegan, 1974), 17. A faction on the left in the 1960s, its salience reinforced by the propaganda of those who feared or exploited it, bruited the notion of a latter-day Leninist minority that would take advantage of the discontents fanned by the Vietnam War. Perhaps a student pseudoproletariat would replace the Old Left, determined to end the war and achieve dramatic social change at home; see Jack Newfield, *A Prophetic Minority* (London: Anthony Blond, 1967), 207–212.

CHAPTER TWO The Social Consensus

1. Curran's involvement is noted in Peter B. Levy, *The New Left and Labor in the 1960s* (Urbana: University of Illinois Press, 1994), 47.

2. See, however, Gary Gerstle's exploration of consensus considered as mythology: "Race and the Myth of the Liberal Consensus," *Journal of American History*, 82 (September 1995), 579–586. There was 85 percent support for Johnson's declared interventionist policy after the Gulf of Tonkin incident in 1964, and 83 percent in February 1965 for the Rolling Thunder bombing campaign. A high number, 65 percent, still backed Nixon's Vietnam policy in November 1969, and 59 percent supported his mining of North Vietnamese ports as late as May 1972. On the principle "our country right or wrong," patriots may support a war even if they disagree with it. So a better gauge might be the answer to another of the pollsters' questions, Do you believe American participation in the Vietnam War to have been a mistake? By October 1969 an estimated 58 percent of Americans thought their country had been in error. However, it is here that a comparative perspective is needed; see the percentages in the text for World War I and the Korean War. These statistics and those in the text are taken from Tom Wells, *The War Within: America's Battle over Vietnam* (Berkeley: University of California Press, 1994), 11, 20, 398, 545, and from Hazel Erskine, "Most War Foes Are over 50." *Washington Post*, May 10, 1970. The figures are for peaks of discontent, and those for World War I derive from polling after the event (there were no opinion polls until the late 1930s). On the prowar consensus in Washington, as distinct from the nation at large, see Joseph G. Morgan, *The Vietnam Lobby: The American Friends of Vietnam, 1955–1975* (Chapel Hill: University of North Carolina Press, 1997), 159.

3. John P. Diggins, "The Italo-American Anti-Fascist Opposition," *Journal of American History*, 54 (December 1967), 581.

4. Walsh quoted in the *Boston Post*, Mar. 17, 1919 (emphasis in the original); Rhodri Jeffreys-Jones, "Massachusetts Labour and the League of Nations Controversy," *Irish Historical Studies*, 19 (September 1975), 90–106.

5. Lodge to Gen. J. H. Sherbourne, Oct. 30, 1919, HCL.

6. The figures are from Philip Taft, *Organized Labor in American History* (New York: Harper and Row, 1964), 162. For a critique of various theories on the rise of organized labor, see Albert A. Blum, "Why Unions Grow," *Labor History*, 9 (Winter 1968), 39–72.

7. Speeches to the House, Apr. 15, 1878, Apr. 6, 1882, Jan. 27, 1883, in Petersburg [Virginia?], Oct. 29, 1885, and McKinley to Henry Cabot Lodge, Sept. 8, 1900—all in McK.

8. Rhodri Jeffreys-Jones, "Massachusetts Labor, Henry Cabot Lodge, and the Abortion of Empire," in Serge Ricard and Hélène

Christol, eds., *Anglo-Saxonism in U.S. Foreign Policy: The Diplomacy of Imperialism, 1899–1919* (Aix: Publications de l'Université de Provence, 1991), 25–47.

9. On the myth of class warfare and on its implications for domestic reform and reaction, see Rhodri Jeffreys-Jones, *Violence and Reform in American History* (New York: New Viewpoints, 1978).

10. For a review of the literature on this tradition and on some of the exceptions to it, see Gregg Andrews, "A Labor Alternative to Corporatist Diplomacy in the Wilsonian Era," *Diplomatic History*, 21 (Winter 1997), 133–137. On this period, see also Simeon Larson, *Labor and Foreign Policy: Gompers, the AFL, and the First World War, 1914–1918* (Rutherford, N.J.: Fairleigh Dickenson University Press, 1975).

11. See Ronald Radosh, *American Labor and United States Foreign Policy* (New York: Vintage, 1970).

12. Unidentified clipping, folder "Committee to Support American Services in Vietnam 1966," Box 13, JKJ.

13. *Wall Street Journal*, Oct. 26, 1967; Meany interview with Dick Cavett (ABC-TV, Dec. 19, 1974) reported in *Dispatcher*, Jan. 10, 1975.

14. Lt. Gen. Joseph M. Heiser, Jr., *Vietnam Studies: Logistic Support* (Washington, D.C.: Department of the Army, 1974), 157.

15. Paul Hall to President, Apr. 22 and May 11, 1965, and Joe Califano to President, Feb. 15, 1966, WHCF, Name File, Hall, Box 35, Gleason to President, Oct. 29, 1965, WHCF, Name File, Gleason, Box 142—all in LBJ.

16. Lee C. White to Hall, May 12, 1965, and LBJ to Hall, Sept. 12, 1966, WHCF, Name File, Hall, Box 35, McGeorge Bundy to Gleason, Nov. 1, 1965, LBJ to Gleason, July 27, 1964, WHCF, Name File, Gleason, Box 142, William S. Mailliard (Rep., Calif.), "An Open Letter to LBJ on Maritime Day" (Remarks before the Propeller Club, Washington, D.C., May 23, 1966), and Anon. memo, Bureau of the Budget, Aug. 10, 1966, WHCF, Name File, Mailliard, Box 40, on the "serious threat in the House" posed by Mailliard and his allies on transportation matters—all in LBJ.

17. Lens thought that both labor and academia had been incorporated into the complex: Sidney Lens, *The Military-Industrial Complex* (London: Stanmore, 1971), 99–138.

18. Roger W. Lotchin, *Fortress California, 1910–1961: From Warfare to Welfare* (New York: Oxford University Press, 1992), xv.

19. *Los Angeles Times*, Oct. 19, 1967.

20. Samuel C. May, "The Postwar Unemployment Problem in Cali-

fornia, 1945–1947" (pamphlet, Berkeley: Bureau of Public Administration, University of California, 1945), p. 1, HI; Robert K. Arnold et al., *The Californian Economy, 1947–1980* (Menlo Park, Calif.: Stanford Research institute, 1961), 15, 16, 247. Roger Lotchin argues that California cities were a product of military investment invited in by urban boosters and that the process started well before World War II: Lotchin, *Fortress California*, xv.

21. Bella Abzug, *Gender Gap* (Boston: Houghton Mifflin, 1984), 90*n*.

22. John E. Mueller, *War, Presidents and Public Opinion* (New York: John Wiley, 1973), 146–147.

23. Quoted in Augusta Genevieve Violette, *Economic Feminism in American Literature Prior to 1848* (New York: Burt Franklin, 1971 [1925]), 37. On the New Jersey election law of 1807, see Willi Paul Adams, *The First American Constitutions*, trans. Rita Kimber and Robert Kimber (Chapel Hill: University of North Carolina Press, 1980), 299.

24. Emily Greene Balch, "The Effect of War and Militarism on the Status of Women," *Publications of the American Sociological Society* (1915), 43.

25. Anna Graves quoted in Harriet Hyman Alonso, *Peace as a Women's Issue: A History of the U.S. Movement for World Peace and Women's Rights* (Syracuse, N.Y.: Syracuse University Press, 1993), 146. Emphasis in the original.

26. A respected historian expressed the reform-and-war adage as follows: "Throughout American history each period of rapid progress toward economic, social and political democracy has been brought to a close by a major war. This is because such periods infect the people with a crusading zeal that makes them willing to fight for their ideals": Ray Allen Billington, *American History After 1865* (Totowa, N.J.: Littlefield, Adams, 1967), 144. The journalists Robert Scheer and Warren Hinckle argue that the "Viet-Nam Lobby," those who agitated for American involvement as part of the anticommunist "Crusade for Democracy," were "liberals": Scheer and Hinckle, "The Viet-Nam Lobby," originally in *Ramparts* (July 1965) and reproduced in Marcus G. Raskin and Bernard B. Fall, eds., *The Viet-Nam Reader: Articles and Documents on American Foreign Policy and the Viet-Nam Crisis* (New York: Vintage, 1965), 80.

27. For a discussion, see Rhodri Jeffreys-Jones, "America's Missing Sisters," *Society for Historians of American Foreign Relations Newsletter*, 26 (September 1995), 16–28.

28. For a summary of some of the foreign policy achievements by American women, see Jeffreys-Jones, *Changing Differences*, 196–197.

29. Claudia Koonz, *Mothers in the Fatherland: Women, the Family, and Nazi Politics* (London: Jonathan Cape, 1987), 30. By 1991 the total number of women elected to both chambers of the Congress since 1916 stood at 134; the House alone has 435 seats and the Senate a further 100: Mildred L. Amer, comp., *Women in the United States Congress* (Washington, D.C.: Congressional Research Service, 1991), 1.

30. Amer, *Women in Congress*, 67. Sirimavo Bandaranaike became prime minister of Ceylon (later Sri Lanka) in 1960, Indira Gandhi of India in 1966, and Golda Meir of Israel in 1969.

31. Smith's standard reply to form letters of protest against the Vietnam War in 1967, in file, "Vietnam War," MCS.

32. Nixon to Luce, July 31, 1968, Box 229, ACBL.

33. Carol Hymowitz and Michaele Weissman, *A History of Women in America* (New York: Bantam, 1978), 344.

34. For a summary of the sets of laws, see Rochelle Gatlin, *American Women Since 1945* (Jackson: University Press of Mississippi, 1987), 200–201.

35. Norman Mailer, *The Armies of the Night: History as a Novel, the Novel as History* (New York: Penguin/Plume, 1994 [1968]), 62.

36. David Kahn, "United States Views of Germany and Japan in 1941," in Ernest R. May, ed., *Knowing One's Enemies: Intelligence Assessment Before the Two World Wars* (Princeton, N.J.: Princeton University Press, 1986), 476–477, 496–497.

37. For various perspectives, see Gary R. Hess, *America Encounters India, 1941–1947* (Baltimore, Md.: Johns Hopkins University Press, 1971), 10–11; W. E. B. Du Bois, *Dusk at Dawn* (New York: Schocken Books, 1968 [1940]), 96; and William R. Scott, *The Sons of Sheba's Race: African-Americans and the Italo-Ethiopian War, 1935–1941* (Bloomington: Indiana University Press, 1993), xiii, 212, 220.

38. Ron E. Armstead, interview with author, Rayburn House Office Building, Washington, D.C., July 18, 1995. At the time of the interview, Armstead was on the Congressional Black Caucus Veterans Braintrust and was a Black Caucus Fellow in the office of Congressman Charles E. Rangel.

39. *Ebony*, 23 (August 1968), 66.

40. Neil A. Wynn, "The 'Good War': The Second World War and Postwar American Society," *Journal of Contemporary History*, 31, iii (1996), 471–474.

41. "Ça vous amuserait de voir tuer un Nègre?" and other clippings assembled in a montage by the Ford Foundation, NAACP. The

author wishes to thank the National Association for the Advancement of Colored People for the use of the referenced NAACP materials. For a compilation of hostile Asian and other foreign reactions to U.S. racism, see Mary Dudziak, "Desegregation as a Cold War Imperative," *Stanford Law Review*, 41 (November 1988), 80–93.

42. For a discussion of how black activists were smeared as Reds, see Brenda Gayle Plummer, *Rising Wind: Black Americans and Foreign Affairs, 1935–1960* (Chapel Hill: University of North Carolina Press, 1996), 172–173.

43. Terrence Lyons, "Keeping Africa off the Agenda," in Warren I. Cohen and Nancy Bernkopf Tucker, eds., *Lyndon Johnson Confronts the World: American Foreign Policy, 1963–1968* (Cambridge: Cambridge University Press, 1994), 245–278.

44. Thomas J. Noer, *Black Liberation: The United States and White Rule in Africa, 1948–1968* (Columbia: University of Missouri Press, 1985), 60.

45. Secretary of State statement, "Concerning the Ford Foundation grant of $600,000 to Howard University in Support of a Program to Prepare Minority Candidates for a Career in Foreign Affairs," Oct. 9, 1963, and John A. Davis, "The Employment of American Negroes in the Foreign Service of the United States (paper read at the 1964 A[merican] N[egro] L[eadership] C[onference on] A[frica] conference)," both in NUL.

46. The singer Paul Robeson had praised Ho Chi Minh and condemned U.S. aid to Vietnamese anti-Communists in 1954, but by the 1960s he was no longer active on the Left: author's interview with Paul Robeson, Jr., July 23, 1995; Martin B. Duberman, *Paul Robeson* (London: Bodley Head, 1989), 713*n*42. For further reflections on the tactical errors of the Communist Party concerning the American race question, see John Patrick Diggins, *The Rise and Fall of the American Left* (New York: Norton, 1992), 170–171.

47. Walter Mosley, *A Red Death* (New York: Pocket Books, 1992), 14.

48. Colin Powell, *My American Journey* (New York: Random House, 1995), 79.

49. The Civil Rights Act became law on July 2, and the Congress adopted the Tonkin Gulf resolution on Aug. 7, 1964.

50. Brian Urquhart, *Ralph Bunche: An American Life* (New York: Norton, 1993), 380–392; Charles W. Hamilton, *Adam Clayton Powell, Jr.: The Political Biography of an American Dilemma* (New York: Atheneum, 1991), 24.

51. See David J. Garrow, *Bearing the Cross: Martin Luther King, Jr., and the Southern Christian Leadership Conference* (New York: Vintage, 1988), 445, 553.

52. Robert W. Mullen, *Blacks in America's Wars: The Shift in Attitudes from the Revolutionary War to Vietnam* (New York: Pathfinder, 1973), 9.

53. Transcript, A. Philip Randolph oral history interview, Oct. 29, 1968, by Thomas H. Baker, p. 17, LBJ.

54. Memo, LBJ to Secretaries of Labor, Defense, and Health, Education and Welfare, and for the Director of the Selective Service System, May 9, 1964, WHCF ND 9-4, Box 147, LBJ.

55. U.S. Commission on Human Rights quoted in Lisa Hsaio, "Project 100,000: The Great Society's Answer to Military Manpower Needs in Vietnam," *Vietnam Generation*, 1 (1989), 22; Wallace Terry, introduction, *Bloods: An Oral History of the Vietnam War by Black Veterans* (New York: Valentine, 1985), xiii.

56. Ragni Lantz, "Dixie Town Fetes War Hero," *Ebony*, 22 (June 1967), 27–36.

57. Thomas H. Johnson, "Black Soldier in 'The Nam,'" *Ebony*, 23 (August 1968), 31; David Llorens, "Why Negroes Re-enlist," *Ebony*, 23 (August 1968), 87; Carolyn DuBose, "'Chappie' James: A New Role for An Old Warrior," *Ebony*, 25 (October 1970), 152.

58. For a corrective to the myth that only the private schools protested, see Kenneth J. Heineman, *Campus Wars: The Peace Movement at American State Universities in the Vietnam Era* (New York: New York University Press, 1993).

59. Wells, *War Within*, 24.

60. The Busch routine also included bussing tables in return for food, as well as—with clockwork regularity in a local bar between two and three in the morning—a debate on Dostoyevsky with one of the English professors at the university. From his part-time work as a self-financed student he had already built a capital sum of about $2,000, which he refused to expend to finish his degree quickly. The author has lost touch with Busch, who was one of his roommates in a house on Catherine Street, Ann Arbor, in 1964–1965.

61. Beisner to Javits, May 28, 1965, Box 85, JKJ.

62. Erskine, "Most War Foes Are over 50"; Richard F. Hamilton, "A Research Note on the Mass Support for 'Tough' Military Initiatives," *American Sociological Review* (June 1969), 439–445, and *Gallup Opinion Index*, "Report No. 40," October 1969, 25, both cited in Harlan Hahn, "Dove Sentiments Among Blue-Collar Workers," *Comments and Opin-*

ions, n.d., 203, in folder "U.S. Public Dissent," box 3 of three boxes marked "1970 Issues: Vietnam," McG.

63. *Crimson*, Sept. 22, 25; Oct. 3, 1916.

64. Henry F. May, *Coming to Terms: A Study in Memory and History* (Berkeley: University of California Press, 1987), 238.

65. Robert Cohen, *When the Old Left Was Young: Student Radicals and America's First Mass Student Movement, 1921–1941* (New York: Oxford University Press, 1993), xiv, xix, 154–157. See also J. Masland, "Attitudes and Activities of the Organized 'Peace' Pressure Groups, 1920-1941" (Mar. 29, 1943), CH; and Anthony J. Badger, *The New Deal: The Depression Years, 1933–1940* (New York: Noonday Press, 1989), 207.

66. For perspectives on this problem, see Ellen Schrecker, *No Ivory Tower: McCarthyism and the Universities* (New York: Oxford University Press, 1986); and Sigmund Diamond, *Compromised Campus: The Collaboration of Universities with the Intelligence Community, 1945–1955* (New York: Oxford University Press, 1992).

67. Terry H. Anderson, *The Movement and the Sixties: Protest in America from Greensboro to Wounded Knee* (New York: Oxford University Press, 1995), 18–19.

68. Gerard T. Rice, "The Federal Government's Harnessing of the Overseas Voluntary Spirit—the Peace Corps," in Rhodri Jeffreys-Jones and Bruce Collins, eds., *The Growth of Federal Power in American History* (DeKalb: Northern Illinois University Press, 1983), 134.

69. Hugh Davis Graham, "The Transformation of Federal Education Policy," in Robert A. Divine, ed., *Exploring the Johnson Years* (Austin: University of Texas Press, 1981), 156–161.

70. Aaron Wildavsky suggests that a radical WASP elite revolted against blue-collar support for the war: Wildavsky, *The Revolt Against the Masses and Other Essays on Politics and Public Policy* (New York: Basic, 1971), 43.

CHAPTER THREE Students

1. "Pigs Shoot to Kill—Bystanders Gunned Down," *Berkeley Barb*, May 12–22, 1969. The episode referred to was alleged to have occurred in the "people's park" campaign (see below).

2. *Los Angeles Times*, Nov. 3, 1970.

3. *Los Angeles Times*, Nov. 1, 1970.

4. Jacob K. Javits, "Non-Violent Change in Our Society," *Dartmouth Alumni Magazine*, July 1968, p. 21.

5. Tom Hayden, *Reunion: A Memoir* (New York: Random House, 1988), 7, 26–27, 31, 34–36.

6. Philip G. Altbach, *Student Politics in America: A Historical Analysis* (New York: McGraw-Hill, 1974), 206*n*9, 230.

7. In the last frame of the *Varsity* cartoon series, the hero is depicted in triumphant mode, posing for American tourists taking photographs of the last "don" (professor) at the university.

8. William J. McGill, *The Year of the Monkey: Revolt on Campus, 1968–69* (New York: McGraw-Hill, 1982), ix.

9. Paul Jacobs and Saul Landau, *The New Radicals: A Report with Documents* (New York: Random House, 1966), 67–72.

10. Two secretaries of state died in office in the earlier period, suggesting that old men really did cling to power in those days, even at risk to their own health. On the other hand, the objection might be raised that the life expectancy of the rich (from whose ranks secretaries of state were drawn) may have changed less over the years than that of the population at large, so the increase from 61.7 to 62.8 may, after all, be significant. See Richard Dean Burns, ed., *Guide to American Foreign Relations Since 1700* (Santa Barbara, Calif.: ABC-CLIO, 1983), Appendix II: Secretaries of State, 1781–1982, pp. 1219–1234; Victoria D. Weisfeld, "Health Care in the United States," in Godfrey Hodgson, ed., *Handbooks to the Modern World: The United States*, 3 vols. (New York: Facts on File, 1992), III, 1613; John A. Hague, "United States—Way of Living," *Encyclopedia Americana*, 30 vols. (New York: Americana, 1968), XXVII, 749.

11. Mary McCarthy, *The Group* (London: Weidenfeld and Nicolson, 1963), 13. William Strauss and Neil Howe point out that more than two generations were involved in the debate over the Vietnam War. They label four: the G.I. elders (born in 1901–1924), the Silent midlifers (1925–1942), the Boomer rising adults (1943–1960), and a youngest generation with no sense of history. They also argue that generational dialectics are a long-running feature of American history. See Strauss and Howe, *Generations: The History of America's Future, 1584–2069* (New York: William Morrow, 1991), 8, 151–154.

12. *MASH* was made into a television series, 1972–1983. Contemporary movies that directly depicted youthful resentment against the Vietnam War include *Alice's Restaurant* (1969) and *The Strawberry Statement* (1970). The historian William Mayer has challenged the view that young people showed a special tendency to rebel against the war, noting that "as late as 1970, the newest entrants into the adult population were evenly divided between advocates of military withdrawal and those who supported

escalation." His own table, however, compiled from data collected at the American Election Studies unit at the Center for Political Studies at the University of Michigan, indicates that the youngest age cohorts consistently produced the highest proportions opposed to the war. The young cohorts were polarized, also showing a tendency to favor drastic military solutions. By whatever means, it would appear, young people wanted out: William G. Mayer, *The Changing American Mind: How and Why American Public Opinion Changed Between 1960 and 1988* (Ann Arbor: University of Michigan Press, 1992), 168–169.

13. McGill, *Year of the Monkey*, 62–99; Paul Breines, "The Mosse Milieu," in Paul Buhle, ed., *History and the New Left: Madison, Wisconsin, 1950–1970* (Philadelphia: Temple University Press, 1990), 249; Everett C. Ladd. "American University Teachers and Opposition to the Vietnam War," *Minerva*, 8 (October 1970), 545; E. M. Schreiber, "Opposition to the Vietnam War Among American University Students and Faculty," *British Journal of Sociology*, 24 (1973), 297.

14. As the novelist Norman Mailer saw it, students defied the draft, and their faculty allies backed them up. See his firsthand account of a speech by the Yale chaplain William Sloane Coffin just before the 1967 march on the Pentagon: Mailer, *The Armies of the Night: History as a Novel, the Novel as History* (New York: Plume, 1994 [1968]), 72–73.

15. Claybourne Carson, *In Struggle: SNCC and the Black Awakening of the 1960s* (Cambridge: Harvard University Press, 1981), 183.

16. See Allan M. Winkler, *Life Under a Cloud: American Anxiety About the Atom* (New York: Oxford University Press, 1993).

17. Sleeve notes, Phil Ochs, *Chords of Fame* (album, 1974).

18. Frank Norris, *The Octopus* (New York: Signet, 1964), 436, 455. Anna Louise Strong, a veteran of the Seattle Central Labor Council, testified to the pedigree of the octopoid image when she told an international labor union conference held in Hanoi in 1965: "In our land, which we love as other people do their native lands, lives a savage beast that threatens the human race. In my youth in Seattle we called it the Octopus": *[Proceedings of the] Second Conference of the International Trade-Union Committee for Solidarity with the Workers and People of Vietnam Against the U.S. Imperialist Aggressors [June 2–7, 1965]* (Hanoi: Vietnam Federation of Trade Unions, 1965), 124.

19. Claude Julien, *L'empire américain* (Paris: Editions Bernard Grasset, 1968), 330.

20. Stuart W. Leslie, *The Cold War and American Science: The Mili-*

tary-Industrial-Academic Complex at MIT and Stanford (New York: Columbia University Press, 1993), 235–249.

21. *The Case Against Dillingham* (Palo Alto: Grass Roots, ca. 1969).

22. *Fire and Sandstone: The Last Radical Guide to Stanford* (Stanford, Calif.: Stanford Radical Caucus and New Left Project, 1970), 2, 35.

23. See James Miller, *Democracy Is in the Streets: From Port Huron to the Siege of Chicago* (Cambridge: Harvard University Press, 1994 [1987]), 172.

24. *Case Against Dillingham*, 4.

25. Lewis S. Feuer, *The Conflict of Generations: The Character and Significance of Student Movements* (London: Heinemann, 1969), 430.

26. The phrase was used ironically and autobiographically by one of the author's graduate students who, in a remarkably swift transition, left the anarchist movement to become a college president in Canada.

27. Interview with Lewis H. Gann, Sept. 15, 1975, Gann being the author of numerous books, including *Burden of Empire: An Appraisal of Western Colonialism in Africa South of the Sahara* (New York: Praeger, 1967).

28. *San Diego Free Press*, Nov. 1–14, 1968.

29. Mailer, *Armies*, 223.

30. Booth quoted in Tom Wells, *The War Within: America's Battle over Vietnam* (Berkeley: University of California Press, 1994), 160. Cf. Booth interview in Miller, *Democracy in the Streets*, 322. Booth served as national secretary in the fall of 1965 and the spring of 1966 (Miller, pp. 246, 258).

31. Author's interview with Leonard Siegel, Sept. 19, 1975.

32. Bunche to Bunche, Jr., Jan. 8, 1969, quoted in Brian Urquhart, *Ralph Bunche: An American Life* (New York: Norton, 1993), 391.

33. Moynihan to Nixon, Mar. 8, 1971, folder "President's Handwriting, January 1971–March 15, 1971," WHCF, POF, Box 9, NPM.

34. Peter B. Levy, *The New Left and Labor in the 1960s* (Urbana: University of Illinois Press, 1994), 46.

35. Javits, "Non-Violent Change in Our Society,"*Dartmouth Alumni Magazine*, July 1968, p. 21.

36. Siegel interview; Melvin Small, *Johnson, Nixon, and the Doves* (New Brunswick, N.J.: Rutgers University Press, 1988), 44; Wells, *War Within*, 107; William Colby, *Honourable Men: My Life in the CIA* (London: Hutchinson, 1978), 289.

37. See Robert S. McNamara, *In Retrospect: The Tragedy and Lessons of Vietnam* (New York: Times Books, 1995).

38. Deborah Shapley, *Promise and Power: The Life and Times of Robert McNamara* (Boston: Little, Brown, 1993), xiii, 381.

39. George Q. Flynn, *The Draft, 1940–1973* (Lawrence: University Press of Kansas, 1993), 2–3, 171.

40. The ranks of the draft offenders were swollen by AWOLs, soldiers absent without leave for a whole variety of reasons ranging from hangovers to emotional problems, as well as discontent with the war. Up to 90 percent of AWOLs returned to their units. The lower figure of 200,000 may be an exaggeration—it is the resistance movement's own approximation of the number of men who by 1974 were fugitives from the draft or the military, were awaiting trial, or were in prison. Lawrence M. Baskir and William A. Strauss, *Chance and Circumstance: The Draft, the War, and the Vietnam Generation* (New York: Knopf, 1978), 5, 23, 27; Renée G. Kasinsky, *Refugees from Militarism: Draft-Age Americans in Canada* (New Brunswick, N.J.: Transaction Books, 1976), 4; Richard Killmer and others, *They Can't Go Home Again: The Story of America's Political Refugees* (Philadelphia: Pilgrim Press, 1971), 109.

41. Kasinsky, *Refugees from Militarism*, 5, 8. According to Kasinsky, "draft dodgers" and "deserters" were the Canadians' descriptive terms, "with no pejorative meaning intended."

42. Killmer, *They Can't Go Home*, 110–111; Kasinsky, *Refugees from Militarism*, 5, 11.

43. Hayden, *Reunion*, 44.

44. "The Port Huron Statement [Port Huron, Michigan, June 11–15, 1962]," reproduced in Miller, *Democracy in the Streets*, 329–374, quotations at 343–344.

45. *San Diego Free Press*, July 11–25, 1969.

46. *San Diego Free Press*, Aug. 6–20, 1969.

47. Levy, *New Left and Labor*, 4–5.

48. See Irwin Unger, *The Movement: A History of the American New Left, 1959–1972* (New York: Dodd, Mead, 1975), chap. 6; and Edward J. Bacciocco, Jr., *The New Left in America: Reform to Revolution, 1956 to 1970* (Stanford, Calif.: Hoover Institution Press, 1974), 146, 147, 216–226.

49. Memo, Bud Krogh and J. F. Lehman to Henry Kissinger, Nov. 11, 1970, "Chronological File, 1970," WHCF, SMOF, EMK, Box 3, NPM.

50. Bao Ninh, *The Sorrow of War: A Novel*, trans. Phan Thanh Hao (London: Minerva, 1994 [Hanoi, 1991]), 6.

51. Gus Tyler, "The Liberal Crisis—Now," *New Leader*, Oct. 7, 1968, p. 5. For a more realistic assessment of the counterculture hippies, see

Terry H. Anderson, *The Movement and the Sixties* (New York: Oxford University Press, 1995), 217–219.

52. Donald E. Phillips, *Student Protest, 1960–1970: An Analysis of Issues and Speeches*, rev. ed. (Lanham, Md.: University Publications of America, 1985), 166.

53. Carson, *In Struggle*, 83.

54. Wells, *War Within*, 13.

55. "The Anti-Vietnam Agitation and the Teach-In Movement: The Problem of Communist Infiltration and Exploitation," *Senate Document*, 89th Cong., 1st sess., no. 72 (Oct. 22, 1965), xi–xii; Carson, *In Struggle*, 184; Wells, *War Within*, 24.

56. "Anti-Vietnam Agitation," 9–11.

57. Michael Barone, Grant Ujifusa, and Douglas Matthews, *The Almanac of American Politics, 1974* (London: Macmillan, 1974), 55.

58. Savio paraphrased in Bacciocco, *New Left*, 149.

59. Record, dustjacket, and text in NLC. On SLATE, see W. J. Rorabaugh, *Berkeley at War: The 1960s* (New York: Oxford University Press, 1990), 15. SLATE is a word, not an acronym.

60. Rorabaugh, *Berkeley at War*, 38–39.

61. Author's interview with Barry M. Silverman (research director, International Longshoremen's and Warehousemen's Union), Sept. 25, 1975; Fred C. Schwarz, *An Analysis of the Rebellion at the University of California as Applied Marxism-Leninism* (Long Beach, Calif.: Christian Anti-Communism Crusade, 1965), 2.

62. Clipping of an article on Bettina Aptheker written by Tom Tiede of the Newspaper Enterprise Association and published in the fall of 1966, in RRGC.

63. Kirkpatrick Sale, *SDS* (New York: Random House, 1973), 237.

64. Author's interview with Seymour M. Lipset, Sept. 17, 1975; William Manchester, *The Glory and the Dream: A Narrative History of America, 1932–1972* (London: Michael Joseph, 1975), 1056. In October 1970, William C. Sullivan, one of J. Edgar Hoover's top aides, admitted that the Communist Party was not at the root of campus disturbances: *Sacramento Bee*, Oct. 13, 1970. There may be another side to the tale of FBI incompetence. According to Morris Hirsch, one of its founders, "Participatory Democracy" left the VDC open to penetration by spies and saboteurs. See Gerard J. De Groot, "The Limits of Moral Protest and Participatory Democracy: The Vietnam Day Committee," *Pacific Historical Review*, 64, i (1995), 107.

65. Author's telephone interview, May 1997, with James Badenoch, Q.C., an English barrister who, as a student, sat on the tracks.

66. Rorabaugh, *Berkeley at War*, 91–94. The provincial nature of the U.S. press (there was no "national" newspaper) complicates the business of assessing the degree of journalistic focus on one region as distinct from another. The historian Melvin Small gives examples of *New York Times* and *Washington Post* coverage of student demonstrations in Washington, D.C.: Small, *Covering Dissent: The Media and the Anti–Vietnam War Movement* (New Brunswick, N.J.: Rutgers University Press, 1994), 43. W. J. Rorabaugh supplies exhaustive evidence of press coverage of events in Berkeley, acknowledging the *Los Angeles Times* and the *New York Times* to have been especially helpful: Rorabaugh, *Berkeley at War*, 259. British newspapers supply a perspective missing from the American scene in that they tend to filter diverse U.S. press reports. To take an extreme example, in 1965 the *Glasgow Herald* covered the Vietnam War extensively but carried no stories on student protest: *Glasgow Herald Index, 1965* (Glasgow: George Outram, 1966). The *Times* (London) may have supplied a more accurate reflection of American media preoccupations. Between March and August 1965, it ran seventeen stories on U.S. protest against the Vietnam War. Twelve were on Berkeley. See *Times Index* (London: The Times), March–April 1965, May–June 1965, July–August 1965.

67. William C. Berman, *William Fulbright and the Vietnam War: The Dissent of a Political Realist* (Kent, Ohio: Kent State University Press, 1988), 44–45; Randall Bennett Woods, *Fulbright: A Biography* (Cambridge: Cambridge University Press, 1995), 422; James F. Hawley to Javits, Oct. 26, 1965, and Javits to Hawley, Nov. 9, 1965, Box 10, JKJ; "Anti-Vietnam Agitation," viii, xiv.

68. Rorabaugh, *Berkeley at War*, 43, 91.

69. Small, *Johnson, Nixon*, 103–104.

70. George C. Herring, *LBJ and Vietnam: A Different Kind of War* (Austin: University of Texas Press, 1994), 125; Rorabaugh, *Berkeley at War*, 92; "Anti-Vietnam Agitation," xii. De Groot, "Limits of Moral Protest," 101.

71. See Sale, *SDS*, 234.

72. Irwin Unger wrote of the period 1965–1968: "As the intensity of the Vietnam War increased, two new trends began to become apparent on the student left. One was a complete break with liberal and reformist groups and a decided movement to the left: the other was a marked shift of attention from the poor, the black, and the relatively inert to middle-class, white college students and their problems on the campuses": Unger,

Movement, 93. But in the same period young men fled to Canada to avoid the draft. It is estimated that one-third of them could have taken the easier options of deferment or exemption. According to the pacifist journalist Sherry Gottlieb, "They refused to cooperate on moral principle": Sherry Gershon Gottlieb, ed., *Hell No, We Won't Go! Resisting the Draft During the Vietnam War* (New York: Viking, 1991), 2.

73. Christian G. Appy, *Working-Class War: American Combat Soldiers and Vietnam* (Chapel Hill: University of North Carolina Press, 1993), 26; Baskir and Strauss, *Chance and Circumstance*, 4, 9.

74. *Opposition West*, June 14, 1966.

75. *Come Vigil Now* (Berkeley: Berkeley Free Press, 1966); *Contra Costa Times*, May 1, 1966, quoted in leaflet distributed during a march down Market Street, San Francisco, on Aug. 6, 1966 ("Hiroshima Day"), entitled "Port Chicago's Where the Action Is"—both in JAC.

76. Anderson, *Movement*, 113; Hayden, *Reunion*, 175–176.

77. The author was faculty adviser to the student-run Ford Dinner Committee at Kirkland House, Harvard University, which issued the invitation to Aptheker to speak. Thirty years later, Diane Aceto Barrios, Assistant to the Master, Kirkland House, did a search of the administrative records of the Ford dinners but found no references to Aptheker. The records were "not complete and at some point skip several years such as 1966–67": E-mail, Barrios to author, Jan. 10, 1996. On the McNamara visit, see Wells, *War Within*, 101.

78. Bettina Aptheker quoted in Wells, *War Within*, 115.

79. On the "military-industrial-university complex," see Stanford chapter, SDS, "Stanford, the Trustees and Southeast Asia" (undated, typewritten pamphlet), RFD. See also Sidney Lens, *The Military-Industrial Complex* (London: Kahn and Averill, 1970), chap. 7, "Academia in Harness," 123–138; and, on the *Ramparts* affair, Rhodri Jeffreys-Jones, *The CIA and American Democracy* (New Haven: Yale University Press, 1989), 157–160.

80. Mailer, *Armies*, 62.

81. This synopsis fails to do justice to one of the great periods of agitation in U.S. history. For treatments of the complexities inherent in just one of the struggles, the Columbia University occupation, see Anderson, *Movement*, 194–203; and Jerry L. Avorn et al., *University in Revolt: A History of the Columbia Crisis* (London: Macdonald, 1968). Jerome Skolnick, director of the Task Force on Violent Aspects of Protest and Confrontation of the National Commission on the Causes and Prevention of Violence, showed an awareness of international context in his report to the

commission. In his view, however, "the worker-student collaboration that surfaced in France in the spring of 1968 seems remote from the American scene." See Skolnick, *Politics of Protest* (New York: Ballantine, 1969), 58, 79, 81–87.

82. "I hope the President does not get maneuvered into being responsible for our past policies in South Viet Nam which many feel were erroneous": Samuel W. Yorty to Walter Jenkins (assistant to the president, White House), Jan. 24, 1964, WHCF, Name File, Yorty, Box 24, LBJ. "I would not favor any dove-like position": Cranston to Joseph L. Rauh, July 13, 1967, JLR. Brown had praised student activism in 1961, welcoming "this new, impatient, critical crop of young gadflies": Brown quoted in unidentified clipping marked "June 1961," RRGC.

83. Frederick G. Dutton to Bill D. Moyers, June 10, 1966, WHCF, Name File, Reagan, Box 59, LBJ. Dutton had chaired the Brown for Governor campaign in 1958 and been deputy national chairman of Citizens for Kennedy and Johnson in 1960 and executive director of the platform organization at the 1964 Democratic National Convention.

84. Keating for Congress Campaign Committee, "Issues" (leaflet, Menlo Park, 1966); and Keating's reply to journalist's question in the Workshop on Peace Candidates and Political Action, in "Proceedings, Regional Vietnam Peace Conference, March 27, 1966," both in JAC.

85. Clippings of an article on Bettina Aptheker written by Tom Tiede of the Newspaper Enterprise Association and published in the fall of 1966, Reagan to Mrs. Gerald H. Hagar of Berkeley, Calif., Oct. 13, 1966, and Reagan quoted in Reagan for Governor Committee press release, Apr. 10, 1966, all in RRGC.

86. Reagan for Governor Committee press release, Apr. 10, 1966, RRGC; *San Francisco Examiner,* May 6, 1966. See also *New York Times,* Oct. 30, 1966.

87. "University community for Brown" (seven-page address issued by a group of UCLA faculty and students in 1966), and "This Week's News from Inside Washington," a clipping from *Human Events* marked "1966," both in RRGC. For a study of Reagan's exploitation of student unrest and of its importance to his political ascent, see Gerard J. De Groot, "Ronald Reagan and Student Unrest in California, 1966–1970," *Pacific Historical Review,* 65, i (1996), 107–129.

88. Skolnick, *Politics of Protest,* 31. Skolnick was director of the abovementioned Task Force on Violent Aspects of Protest and Confrontation of the National Commission on the Causes and Prevention of Violence, established in the Johnson administration.

89. Woods, *Fulbright*, 423; Berman, *Fulbright and Vietnam*, 63–64; William Fulbright, *The Arrogance of Power* (New York: Random House, 1966).

90. Joseph L. Rauh, Jr., "A Proposal to Maximize Political Support for an End to the War in Vietnam," typescript circa July 1967, Cranston to Rauh, July 13, 1967, Wyman to Rauh, Aug. 9, 1967, all in Box 30, JLR; Rauh, "Writing the Democratic Platform," *New Republic*, Oct. 14, 1967, pp. 11–12. On the problems facing the Democrats of California, see Lewis Chester, Godfrey Hodgson, and Bruce Page, *An American Melodrama: The Presidential Campaign of 1968* (New York: Viking, 1969), 323.

91. Flynn, *Draft*, 203–205, 215, 221; Appy, *Working-Class War*, 36.

92. *Washington Post*, Jan. 21, 1967.

93. Memo, Dick Moose to Walt Rostow, May 19, 1967, folder "Vietnam, Protest Petitions," Country File, Vietnam, NSF, Box 191, WHCF, LBJ.

94. Memo, Helms to president, Nov. 15, 1967, enclosing partially sanitized CIA report of the same date, "International Connections of U.S. Peace Groups," folder "U.S. Peace Groups—International Connections," Agency File, Intelligence, NSF, Box 10, WHCF, LBJ. See also Jeffreys-Jones, *CIA and American Democracy*, 167–168; and Wells, *War Within*, 183–191.

95. Memo, SAC (special agent in charge), Cincinnati to Director, FBI, June 3, 1968, and memo, Director, FBI to SAC, Cincinnati, June 18, 1968, reproduced in "Federal Bureau of Investigation," *Hearings Before the Select Committee to Study Governmental Operations with Respect to Intelligence Activities of the United States Senate*, 94th Cong., 1st sess., pursuant to S. res. 21, 7 vols., vol. 6, Nov. 18 and 19, Dec. 2, 3, 9, and 11, 1975, pp. 434–439. Background information is from William A. Little, "Radicals and Racists: The Church Committee's Investigation of the FBI's COINTELPRO" (M. Sc. diss., Edinburgh University, 1975), 38–47.

96. Chester et al., *American Melodrama*, 98, 738; William H. Chafe, *Never Stop Running: Allard Lowenstein and the Struggle to Save American Liberalism* (New York: Basic, 1993), 262–266.

97. Anderson, *Movement*, 225.

98. *New York Times*, May 16, 1968.

99. Stephen E. Ambrose, *Nixon: The Triumph of a Politician, 1962–1972* (New York: Simon and Schuster, 1989), 167–168.

100. *New York Times*, Oct. 17, 1968. By 1970, Semple was one of the very few journalists whom Nixon trusted. See Wells, *War Within*, 449.

101. Baskir and Strauss, *Chance and Circumstance*, 27.

102. Douglas S. Blaufarb, *The Counter-Insurgency Era: U.S. Doctrine and Performance, 1950 to the Present* (New York: Free Press, 1977), 292; Joan Hoff, *Nixon Reconsidered* (New York: Basic, 1994), 164–165.

103. Other affected officials in the Nixon administration included the senior White House staffers H. R. Haldeman and John Ehrlichman (Susan Haldeman and Peter Ehrlichman were both at Stanford), Secretary of the Treasury George Shultz, Director of the Office of Management and Budget Caspar Weinberger, and Vice President Spiro Agnew (who prevented his fourteen-year-old daughter from attending the moratorium demonstration in 1969): Wells, *War Within*, 366, 374; Small, *Johnson, Nixon*, 11, 184. See also Hoff, *Nixon Reconsidered*, 164; and Wells, *War Within*, 287–289.

104. Small, *Johnson, Nixon*, 186; Charles DeBenedetti, *An American Ordeal: The Antiwar Movement of the Vietnam Era* (Syracuse, N.Y.: Syracuse University Press, 1990), 248.

105. Nixon's biographer Stephen Ambrose challenges Nixon's estimation of the importance of the Silent Majority speech, arguing that it was bullying in intent and divisive in its effects: Ambrose, *Nixon: Triumph*, 310. See also *The Memoirs of Richard Nixon*, 2 vols. (New York: Warner, 1979), I, 496, 498, 506; and Ronald Reagan, "The Knowledge Factory: A Source of Student Rebellion," reproduced in Immanuel Wallerstein and Paul Starr, eds., *The University Crisis Reader*, 2 vols. (New York: Random House, 1971), I, 130–132.

106. Lists of student demands in 1969 are reproduced in Wallerstein and Starr, *Reader*, II, 491–493.

107. *New York Times*, Jan. 14, 1970.

108. "People's Parkers Name Their Real Goals," *San Francisco Sunday Examiner and Chronicle*, June 8, 1969; "Pigs Shoot to Kill—Bystanders Gunned Down," *Berkeley Barb*, May 12–22, 1969; 1969 Berkeley ephemera in NLC.

109. DeBenedetti, *American Ordeal*, 251. See also Wells, *War Within*, 148, 202, 253, 328.

110. *New Republic*, Mar. 15, 1969, quoted in Leslie, *Cold War and Science*, 234.

111. *Stanford Daily*, May 16, 1969; Stanford chapter, SDS, "Stanford, the Trustees and Southeast Asia" (undated, typewritten pamphlet), RFD; Leonard Siegel, *From Our Own Backyard: Old Wars Never Fade Away* (East Palo Alto, Calif.: Pacific Studies Center, 1972).

112. Memo, Fred Fielding to Charles Colson, Jan. 18, 1971, folder "Campus Unrest," WHCF, SMOF, CC, Box 44, NPM.

113. Memo with attachment, Krogh to H. R. Haldeman, Sept. 25, 1970, Chronological File, 1970, WHCF, SMOF, EMK, Box 3, NPM.

114. "Law Students Against the War: History and Purposes," a statement enclosed with Bradley R. Bank, co-chairman's circular to the legal profession, May 27, 1970, and state-by-state lists of candidates with interview-based details of their Vietnam War stances, May 25 and June 26, 1970, NCJW.

115. Mona G. Jacquenay, *Radicalism on Campus, 1969–1971: Backlash in Law Enforcement and in the Universities* (New York: Philosophical Library, 1972), 19.

116. *The Report of the President's Commission on Campus Unrest* (New York: Arno, 1970), 45.

117. George H. Gallup, *The Gallup Poll: Public Opinion 1935–1971*, 3 vols. (New York: Random House, 1972), III, 2250, 2251.

118. *Nixon Press Conferences* (London: Heyden, 1978), May 8, 1970, pp. 101–102.

119. Memo, Len Smith to Leonard Garment, enclosing memo by Noble Melencamp, Apr. 16, 1970, folder "Students and Campus Unrest," WHCF, SMOF, LG, Box 150, NPM; memo, stamped "the president has seen," Colson to president, Mar. 22, 1971, folder "President's Handwriting, March 16–May 10, 1971," WHCF, POF, Box 10, NPM. For an analysis of "Campus Opinion in May 1970," see *Report on Campus Unrest*, 47–49.

120. Memo, Jeb S. Magruder to Haldeman, Apr. 30, 1970, folder "Young Americans for Freedom," WHCF, SMOF, CC, Box 125, NPM. See also Mayer, *Changing American Mind*, 168–169.

121. Reports by Campus Opinion Poll, *New York Times*, and *Harvard Crimson* summarized in Huntington, W.Va., *Herald-Dispatch*, Oct. 30, 1970; Ronald B. Dear, director of regional and state activities, Young Americans for Freedom, to Robert Odle, White House, Apr. 30, 1970, folder "White House Conference on Youth," WHCF, SMOF, CC, Box 125, NPM.

122. [CIA] Inspector General Memorandum of Sept. 11, 1972, in "Intelligence Activities and the Rights of Americans" (Final Report of the Select Committee to Study Governmental Operations with Respect to Intelligence Activities, 5 Books, Book 2), *Senate Report*, 94th Cong., 2d sess., no. 94-755 (Apr. 26, 1976), 102.

123. Executive Order Establishing the President's Commission on Campus Unrest, and press release, "Statement by the President Creating a Commission on Campus Unrest," both in June 13, 1970, folder "Students and Campus Unrest," WHCF, SMOF, LG, Box 150, NPM.

124. Reagan press conferences, Dec. 2 and Nov. 18, 1969, Reagan address at Eisenhower College, Washington, D.C., Oct. 14, 1969, and Reagan remarks at a Republican fundraising dinner in Colorado, Oct. 24, 1969, all in RRGC.

125. *Los Angeles Times*, Nov. 1, 1970.

126. Quoted in De Groot, "Reagan and Student Unrest," 128.

127. Some caution is required here. Parties in control of the White House rarely do well in midterm contests. The Republicans, and perhaps conservatism, had peaked in California in 1968 (significantly, according to the theory that California is a leader state, because this was four years before Nixon's landslide presidential victory of 1972). Movement is inevitable in politics, and movement from a peak can only be downward. Against this background, Reagan and his supporters did hold their own. The *Los Angeles Times* was ambivalent on his fortunes, pointing out that the loss of the California legislature was a blow to his prestige but noting that he otherwise "led a phalanx of Republicans to victory": *Los Angeles Times*, Nov. 4, 5, 1970.

128. Memo, Lew Evans, Jr., to Haldeman, July 20, 1970, folder "White House Conference on Youth," WHCF, SMOF, CC, Box 124, NPM. The Twenty-sixth Amendment to the U.S. Constitution lowered the right to vote to age eighteen in 1971.

129. Memo, President to Bob Finch, Jan. 18, 1971, folder "Memos—January 1971," WHCF, PPF, memoranda for the President, 1969–74, Box 3, NPM.

130. Memo, Bob Finch to Haldeman, Feb. 2, 1971, WHCF, SMOF, CC, Box 124, NPM.

131. McGovern's address at Wheaton Methodist College, Wheaton, Ill., Oct. 11, 1972, folder "Vietnam: Miscellany 1972—I," Box 25, McG, published with permission of Princeton University Library. See also George McGovern, *An American Journey: The Presidential Campaign Speeches of George McGovern* (New York: Random House, 1974), 170, 191, 205.

CHAPTER FOUR African Americans

1. Muhammad Ali in Sherry G. Gottlieb, ed., *Hell No, We Won't Go! Resisting the Draft During the Vietnam War* (New York: Viking, 1991), 194, 196–197.

2. Author's interview with Ron E. Armstead, July 18, 1995. At the time of the interview, Armstead was a Congressional Black Caucus con-

gressional fellow in the office of Harlem congressman Charles B. Rangel and was involved in the Black Caucus Veterans Braintrust. He served in Vietnam as a medic and later became a community activist in the Roxbury area of Boston.

3. According to Paul Robeson, Jr., who believes the Communist Party helped African Americans in his father's generation, black radicals would have nothing to do with the left by the end of the 1960s. Gus Hall, general secretary of the Communist Party of the United States since 1959, was a "bigot"; Trotskyism had an appeal, but that was mainly confined to blacks of Caribbean extraction; the Jamaican C. L. R. James commanded respect among African Americans only as an individual, not as a socialist: author's interview with Paul Robeson, Jr., July 23, 1995. Angela Davis was a respected African American West Coast Communist who did take a stance against the war; and Communists did run black candidates on antiwar tickets—for example, Rasheed Storey for the governorship of New York in 1970: see the *New York Daily World*, Oct. 8, 1970. But on the whole—whatever J. Edgar Hoover and his presidential acolytes may have believed—black radicals followed a nonsocialist path in the sixties.

4. Although I follow Mullen's categories, the definitions are my own. See Robert W. Mullen, *Blacks and Vietnam* (Washington, D.C.: University Press of America, 1981), 13–29.

5. Eldridge Cleaver, *Soul on Ice* (London: Jonathan Cape, 1968), 123.

6. Malcolm X, "Prospects for Freedom in 1965" (talk in Palm Gardens, N.Y., Jan. 7, 1965, sponsored by the Militant Labor Forum), in George Breitman, ed., *Malcolm X Speaks: Selected Speeches and Statements* (London: Secker and Warburg, 1965), 148.

7. Donald Jackson, "Unite or Perish," *Liberator* (February 1967), 161-168, summarized in Mullen, *Blacks and Vietnam*, 53–59 at 54.

8. Mullen, *Blacks and Vietnam*, 8, 64, 68; L. Deckle McLean, "The Black Man and the Draft," *Ebony*, 23 (August 1968), 61.

9. Wilkins quoted in Alexander DeConde, *Ethnicity, Race, and Foreign Policy: A History* (Boston: Northeastern University Press, 1992), 151. On Wilkins's self-characterization as a token Negro, see Roger Wilkins, *A Man's Life: An Autobiography* (Woodbridge, Conn.: Ox Bow Press, 1991 [1982]), 246–248.

10. Report on King in the *New York Times*, Apr. 2, 1967, quoted in Robert Weisbrot, *Freedom Bound: A History of America's Civil Rights Movement* (New York: Norton, 1990), 247.

11. Shirley Chisholm, *Unbought and Unbossed* (Boston: Houghton Mifflin, 1970), 96.

12. Weisbrot, *Freedom Bound*, 189.

13. Whitney M. Young, Jr.'s testimony (as executive director of the NUL) to the Ad Hoc Subcommittee on the War on Poverty Program of the House Committee on Education and Labor, Apr. 14, 1964, in August Meier, Elliott Rudwick, and Francis L. Broderick, eds., *Black Protest Thought in the Twentieth Century*, 2d ed. (Indianapolis: Bobbs-Merrill, 1971), 431; Thomas L. Blair, *Retreat to the Ghetto: The End of a Dream?* (London: Wildwood, 1977), 164–165.

14. Transcript, James Farmer oral history interview, July 20, 1971, by Paige Mulhollan, pp. 25–26, LBJ.

15. Transcript, Clifford L. Alexander, Jr., oral history interviews by Joe B. Frantz, Nov. 1, 1971, pp. 25, 41, and Feb. 17, 1972, p. 15, LBJ.

16. Extract from Congressional Black Caucus (CBC) recommendations enclosed with memo, Leonard Garment to Secretary of State William Rogers, Apr. 9, 1971, folder "Black Caucus—Report and Review [3 of 6]," WHCF, SMOF, LG, Box 47, NPM.

17. Maya Angelou, *I Know Why the Caged Bird Sings* (London: Virago, 1984 [1969]), 208.

18. *New York Times*, Oct. 2, 1966, cited in Weisbrot, *Freedom Bound*, 247.

19. McLean, "Black Man," 66.

20. McLean, "Black Man," 63.

21. *Newsweek*, June 30, 1969, p. 20, cited in Mullen, *Blacks and Vietnam*, 2.

22. Brian Urquhart, *Ralph Bunche: An American Life* (New York: Norton, 1993), 380.

23. Powell quoted in Charles W. Hamilton, *Adam Clayton Powell, Jr.: The Political Biography of an American Dilemma* (New York: Atheneum, 1991), 24.

24. Transcript, James Farmer oral history interview, October 1969, by Harri Baker, p. 9, LBJ; Urquhart, *Ralph Bunche*, 391.

25. *New York World Journal Tribune*, Apr. 18, 1967; memo, Alexander to the president, citing an eyewitness account by his father, Clifford Alexander, Sr., Apr. 28, 1967, WHCF, Name File, King 1966, Box 144, LBJ.

26. Norman Mailer, *The Armies of the Night: History as a Novel, the Novel as History* (New York: Plume, 1994 [1968]), 109.

27. *Report of the National Advisory Commission on Civil Disorders* (New York: Bantam, 1968), 135.

28. Mullen, *Blacks and Vietnam*, 18–19.

29. Clayborne Carson, *In Struggle: SNCC and the Black Awakening of*

the 1960s (Cambridge: Harvard University Press, 1981), 174, 176, 184, 188; Terry H. Anderson, *The Movement and the Sixties: Protest in America from Greensboro to Wounded Knee* (New York: Oxford University Press, 1995), 158.

30. Christian G. Appy, *Working-Class War: American Combat Soldiers and Vietnam* (Chapel Hill: University of North Carolina Press, 1993), 20.

31. Black Panther Party platform quoted in Mullen, *Blacks and Vietnam*, 66.

32. Vanik to Valenti, Aug. 18, 1965, WHCF, ND 9-4, Box 147, LBJ.

33. Bryant in Wallace Terry, ed., *Bloods: An Oral History of the Vietnam War by Black Veterans* (New York: Ballantine, 1985), 18.

34. Department of Defense Fact Sheet, Jan. 18, 1967, folder "Negro Participation in the Armed Forces and in Vietnam," Country File, Vietnam, NSF, Box 191, WHCF, LBJ.

35. Richard J. Ford in Terry, *Bloods*, 38.

36. Alex Poinsett, "The Negro Officer," *Ebony*, 23 (August 1968), 136. The two African American generals were Brig. Gen. Frederic E. Davison and Lt. Gen. Benjamin O. Davis. According to U.S. military headquarters in Saigon, the highest-serving black officers on duty in Vietnam in early 1967 were twenty-one lieutenant colonels, two of whom, Harry W. Brooks and Felix Salvadore, commanded combat battalions. Brooks went on to become a brigadier general and served as a role model for Colin Powell. See the *Washington Post*, Apr. 3, 1967; and Colin Powell, *My American Journey* (New York: Random House, 1995), 185–186.

37. For a discussion of this point, see James E. Westheider, *Fighting on Two Fronts: African Americans and the Vietnam War* (New York: New York University Press, 1997), 3.

38. Edwards in Terry, *Bloods*, 11.

39. *Washington Post*, Apr. 3, 1967.

40. According to Robert J. Ellison, in 1967 the "Negro male median age [was] 20.4 years and the white male [was] 28.2": Ellison, "Viet Nam: Every Youth Must Face the Fact of Involvement," *Ebony*, 22 (August 1967), 27. Some of the contemporary debate focused on the issue of which branches of the armed forces were more integrated than others—for example, the Marines were held to have started integrating late, and the Army was more progressive than the Navy and Air Force. On the attempts to exculpate the military in general terms, see Hanson Baldwin of the *New York Times* quoted in McLean, "Black Man," 61; Bernard C. Nalty, *Strength for the Fight: A History of Black Americans in the Military* (New York: Free Press, 1986), 297; Appy, *Working-Class War*, 21–22.

41. "Excerpt from the transcript of Monday, March 1, 1965, page 59, Secretary McNamara," "Excerpt from transcript of Thursday, Apr. 8, 1965, page 758, General Cantwell," "Statement of Senator Margaret Chase Smith, United States Senate, Aug. 11, 1967," Robert S. McNamara to Smith, Aug. 11, 1967, all in file "Armed Services Committee, Secretary of Defense," folder "McNamara, Robert," MCS. For a table showing the black representation in the National Guard on Dec. 31, 1966, on a state-by-state basis, see the *Washington Post*, Aug. 11, 1967. On other Smith-McNamara difficulties, see Rhodri Jeffreys-Jones, *Changing Differences: Women and the Shaping of American Foreign Policy, 1917–1994* (New Brunswick, N.J.: Rutgers University Press, 1995), 122, 124.

42. Memo, Alexander for the President, Jan. 7, 1966, WHCF, Name File, King 1966, Box 144, LBJ.

43. Diggs to Lewis B. Hershey, Feb. 7, 1966, NAACP.

44. Weisbrot, *Freedom Bound*, 193.

45. McNamara quoted in Appy, *Working-Class War*, 32.

46. Lisa Hsiao, "Project 100,000: The Great Society's Answer to Military Manpower Needs in Vietnam," *Vietnam Generation*, 1 (1989), 16.

47. W. Willard Wirtz to the president, Jan. 1, 1964, WHCF National Security-Defense (ND) 9–4, Box 147, LBJ. President Kennedy appointed a Committee on Equal Opportunity in the Armed Forces with the attorney Gerhard A. Gessell as chair. See Nalty, *Strength for the Fight*, 281.

48. Hsiao, "Project 100,000," 16, 23, 30; George Q. Flynn, *The Draft, 1940–1973* (Lawrence: University Press of Kansas, 1993), 209.

49. Melvin Small, *Covering Dissent: The Media and the Anti–Vietnam War Movement* (New Brunswick, N.J.: Rutgers University Press, 1994), 66.

50. Salient points are taken from a standardized petition to the president in support of King's position, Apr. 27, 1967, WHCF, Name File, King 1967, Box 144, LBJ.

51. Carl T. Rowan, "Martin Luther King's Tragic Decision," in David J. Garrow, ed., *Martin Luther King, Jr.: Civil Rights Leader, Theologian, Orator*, 3 vols. (Brooklyn, N.Y.: Carlson, 1989), III, 2.

52. Rowan, "Tragic Decision," 4–5; David L. Lewis, *King: A Biography*, 2d ed. (Urbana: University of Illinois Press, 1978), 363.

53. David J. Garrow, *Bearing the Cross: Martin Luther King, Jr., and the Southern Christian Leadership Conference* (New York: Vintage, 1988), 543, 552.

54. Telegram, King to President, Jan. 13, 1966, WHCF, Name File, King 1966, Box 144, LBJ. Typos corrected.

55. King quoted in Garrow, *Bearing the Cross*, 551; and in Mullen, *Blacks and Vietnam*, 79. See also Adam Fairclough, *Martin Luther King* (London: Cardinal, 1990), 107.

56. Thomas Powers, *The War at Home: Vietnam and the American People, 1964–1968* (New York: Grossman, 1973), 163.

57. Memos, Fred Panzer to President, May 19, 20, June 11, 1967, WHCF, Name File, King 1967, Box 144, LBJ.

58. Joseph L. Rauh, Jr., "Writing the Democratic Platform," *New Republic*, Oct. 14, 1967.

59. Jackie Robinson, "Want to Hear from Dr. King," *New Courier*, Apr. 15, 1967; editorial, "Where We Stand," *New York Amsterdam News*, Apr. 15, 1967.

60. Transcript, Clifford L. Alexander, oral history interview, Feb. 17, 1972, by Joe B. Frantz, pp. 15–16, LBJ.

61. White to Meyer, Sept. 3, 1952, and Wilkins to Philadelphia businessman Joel I. Judovich, Aug. 25, 1958, both in NAACP.

62. *New York Times*, Nov. 26, 1962; ANLCA conference resolution sent to President John F. Kennedy on Nov. 24, 1962, ANLCA leaders' conversation with Kennedy on Dec. 17, 1962, and Wilkins to Kennedy (telegram), Jan. 2, 1963, all referred to in Wilkins to conference participant (circular), Jan. 8, 1963, NUL.

63. Wilkins to Diggs, Mar. 2, 1966, NAACP.

64. King, "Statement on Vietnam" (at the SCLC board meeting in Miami), Apr. 13, 1966, and memo, Current to Wilkins and other senior NAACP officials, Apr. 14, 1966, both in NAACP.

65. Wilkins quoted in Manfred Berg, "Guns, Butter, and Civil Rights: The National Association for the Advancement of Colored People and the Vietnam War, 1964–1968," in David K. Adams and Cornelis Van Minnen, eds., *Aspects of War in American History* (Keele, England: Keele University Press, 1997), 228.

66. Wilkins to Johnson, May 4, 1966, together with typescript of pages 5 and 6 of an earlier draft of the letter, corrected by hand and signed by Wilkins, NAACP; Roy Wilkins, *Standing Fast: The Autobiography of Roy Wilkins* (New York: DaCapo Press, 1994 [1982]), 299.

67. Memo, Current to Wilkins, Apr. 16, 1967, Wilkins speech at Yale University, Apr. 18, 1967, quoted in United Press International report (clipping from an unidentified newspaper), Wilkins to Daniel A. Davis, June 19, 1967, all in NAACP. The political scientist Rob Singh, in comments on the manuscript of this book, drew attention to the absence of black foreign-policy lobbies that might have deterred Wilkins from his

course. Such organizations lay in the future. Transafrica, to name one, was established in 1977.

68. Robert J. Donovan (Washington bureau chief), "Civil Rights Fervor Getting Lost in Clamor for End to Viet War," *Los Angeles Times*, Apr. 16, 1967; Thelma W. Babbit to Wilkins, Apr. 14, 1967 (noting strictures in the *Boston Globe* on the NAACP's "scurrilous attack" and containing a postscript on her ashtray friend), Clyde R. Taylor to Wilkins, Apr. 17, 1967, numerous other letters, for and against King, all in NAACP.

69. President Johnson's paraphrase of Brooke's position in Memorandum of Conversation, The President and Dr. Walter Judd, Oct. 16, 1967, folder "Vietnam 7E (1)b 9/67–10/67—Public Relations Activities," Country File, Vietnam, NSF, Box 99, WHCF, LBJ; Jacob K. Javits, "Vietnam and the U.S. Economy," press release, Feb. 10, 1968, Box 40, JKJ.

70. Terry, *Bloods*, "Introduction," xiv. Used in this context, the term *Blood* denoted racial militancy and brotherhood. More generally, African Americans used it to identify anyone of their race. It was being used in the more militant sense by mid-1966, so a new language was already in place by the time of the change described by Terry. William King gives an example of earlier usage in "'Our Men in Vietnam': Black Media as a Source of the Afro-American Experience in Southeast Asia," *Vietnam Generation*, 1 (Spring 1989), 96.

71. Richard R. Moser, *The New Winter Soldiers: GI and Veteran Dissent During the Vietnam Era* (New Brunswick, N.J.: Rutgers University Press, 1996), 65; Robert W. Mullen, *Blacks in America's Wars* (New York: Pathfinder, 1973), 80; Glen Gendzel, "Fragging," in Stanley I. Kutler, ed., *Encyclopedia of the Vietnam War* (New York: Scribner's, 1996), 199.

72. Tom Wells, *The War Within: America's Battle over Vietnam* (Berkeley: University of California Press, 1994), 282–283. Telegrams, Rostow to President, Aug. 30, 31, 1968, and Memoranda to the President, Walt Rostow, vol. 92, Aug. 22–31, NSF, Box 39, WHCF, LBJ; Nalty, *Strength for the Fight*, 305.

73. Steven Morris, "How Blacks Upset the Marine Corps: 'New Breed' Leathernecks Are Tackling Racial Vestiges," *Ebony*, 25 (December 1969), 55, 57. See also Mullen, *Blacks in America's Wars*, 82–83.

74. Ulf Nilson, "Deserters in Sweden: Fourteen Black Ex-GIs Find Refuge from Vietnam War," *Ebony*, 23 (August 1968), 121–122; Terry Whitmore, *Memphis, Nam, Sweden: The Autobiography of a Black American Exile* (Garden City, N.Y.: Doubleday, 1971), 85, 188. On the effectiveness

of Hanoi Hannah's appeal to black soldiers, see Myra MacPherson, *Vietnam and the Haunted Generation* (New York: Doubleday, 1993), 555.

75. Author's interview with Jack Calhoun (an organizer of AMEX, representing American military exiles in Canada, and later an investigative journalist), July 28, 1995; Roger N. Williams, *The New Exiles: American War Resisters in Canada* (New York: Liveright, 1971), 339; David S. Surrey, *Choice of Conscience: Vietnam Era Military and Draft Resisters in Canada* (New York: Praeger, 1982), 76.

76. Thomas A. Johnson, "Negro Has New Role in Southeast Asia," *New York Times*, Apr. 30, 1968; Sol Stern, "When the Black G.I. Comes Home from Vietnam," *New York Times*, Mar. 24, 1968; Russell quoted in Williams, *New Exiles*, 340; Calhoun interview.

77. The quotation is a paraphrase of Smith's stated position by the interviewer Jim Clarke in a transcript, "Close-Up: Howard K. Smith," interview by Clarke for Television Seven News, WMAL-TV, Mar. 30, 1968, folder "Vietnam 7D (2) 12/67–3/68 News Media Coverage of Vietnam," Country File, Vietnam, NSF, Box 98, WHCF, LBJ.

78. Ilya V. Gaiduk, "Soviet Policy Towards U.S. Participation in the Vietnam War," *History*, 81 (January 1996), 47–48; Small, *Covering Dissent*, 161. Ilya Gaiduk of the Institute of World History in Moscow points to evidence, in Communist Party archives, of Soviet exploitation of the African American issue and of "Soviet penetration into and support of" the Black Panthers and similar movements: E-mail, Gaiduk to author, Jan. 24, 1996.

79. Excerpt from David Parks, *G.I. Diary* (New York: Harper and Row, 1968), in Jay David and Elaine Crane, eds., *The Black Soldier: From the American Revolution to Vietnam* (New York: William Morrow, 1971), 210, 213–214. The Parks diary was quoted in August 1968 in McLean, "Black Man," 62.

80. Sol Stern, "When the Black G.I. Comes Home from Vietnam," *New York Times*, Mar. 24, 1968. Stern was an editor of *Ramparts* magazine.

81. *Washington Star*, May 6, 1968.

82. Johnson's series "The U.S. Negro in Vietnam," *New York Times*, Apr. 29, May 1, July 29, 1968, was more supportive of the war than his later summary "Negroes in 'The Nam': Brothers are Found in Every Corner of the Beleaguered Countryside," *Ebony*, 23 (August 1968), 31–33. The *Sepia* quotations are from King, "Our Men in Vietnam," 94, 103. The historian Christian G. Appy notes the spate of articles on "the Negro in Vietnam"; he discerns an ironic tone in articles by African American journalists, but

also their tendency to portray black soldiers as "highly motivated, enthusiastic troops," a judgment with which he agrees: Appy, *Working-Class War*, 21. It is true that racial pride in black valor is consistently evident in the African American journalism of the time, as is fraternal concern for the black soldier in the firing line. Although it is hazardous to generalize about a magazine like *Ebony*, every issue of which contained a variety of individual perceptions, it is nevertheless possible to discern a hardening of the antiwar line in articles on the African American soldier. This hardening was not yet evident in mid-1967. In June, for example, Ragni Lantz contributed a sanguine article about the homecoming of Congressional Medal of Honor winner Lawrence Joel. To be sure, it contained the acid comment that Joel's father was a self-improving man who could not afford to buy a copy of the *New York Times*. Nevertheless, its commendatory tone would have seemed out of place in 1968. The same could be said of an August 1967 article by Robert J. Ellison, who seemed resigned to the injustice of the selective service system. By 1968, however, *Ebony* was distinctly critical of the role and treatment of the black soldier. Of the nineteen articles in its special issue on the subject, eight were mainly on Vietnam, and although all the contributors tried to be objective, half the Vietnam articles contained material that would have influenced readers to be hostile to the war. To make a comparison with the world of white journalism, it was as if *Life* magazine had become heavily radicalized. See Ragni Lantz, "Dixie Town Fetes War Hero," *Ebony*, 22 (June 1967), 27–36; Ellison, "Viet Nam: Every Youth Must Face the Fact of Involvement," *Ebony*, 22 (August 1967), 23–28; and the whole issue of *Ebony*, 23 (August 1968); see also "Report from Black America—a Newsweek Poll," *Newsweek*, June 30, 1968, pp. 16–35; and Raymond R. Coffey, "When the Blacks Come Home," *The Progressive* (November 1968).

83. "File references to the importance of 'destroying' him as a public figure decreased sharply": David J. Garrow, *The FBI and Martin Luther King, Jr.* (New York: Penguin, 1981), 206.

84. Telegram, director, FBI, to White House, May 19, 1967, folder "Vietnam, Protest Petitions," Country File, Vietnam, NSF, Box 191, WHCF, LBJ; quotation in Garrow, *FBI and King*, 183.

85. Memo, Panzer for President, May 19, 1967, WHCF, Name File, King 1967, Box 144, LBJ; Harrisburg, Pa., *Patriot*, June 1, 1967; *New York Post*, June 1, 1967; *Washington Post*, June 1, 1967.

86. Memo, Joseph A. Califano for Bureau of the Budget Director Charles L. Schultze, Nov. 3, 1967, enclosing E. H. Rastatter, "Have the Great Society . . . ?" (Oct. 13, 1967), memo, Schultze for Cali-

fano, Nov. 14, 1967, all in "Presidential Task Force on Accomplishments of the Johnson Administration," folder "Facts and Figures: Vietnam," OFWHA, JCG, Box 290, LBJ.

87. Memo, Panzer for President, June 9, 1967, WHCF, Name File, King 1967, Box 144, LBJ.

88. Meany to president, Dec. 29, 1967, WHCF, Name File, Meany, Box 337, LBJ.

89. See Murray Friedman, *What Went Wrong? The Creation and Collapse of the Black-Jewish Alliance* (New York: Free Press, 1995), 243.

90. In 1956, Fulbright had been a signatory of the Southern Manifesto, which opposed the integration of schools on the eve of the sensational Little Rock confrontation in his own state. By 1965, persuaded by the expansion of the African American electorate in Arkansas, Fulbright had changed his mind on civil rights, but his reformed stance may not have been an entirely convincing spectacle for black voters, because, according to his biographer Randall B. Woods, "it is indisputable that J. William Fulbright was a racist": Woods, "Dixie's Dove: J. William Fulbright, the Vietnam War, and the American South," *Journal of Southern History*, 40 (August 1994), 538. See also Woods, *Fulbright: A Biography* (Cambridge: Cambridge University Press, 1995), 207–211. The historian Joan Hoff has mounted a spirited defense of President Nixon's civil rights record. She also argues, on the basis of an examination of the presidential tapes, that racist slurs were absent in the private conversations of what was, after all, a notoriously profane White House: Joan Hoff, *Nixon Reconsidered* (New York: Basic, 1994), 77–114, 319–320. For examples of the extensive academic discussions of the African American vote from the mid-1960s on, see Frances Fox Piven, *Why Americans Don't Vote* (New York: Pantheon, 1989), 144–148; and Chandler Davidson, "Minority Vote Dilution: An Overview," in Davidson, ed., *Minority Vote Dilution* (Washington, D.C.: Howard University Press, 1989), 3–9.

91. Small, *Covering Dissent*, 97.

92. Department of Defense report, "ARPA Troop Relations Project," circa March 1970, and memo, Dave Miller for Bud Krogh, Mar. 16, 1970, both in folder "Racial Unrest in the Military," WHCF, SMOF, LG, Box 124, NPM.

93. Fred Halstead, *GIs Speak Out Against the War: The Case of the Ft. Jackson 8: Interviews of Participants* (New York: Pathfinder Press, 1970), 9, 20.

94. Norman's paraphrase of his commanding officer's remarks in Terry, *Bloods*, 186–187.

95. *New York Times*, Feb. 2, 1970, and memo, Dave Miller for Bud Krogh, Mar. 16, 1970, both in folder "Racial Unrest in the Military," WHCF, SMOF, LG, Box 124, NPM. Corson's criticisms of the conduct of the Vietnam War, though not of its racial dimensions, appear in his book *The Armies of Ignorance: The Rise of the American Intelligence Empire* (New York: Dial, 1977), 399–402, 406–409.

96. For a thoughtful treatment of this problem, see Jon Nordheimer's account of Congressional Medal of Honor winner Dwight Johnson. Unable to readapt to the racial inequalities back home, Johnson was shot dead attempting an armed robbery of a grocery store: Nordheimer, "From Dakto to Detroit: Death of Troubled Hero," *New York Times*, May 25, 1971. Compare the story of Eldson McGhee, too poor to go to college, wounded, drugged up, criminalized, and radicalized in Vietnam, who ended up a self-educated ex-con, as related in MacPherson, *Haunted Generation*, 552–558.

97. *Protest the Jailing of Walter Collins and the Situation of Black Draft Resisters* (pamphlet, Louisville, Ky.: Southern Conference Education Fund, 1970) and *An Enemy of the People: How the Draft Is Used to Stop Movement for Social Change* (pamphlet, Louisville, Ky.: Southern Conference Education Fund, 1970), both in folder "Situation of Black Draft Resisters," WHCF, SMOF, LG, Box 18, NPM. A left-wing civil rights organization founded in the 1930s, the Southern Conference Education Fund had enjoyed the support of Eleanor Roosevelt and, in the 1960s, cooperated with SNCC: Carson, *In Struggle*, 51. The SCEF cited the following examples of black radicals persecuted through the draft system: Cleveland Sellers (SNCC's program secretary, sentenced to five years in prison in April 1968), Fred Brooks (a student leader who went into exile after being sentenced to four years in March 1968), Raymond DuVernay (appealed the decision of his all-white Louisiana draft board to the Supreme Court, lost, and went to prison), Eddie Oquendo (Youth Against War and Fascism, went to prison after losing in the Supreme Court), J. O. Sumrall, Jr. (a Mississippi civil rights worker who went into exile after the Supreme Court refused to hear his case), Michael Simmons (sentenced both for draft refusal and for protesting against his induction in August 1966; ten of his fellow SNCC workers in Atlanta, Ga., were also imprisoned on charges arising from their participation in the Simmons induction protest demonstration), Mickey Booth (a SNCC leader in Memphis charged with perjury during his earlier trial for refusing to accept the draft, in which the jury had acquitted him), and Muhammad Ali (sentenced to five years after running foul of the Louisville, Ky., draft

board): *Black Draft Resisters: Does Anybody Care? A Fact Sheet* (Louisville, Ky.: Southern Conference Education Fund, 1970), in folder "Situation of Black Draft Resisters," WHCF, SMOF, LG, Box 18, NPM.

98. Memo, "Response to Black Caucus Recommendations and Comments," Laird for Garment, Apr. 17, 1971, folder "Black Caucus—Report and Review," WHCF, SMOF, LG, Box 47, NPM.

99. Eric Joyce, *Arms and the Man—Renewing the Armed Services* (London: Fabian Society, 1997), 9, 10, 15; Appy, *Working-Class War*, 19. James Westheider believes that, over the course of the war, black battle mortalities were 30 percent higher than the overall figure for U.S. combat forces in Vietnam: Westheider, *Fighting on Two Fronts*, 13.

100. According to Doris K. Reed, a research associate at the Southern Regional Council (a privately financed liberal foundation based in Atlanta, Ga.), as of March 1969 "Negro combat deaths" since 1961 were 13.3 percent of the total: Reed to Gwendolyn Patton of the National Association of Black Students, Oct. 23, 1969, folder "Vietnam 1969," Box 203, EWB. Tables produced by the Office of the Deputy Assistant Secretary of Defense, Equal Opportunity, do not really uphold the view that racial imbalances had disappeared by the later stages of the war. On March 31, 1971, African Americans composed 11.1 percent of the enlisted men in the armed forces but only 2.2 percent of the officers; they still made up 11.2 percent of the armed forces in Vietnam, and, in the war to date, they accounted for 5,570 of the 44,888 killed in action, or 12.4 percent. The tables are in Morris J. Macgregor and Bernard C. Nalty, eds., *Blacks in the United States Forces: Basic Documents*, vol. 13, *Equal Treatment and Opportunity: The McNamara Doctrine* (Wilmington, Del.: Scholarly Resources, 1977), 439.

101. Roy Wilkins's calculation cited in Nick Thimmesch, "Black Progress Increases with Less Fanfare," Newsday/Los Angeles Times syndicated column, July 24, 1971, in folder "Black Congressmen," WHCF, SMOF, LG, Box 49, NPM; Milton D. Morris, "Black Electoral Participation and the Distribution of Public Benefits," in Davidson, *Minority Vote Dilution*, 274.

102. Robert Singh, *The Congressional Black Caucus: Racial Politics in the U.S. Congress* (Thousand Oaks, Calif.: Sage, 1998), 55.

103. Robert S. Singh, "The Congressional Black Caucus: Representation and Policy-Making in the United States Congress, 1971–1990" (D.Phil. diss., Oxford University, 1993), 371–372.

104. *Philadelphia Inquirer*, Feb. 3, 1971; *Washington Post*, Mar. 26, 27, 1971, and subsequently (the story of sixty demands was still running in the

Post and the *Star* at the end of May); memo, Leonard Garment for secretary of defense, Apr. 8, 1971, enclosing Foreign Policy Recommendation 1 and the Black Caucus comments on it, in folder "Black Caucus—Report and Review," WHCF, SMOF, LG, Box 47, NPM; transcript, NBC, Meet the Press, May 23, 1971, in folder "Black Caucus—Spring '71, Report and Review," WHCF, SMOF, LG, Box 48, NPM.

105. Charles C. Diggs, Jr. (as chair, Congressional Black Caucus), to president, Apr. 5, 1971, in folder "Black Caucus—Report and Review," WHCF, SMOF, LG, Box 47, NPM.

106. W. J. Rorabaugh, *Berkeley at War: The 1960s* (Oxford: Oxford University Press, 1989), 166; Thimmesch, "Black Progress"; Carol M. Swain, *Black Faces, Black Interests: The Representation of African Americans in Congress* (Cambridge: Harvard University Press, 1993), 134.

107. To Manning Marable, Dellums was "the most articulate opponent of the U.S. war effort, black or white": Marable, *Race, Reform, and Rebellion: The Second Reconstruction in Black America, 1945–1990* (London: Macmillan, 1991), 101.

108. The quotation is from Guenter Lewy, *America in Vietnam* (Oxford: Oxford University Press, 1978), 299, 317. See also Rorabaugh, *Berkeley at War*, 75; Anderson, *Movement*, 297, 369; Citizens Commission of Inquiry, ed., *The Dellums Committee Hearings on War Crimes in Vietnam: An Inquiry into Command Responsibilities in Southeast Asia* (New York: Vintage, 1972), viii, 3. Further information is from Bertrand Russell, *War Crimes in Vietnam* (London: Allen and Unwin, 1967); and two papers delivered at the biennial conference of the European Association for American Studies in 1994: Sylvia A. Ellis, "British Opposition to the Vietnam War, 1964–68," and Kim Salomon, "The Great Satan: The Anti-Vietnam-War Movement in Sweden and Protests Against the United States."

109. Donald C. Bacon, Roger H. Davidson, and Morton Keller, eds., *The Encyclopedia of the United States Congress*, 4 vols. (New York: Simon and Schuster, 1995), I, 175. Robert Singh argues that the Congressional Black Caucus did not, in fact, have a major impact. Debating the issue over lunch in the Kalpna Restaurant in Edinburgh on Oct. 23, 1997, the author suggested that the caucus may have enjoyed a honeymoon period during which the White House afforded it provisional respect, as in the case of newly enfranchised women in the early 1920s, but Singh believes that Nixon could not afford this luxury, because of the overriding problem of the Wallace movement in the South.

110. Press release, National Black Silent Majority Committee, July 6, 1970, Nixon to Clay J. Claiborne, Oct. 7, 1970, unsigned Nixon life

membership card, National Republican Congressional Committee, *Black Leadership in the Nixon Administration*, n.d., all in folder "National Black Silent Majority," WHCF, SMOF, CC, Box 88, NPM.

111. "Wall Street" (undated text of speech) in file "1970 Campaign," Box 1, JLB. In the concluding stages of his campaign, Buckley appealed for Jewish support on the basis of his support for Israel and his hostility to the "anti-semitic," "New Left" Black Panther Party. He admitted he still had little support in the black community, which misunderstood conservatism for "semantic" reasons, but in a last-minute appeal promised to appoint a black staff liaison officer if elected: *New York Times*, Oct. 30, 1970; and advertisement by Concerned Citizens for Buckley, *New York Times* on the same day and *Long Island Press*, Oct. 31, 1970.

112. Garment preferred to be compared with another Democratic gray eminence and proudly recalled that Nixon called him the "Clark Clifford of the Republican Party." See Leonard Garment, *Crazy Rhythm: My Journey from Brooklyn, Jazz, and Wall Street to Nixon's White House, Watergate, and Beyond . . .* (New York: Times Books / Random House, 1997), 146, 149, 151, 156. Garment played a role in Nixon's second term, too. In relation to Watergate, he advised the beleaguered president to come clean, then urged him to resign, and finally pressured the incoming president, Gerald Ford, to pardon the resigning chief executive: Stephen E. Ambrose, *Nixon: Ruin and Recovery, 1973–1990* (New York: Touchstone, 1991), 118, 143, 264, 278, 455. Further biographical details are from the finding aid for the Leonard Garment materials in SMOF, WHCF, NPM; and from Ambrose, *Nixon: The Triumph*, 82.

113. Memo, Leonard Garment for the President, Nov. 23, 1970, and (with a positive response) memo, John Erlichman for Len Garment, Dec. 16, 1970, both in Box 6, LGP.

114. Hoff, *Nixon Reconsidered*, 92–93; Thimmesch, "Black Progress"; administration response to Black Caucus recommendation 1 under the heading "Justice and Civil Rights / Veterans's Affairs," and memo, Shultz for the president, May 15, 1971, both in folder "Black Caucus I," WHCF, SMOF, LG, Box 46, NPM; report (undated but from early 1971 on the basis of internal evidence) marked "VA Internal," in folder "Black Congressmen," WHCF, SMOF, LG, Box 49, NPM.

115. Brooke quoted in the *Boston Record-American*, Mar. 25, 1967.

116. Brooke to the Rev. James R. Bruno, May 17, 1971, in folder "Vietnam 1971," Box 210, and a 1972 compilation, "Record of Senator Edward W. Brooke on Vietnam," in folder "Vietnam Position 71–73," Box 497, both in EWB.

117. Memo, W. Richard Howard for Steve Karalekas, Sept. 29, 1972, in folder "Sen. Edward Brooke, Mass.," WHCF, SMOF, CC, Box 40, NPM.

118. Memo, Colson for H. R. Haldeman, Mar. 17, 1971, and memo, Colson for Larry Higby, Apr. 16, 1971, enclosing a photocopy of the *Congressional Record* for Apr. 15, 1971, in folder "Meeting w. Sen. Brooke, May 14, 1971," WHCF, SMOF, CC, Box 23, NPM.

119. Transcript, prepared by the University of Massachusetts, of Brooke speech, n.d., enclosed with memo, Howard A. Cohen for Colson, May 30, 1972, with remark scribbled over indecipherable initials, in folder "Sen. Edward Brooke, Mass.," WHCF, SMOF, CC, Box 40, NPM.

120. "Black Veterans Issue Paper," n.d., and McGovern press release "Vietnamization and Asian Lives," May 25, 1972, both in folder "Vietnam: Miscellany—I," Box 25, McG, published with permission of Princeton University Library.

121. Woods's paraphrase of Fulbright's view, based on separate interviews with Dean Rusk and Walt Rostow: Woods, "Dixie's Dove," 537.

122. Hanoi radio quoted in Leonard Marks, comp., "War Protests in U.S. Encourage Hanoi to Reject Peace-Talk Proposals," enclosed with memo, Walt Rostow for president, Nov. 17, 1967, in folder "Vietnam 7A 8/67–9/68," Country File, Vietnam, NSF, Box 97, WHCF, LBJ.

123. Parimal Kumar Das, *India and the Vietnam War* (New Delhi: Young Asia Publications, 1972), vi.

124. Thomas B. Morgan, *The Anti-Americans* (London: Michael Joseph, 1967), 9–10; Marks, "War Protests."

125. Excerpt from *Manchester Guardian*, May 7, 1970, in "Selected Reactions of Foreign Press to Vietnam War," in folder "World Reaction," in Box 2 of three unprocessed boxes marked "Vietnam," McG.

126. Joseph M. Siracusa and Yeong-Han Cheong, *America's Australia, Australia's America: A Guide to Issues and References* (Claremont, Calif.: Regine, 1997), 54–55; Salomon, "Anti-Vietnam War Movement in Sweden."

CHAPTER FIVE Women

1. See Helen Laville, " 'A Woman's Place Is in the Cold War': American Women's Organizations and International Relations" (Ph.D. diss., University of Nottingham, 1998); and Laville, "The Committee of Correspondence-CIA Funding of Women's Groups, 1952–1967," *Intelligence and National Security*, 12 (January 1997), 104–121. The very notion of mi-

nority status was repugnant to some women. In the debate on the Civil Rights Act of 1964, Congresswoman Frances Bolton (Rep., Ohio) bridled at and rejected its sponsor's categorization of women as a "minority" when, in fact, they outnumbered men in the population by 2.5 million: Irving Bernstein, *Guns or Butter: The Presidency of Lyndon Johnson* (New York: Oxford University Press, 1996), 54.

The term *minority* meant different things to different people. When the prowar journalist Marguerite Higgins described her book *Our Vietnam Nightmare* (New York: Harper, 1965) as a "minority report" on the war, she was thinking not as a feminist but as a maverick who happened to be a woman (the phrase "minority report" is from the dust jacket; thus it may not have been coined by Higgins but would presumably have had her approval). Higgins's book was the only popular journalistic account supportive of the war. Four other prominent female journalists were Gloria Emerson, Frances Fitzgerald, Mary McCarthy, and Martha Gellhorn. Freelance writers, they were more critical of the war than Higgins was, although, like her, they tended to avoid explicitly feminist interpretations. See Gloria Emerson, *Winners and Losers: Battles, Retreats, Gains, Losses, and Ruins from a Long War* (New York: Random House, 1977); Frances Fitzgerald, *Fire in the Lake: The Vietnamese and Americans in Vietnam* (Boston: Little, Brown, 1972); Mary McCarthy, *Hanoi* (London: Weidenfeld and Nicolson, 1968); Martha Gellhorn, *A New Kind of War* (Manchester, England: Manchester Guardian and Evening News, 1966); and, for commentary, David W. Levy, *The Debate over Vietnam* (Baltimore, Md.: Johns Hopkins University Press, 1991), 89–90.

2. Gunnar Myrdal, "Appendix 5: A Parallel to the Negro Problem," in Myrdal, *An American Dilemma: The Negro Problem in Modern Democracy*, 2 vols. (New York: Harper, 1944), II, 1073, 1078. The author of a more recent book, too, equates women with ethnic and racial "minorities": James E. Westheider, *Fighting on Two Fronts: African Americans and the Vietnam War* (New York: New York University Press, 1997), 7.

3. Shirley Chisholm, *Unbought and Unbossed* (Boston: Houghton Mifflin, 1970), xii.

4. The emphasis is added but is consistent with McCarthy's character critique: Mary McCarthy, *The Group* (London: Weidenfeld and Nicolson, 1963), 242.

5. This myth is discussed in Rhodri Jeffreys-Jones, *Changing Differences: Women and the Shaping of American Foreign Policy, 1917–1994* (New Brunswick, N.J.: Rutgers University Press, 1995).

6. In a periodization of the antifeminist backlash, Susan Faludi pre-

sents the 1970s as a decade of remission: Faludi, *Backlash: The Undeclared War Against American Women* (New York: Doubleday, 1991), 55.

7. Transcript, India Edwards oral history interview, Feb. 4, 1969, by Joe B. Franz, pp. 12, 34, LBJ. See also figures for the Eighty-seventh and Ninety-first Congresses in Mildred Amer, comp., *Women in the United States Congress* (Washington, D.C.: Congressional Research Service, 1991), 67; Homer L. Calkin, *Women in the Department of State: Their Role in Foreign Affairs* (Washington, D.C.: Department of State, 1977), 150; and Nancy E. McGlen and Meredith Reid Sarkees, *Women in Foreign Policy: The Insiders* (New York: Routledge, 1993), 76.

8. Blanche Linden-Ward and Carol Hurd Green, *Changing the Future: American Women in the 1960s* (New York: Twayne, 1993), 134, 137.

9. Kathryn Marshall, *In the Combat Zone: An Oral History of American Women in Vietnam, 1966–1975* (Boston: Little, Brown, 1987), 405; Joe P. Dunn, "The Vietnam War and Women," in Dunn, *Teaching the Vietnam War: Resources and Assessments* (Los Angeles: Center for the Study of Armament and Disarmament, 1990), 47.

10. See the account given by a prominent spokeswoman for veteran nurses, Rose Sandecki: "A Nurse's View," in Walter Capps, ed., *The Vietnam Reader* (New York: Routledge, 1991), 227. Cf Dunn, "Vietnam War and Women," 51–52.

11. Adams in Marshall, *Oral History*, 220.

12. Dullea quoted in Jean Bethke Elshtein, *Women and War* (Brighton: Harvester, 1987), 10. Reliable information on the women who served in Vietnam is scarce. Linden-War and Green do offer the observation that "feminism had little impact on the 'soldiers in skirts,' who were often from working-class backgrounds, and had chosen service to escape from limited opportunities at home," circumstances that inhibited their protest against the war: *Changing the Future*, 137. Another significant factor may be the number of military nurses who came from military families with a tradition of never questioning orders.

13. Virginia Elwood-Akers, *Women War Correspondents in the Vietnam War, 1961–1975* (Metuchen, N.J.: Scarecrow, 1988), 1, 7.

14. Higgins, *Nightmare*, 7, 278–288, 291; Elwood-Akers, *Women War Correspondents*, 17, 38.

15. Michael R. Beschloss, ed., *Taking Charge: The Johnson White House Tapes, 1963–1964* (New York: Simon and Schuster, 1997), 417.

16. Higgins, *Nightmare*, 170; Ngô Viñh Long, "Ngo Dinh Nhu," in Stanley I. Kutler, ed., *Encyclopedia of the Vietnam War* (New York: Charles Scribner's Sons, 1996), 359.

17. Undated letter, Madame Nhu to Luce, January 1964, and Luce to Nhu, Feb. 24, 1964, ACBL; Wilfrid Sheed, *Clare Boothe Luce* (New York: Dutton, 1982), 130.

18. *New York Times*, May 20, 1973.

19. "Don't Bring Flowers" (leaflet, Jan. 15, 1968), reproduced in *Vietnam Generation*, 1 (Summer–Fall 1989), 207.

20. Linden-Ward and Green, *Changing the Future*, 117–118; William H. Chafe, *The Paradox of Change: American Women in the Twentieth Century*, 48–51; Ruth B. Mandel, *In the Running: The New Woman Candidate* (Boston: Beacon, 1981), 137.

21. Douglas to Mrs. J. R. Illick, Aug. 10, 1965, telegram, Stuart to LBJ, Apr. 8, 1965, LBJ to Stuart, Apr. 12, 1965, Stuart to LBJ, July 30, 1965, all in folder "International Relations—Vietnam, 1965-66," in Container 1901, LWV.

22. Susan Lynn, *Progressive Women in Conservative Times: Racial Justice, Peace, and Feminism, 1945 to the 1960s* (New Brunswick, N.J.: Rutgers University Press, 1992), 171.

23. Mills to Mrs. S. W. Chilton, Mar. 8, 1966, in folder "International Relations—Vietnam, 1965–66," in Container 1901, LWV; Teska to Mrs. John Crossen, June 2, 1967, in folder "International Relations—Vietnam, 1965–67," Teska to Mrs. John Stoddard, Sept. 25, 1967, in folder "International Relations—Vietnam, 1967," Mrs. John A. Ahern (director and foreign policy chair, LWV) to Mrs. Rose Fajans, June 1, 1971, and Mrs. Mabel M. Long (organization coordinator, LWV) to Mrs. Albert B. Glaser, May 16, 1972, in folder "International Relations—Vietnam," all in Container 1902, LWV.

24. The following information on congresswomen is from Amer, *Women in Congress*, 53; *Women in Congress, 1917–1900* (Washington, D.C.: Office of the Historian, U.S. House of Representatives, 1991); and Donald C. Bacon et al., eds., *The Encyclopedia of the United States Congress*, 4 vols. (New York: Simon and Schuster, 1995).

25. Linden-Ward and Green, *Changing the Future*, 23.

26. The quotation is from the *Congressional Record*, Feb. 23, 1967, S2498; and the account is from Jeffreys-Jones, *Changing Differences*, 121–126.

27. On the Denver protest, see Terry F. Anderson, *The Movement and the Sixties: Protest in America from Greensboro to Wounded Knee* (New York: Oxford University Press, 1995), 166. On women's adoption and abandonment of anti-inflationary principles in foreign policy, see Jeffreys-Jones, *Changing Differences*, chaps. 3 and 6.

28. On Vietnamese women, see Ellen Baker, "Prostitution," and Sandra C. Taylor, "Women, Vietnamese," in Kutler, *Encyclopedia of the Vietnam War.* According to Arlen Eisen, Vietnamese women "came to symbolize not only the strength of national liberation movements, but also the potential of women": Eisen, *Women and Revolution in Vietnam* (London: Zed, 1984), 3. Vietnamese war literature brings out graphically the role of women on the communist side. Duong Thu Huong, author of *Novel Without a Name* (London: Pan, 1995), based her novel on her seven-year ordeal on the front line for North Vietnam. Women feature prominently in *The Sorrow of War* (London: Minerva, 1994) by the (male) novelist Bao Ninh, one of only ten survivors of the Glorious Twenty-seventh Youth Brigade, which went to war in the communist cause in 1969.

29. For a variety of evidence on male domination and chauvinism in the peace movement, see Lynn, *Progressive Women*, 170–171 (on the Quakers); Anderson, *Movement*, 314–315; and W. J. Rorabaugh, *Berkeley at War: The 1960s* (New York: Oxford University Press, 1989), 132. On Hayden, see Tom Hayden, *Reunion: A Memoir* (New York: Random House, 1988), 96; Myra MacPherson, *Long Time Passing: Vietnam and the Haunted Generation* (New York: Doubleday, 1984), 467; Tom Wells, *The War Within: America's Battle over Vietnam* (Berkeley: University of California Press, 1994), 550. According to Amy Swerdlow, male chauvinism continues to affect the attitudes of historians of the sixties, who tend to belittle the women's peace movement: Swerdlow, *Women Strike for Peace: Traditional Motherhood and Radical Politics in the 1960s* (Chicago: University of Chicago Press, 1993), 10, 12, 245–246*n*10. Alice Echols levels a similar charge, also noting that the New Left was more tolerant of black radicals than of women and that women were initially used as "sexual bait" in the G.I. coffeehouse movement: Echols, " 'Women Power' and Women's Liberation: Exploring the Relationship Between the Antiwar Movement and the Women's Liberation Movement," in Melvin Small and William D. Hoover, eds., *Give Peace a Chance: Exploring the Vietnam Antiwar Movement: Essays from the Charles DeBenedetti Memorial Conference* (Syracuse: Syracuse University Press, 1992), 171, 173, 178.

30. Recollection of Leslie Cagan, "Women and the Anti-Draft Movement," *Radical America*, 14 (May 1980), 9.

31. LBJ quoted in Michael Kimmel, *Manhood in America: A Cultural History* (New York: Free Press, 1996), 270. For further evidence of LBJ's attitude toward women, see Susan M. Hartmann, "Women's Issues and the Johnson Administration," in Robert A. Divine, ed., *The Johnson Years*,

vol. 3: *LBJ at Home and Abroad* (Lawrence: University Press of Kansas, 1994), 56. On American officers in Vietnam, see Sandecki, "Nurse's View," 224.

32. Norman Mailer, *The Armies of the Night* (New York: Penguin, 1994 [1968]), 276–277. Mailer stabbed his first wife, Adele, with a penknife; his inebriety and violence are recorded in Adele Mailer, *The Last Party: Scenes from My Life with Norman Mailer* (New York: Barricade, 1997).

33. Joan Baez, *And a Voice to Sing With: A Memoir* (London: Century, 1988), 152, 254.

34. Hayden, *Reunion*, xix, 96.

35. Anna Louise Strong wrote an early attack on the Southeast Asia policy of the United States: Strong, *Cash and Violence in Laos and Vietnam* (New York: Mainstream, 1962). "Fuck the Army" was the acronymically derived alternative title for the alternative newspaper *Fun, Travel, and Adventure.* There was also a G.I. coffeehouse movement against the war that affected Army women. Helga Alice Herz set herself alight on March 16, 1965, to protest the bombing of North Vietnam. In 1965 the journalist Carol Brightman started the thrice-annual publication of her antiwar *Viet Report*, with 12,000 paid subscriptions and a printrun of 80,000. See Linden-Ward and Green, *Changing the Future*, 137, 168.

36. Frances Fox Piven and Richard A. Cloward, *Poor People's Movements: Why They Succeed, How They Fail* (New York: Pantheon, 1977), xii; Melvin Small, *Covering Dissent: The Media and the Anti–Vietnam War Movement* (New Brunswick, N.J.: Rutgers University Press, 1994), 8, 35. Piven was a Columbia University political scientist who had climbed through a window to help occupy the Mathematics Building in the strike of 1968: Hayden, *Reunion*, photo on p. 236 ff.

37. Author's interview with Amy Swerdlow, Nov. 2, 1991.

38. Swerdlow, *Women Strike for Peace*, 3, 95–96; Charles DeBenedetti, *An American Ordeal: The Antiwar Movement of the Vietnam Era* (Syracuse, N.Y.: Syracuse University Press, 1990), 54.

39. Anderson, *Movement*, 167; Linden-Ward and Green, *Changing the Future*, 167–169.

40. The press appears to have exaggerated the numbers involved in early WSP protests; see Swerdlow, *Women Strike for Peace*, 247*nn*1&4.

41. Linden-Ward and Green, *Changing the Future*, 168.

42. Petition, enclosed with memo, Ned to Dick, May 6, 1966, Box 86, JKJ.

43. Author's interview with Bella Abzug, Nov. 1, 1991. For an appraisal of Abzug in relation to foreign policy, including the Vietnam War, see Jeffreys-Jones, *Changing Differences*, chap. 8.

44. Swerdlow, *Women Strike for Peace*, 150–153.

45. Linden-Ward and Green, *Changing the Future*, 172; Harriet Hyman Alonso, *Peace as a Woman's Issue: A History of the U.S. Movement for World Peace and Women's Rights* (Syracuse, N.Y.: Syracuse University Press, 1993), 216–217.

46. Linden-Ward and Green, *Changing the Future*, 172; Alonso, *Peace as a Woman's Issue*, 218; *Philadelphia Evening Bulletin*, Mar. 9, 1971.

47. *Philadelphia Evening Bulletin*, Mar. 9, 1971; and materials in BSA.

48. Linden-Ward and Green, *Changing the Future*, 172; Alonso, *Peace as a Woman's Issue*, 216. All the women listed were well-known stage/screen/television personalities and were included in *Who's Who in America*. McCambridge and Woodward had won Academy Awards, and Winters an Emmy.

49. Baez, *Voice to Sing With*, 24, 69, 146; DeBenedetti, *American Ordeal*, 207.

50. John Ranelagh, *The Agency: The Rise and Decline of the CIA—From Wild Bill Donovan to William Casey* (New York: Simon and Schuster, 1986), 223.

51. McCarthy, *Hanoi*, 88. See also Elwood-Akers, *Women War Correspondents*, 72, 105, 124–125; and Deborah A. Butler, *American Women Writers on Vietnam: Unheard Voices: A Selected Annotated Bibliography* (New York: Garland, 1990), 102.

52. Rankin quoted in Joan Hoff Wilson, "'Peace Is a Woman's Job . . .': Jeannette Rankin and American Foreign Policy: Her Lifework as a Pacifist," *Montana*, 30 (Spring 1980), 50. See also Wells, *War Within*, 228.

53. Linden-Ward and Green, *Changing the Future*, 170; Echols, "Power and Liberation," 176.

54. Friedan quoted in Echols, "Power and Liberation," 176. See also Hoff Wilson, "Rankin," 52; and James Miller, *"Democracy Is in the Streets": From Port Huron to the Siege of Chicago* (Cambridge: Harvard University Press, 1994 [1987]), 257.

55. Alonso, *Peace as a Woman's Issue*, 223. See also Ruth Rosen, "The Day They Buried 'Traditional Motherhood': Women and the Politics of Peace Protest," *Vietnam Generation*, 1 (Summer–Fall, 1989), 209.

56. *Washington Sunday Star*, Jan. 21, 1968.

57. Kelly was the second of twenty-four supportive callers to the First Lady's office on Jan. 19, 1968: "[Log of] Telephone calls—Liz Carpen-

ter—January 19, 1968," in folder "Johnson, Lady Bird 9/13/67–1/29/68," EX PP 5, Box 63, WHCF, LBJ.

58. *Washington Sunday Star*, Jan. 21, 1968. See also Liz Carpenter in *Variety*, Jan. 24, 1968; and Mezzack, "Without Manners," 751–752.

59. Emphasis added. The caller was a Mrs. Remington from Bethesda, Md., the widow of an Army officer, the mother-in-law of a Navy officer, and the mother of an Air Force man: "[Log of] Telephone calls—Liz Carpenter—January 19, 1968," in folder "Johnson, Lady Bird 9/13/67–1/29/68," EX PP 5, Box 63, WHCF, LBJ.

60. Jack Kofoed in *Miami Herald*, Jan. 20, 1968.

61. Report by Les Carpenter in *Variety*, Jan. 24, 1968.

62. Representative George E. Brown, Jr. (Dem., Calif.), agreed with Kitt but not with her chosen venue; Representative Robert Kastenmeier (Dem., Wis.) agreed with both the sentiment and the location: *Washington Evening Star*, Jan. 20, 1968.

63. Levy, *Debate over Vietnam*, 109. As early as 1962, a survey of college students predicted that women would take a more assertive antiwar stance than men: DeBenedetti, *American Ordeal*, 55. Senator Jacob Javits's correspondence in January 1968 reveals more male than female letters against the war; on the other hand, women had not bothered to write to him on the subject at all in the past and were now doing so in increasing numbers: Box 96, JKJ.

64. Maureen Ryan, "The Other Side of Grief: American Women Writers and the Vietnam War," *Critique*, 36 (Fall 1994), 45; MacPherson, *Long Time Passing*, 461; Echols, "Power and Liberation," 171.

65. Hartmann, "Women's Issues," 63.

66. Edwards interview, p. 38.

67. Paul K. Conkin, *Big Daddy from the Padernales: Lyndon Baines Johnson* (Boston: Twayne, 1986), 180; emphases added. Irving Bernstein's account of social reform during Johnson's presidency is sympathetic, but he finds little to say about women: Bernstein, *Guns or Butter*, 52–55. Hugh Davis Graham and Susan Hartmann both suggest that the legacy of the Johnson administration was less legislative achievement than a raised level of women's expectations: Graham, *Civil Rights and the Presidency: Race and Gender in American Politics, 1960–1972* (New York: Oxford University Press, 1992), 7; Hartmann, "Women's Issues," 75.

68. Transcript, Patricia Roberts Harris oral history interview, May 19, 1969, by Steve Goodell, p. 40, LBJ. Harris may have been less than happy with America, but she also found that male chauvinism was rampant in European diplomatic circles.

69. On FDR's reluctance to meet the WILPF in the spring of 1933, see Jeffreys-Jones, *Changing Differences*, 72. Two extenuating arguments might be made: FDR heard rather than listened to the WILPF, although he went along with their neutrality campaign in the short term; and LBJ had a war on, which FDR did not, so listening to peace lobbyists might have sent out the wrong signal to American soldiers and communist negotiators.

70. Cooper to Mrs. Philip Good, July 2, 1965, memo, Perry Barber for Valenti, July 23, 1965, and memo, Valenti for Bundy, July 23, 1965, all in WHCF, Name File, Women's, Box 453, LBJ.

71. Mezzack, "Without Manners," 755–756. On Johnson's affairs, see Hartmann, "Women's Issues," 56.

72. See Stephen Kneeshaw, "Voices from Vietnam: The New Literature from America's Longest War," *Teaching History*, 13, i (1988), 25–26.

73. Fitzgerald, *Fire in the Lake;* Elwood-Akers, *Women War Correspondents*, 197.

74. Hoff Wilson, "Rankin," 52.

75. Hayden's transformation is indicated by the title of his memoir, *Reunion*. See also DeBenedetti, *American Ordeal*, 337: Hayden "in a sense had come back to America."

76. DeBenedetti, *American Ordeal*, 338; MacPherson, *Long Time Passing*, 466.

77. MacPherson, *Long Time Passing*, 466. The discussion group was VWAR-L on LISTSERV@UBVM.BITNET.

78. Marvin quoted in "Activity Cues: An Emergency Convocation to End the War," Washington, D.C., May 10–11, 1972, and memo, Olyn Margolin for Eli Fox, June 2, 1972, both in folder "Vietnam, 1972, n.d.," NCJW; copy of telegram, Rabbi Arthur L. Lelyveld to President, Jan. 8, 1968, enclosed with memo, Bromley Smith for Walt Rostow, Jan. 8, 1968, folder "Public Relations Activities (2 of 2)," Country File, Vietnam, NSF, Box 100, WHCF, LBJ.

79. Seven polls conducted by Louis Harris and Associates for various clients, question IDs 70VSM2 RM09D, 71VASL R17A, 72VS2 R14A20, 72VS1 R14B, 72VS1 R14C, 72VS2 R15C02, and 72VS1 R26A, all accessed via the DIALOG/POLL Internet facility, Public Opinion Online 1940–93.

80. The McGovern count was up to the point where both genders had reached a minimum of 25 letters, yielding 25 female doves and 46 male, 25 female hawks and 60 male. The Javits sex-differentiated count in 1968 was conducted on a similar basis: 25 female and 37 male in an

overwhelmingly antiwar bag (in a response to the *New York Times* in 1967, Javits had estimated that over a period of six months his mail ran fifty to one against the Vietnam War). An entire folder in the Smith correspondence contained 54 female and 76 male writers on Vietnam (only a portion of the Smith letters was preserved for the Smith Library in Skowhegan, Maine, and the basis of selection is unknown). The Abzug percentage is based on a small number of cards, 11 female and 6 male, but the proportion is similar to that in the case of her replies to letters in 1974 complaining about excessive levels of military expenditure: 14 to women and 7 to men.

Sources: Letters (first 156 examined) in folder "Vietnam Speech—pro McG.," and letters (first legible 85 examined) in folder "Hawk letters out-of-state Vietnam speech," both Accession No. 7183482, Box 7, McG; 17 "Dear Congressman" standard antiwar cards sent to Bella Abzug in 1971, Box 499, and Abzug to Michele Mooney, Sept. 4, 1974, and 20 similar letters (totals: 14 female, 7 male), Box 620, all in BSA; absence of female correspondents in Box 85, and letters (first 62 examined), in folder "Vietnam—1968," together with reply to *New York Times* questionnaire sent by John Finney and William M. Blair of the Washington Bureau of the *New York Times*, Sept. 29, 1969, in folder "Vietnam—1967," all in Box 86, JKJ; letters (first 130 examined, consisting of just over one-fourth of the total retained in Skowhegan) in the Vietnam/Cambodia files, MCS.

81. Anderson, *Movement*, 369. See also Stephen E. Ambrose, *Nixon: The Triumph of a Politician, 1962–1972* (New York: Simon and Schuster, 1989), 396.

82. *Washington Post*, Dec. 3, 1970.

83. Joan Michel, "For Women's Votes or Rights?" *Middletown Times Herald-Record*, Aug. 23, 1970; Ellen Fleysher, "Gals Deny Political Suitors," *New York News*, Oct. 30, 1970; Nancy Hartnagel and Mary E. Stoll, "Beauty Shops Polled: Rocky-Buckley 'Wave,' " *Schenectady Union-Star*, Oct. 30, 1970. Apparently, President Nixon had a high regard for Buckley's inspirational appeal with women, requesting at one stage that he be dispatched to a women's meeting to "upstage" his political rival Nelson Rockefeller: Haldeman paraphrase of Nixon in H. R. Haldeman Diary, CD-ROM version (Santa Monica, Calif.: Sony Imagesoft, 1994), Jan. 16, 1971.

84. Swerdlow, *Women Strike for Peace*, 153–154.

85. Bella Abzug, *Gender Gap: Bella Abzug's Guide to Political Power for American Women* (Boston: Houghton Mifflin, 1984), 29.

86. In 1972 the House adopted the Equal Rights Amendment by a vote of 354 to 23, and the Senate by a vote of 84 to 8, but the states failed

to ratify it with the required three-fourths majority by the deadline of June 1982. For a list of further measures and the Abzug quotation, see Anderson, *Movement*, 405.

87. Jeffreys-Jones, *Changing Differences*, 138.

88. Abzug, *Gender Gap*, 163.

89. Transcript, ABC interviews with five political guests, including Shirley Chisholm, June 4, 1972, folder "Vietnam: Miscellany 1972—I," Box 25, McG; H. Bruce Franklin, *M.I.A., or, Mythmaking in America* (New York: Lawrence Hill, 1992), 13–14, 74, 93–95.

90. Haldeman Diary, CD-ROM, Apr. 17, 1969.

91. Memo, Moynihan for the president, Aug. 20, 1969, enclosed with memo, "Female Equality," Erlichman for the president, Sept. 29, 1969, WHCF, Subject Files, Human Rights, folder "[Ex] HU2-5 Women. Beginning—12/31/69," Box 2, NPM.

92. Joan Hoff, *Nixon Reconsidered* (New York: Basic, 1994), 100–101; memo, "The Feminine Revolution," Hauser for Safire, Mar. 2, 1970, WHCF, Subject Files, Human Rights, folder "[Ex] HU2-5 Women. Beginning—12/31/69," Box 2, NPM.

93. Memo, Hauser for President, Apr. 12, 1971, enclosed with memo, Hauser for Rose Mary Woods (Nixon's secretary), Apr. 12, 1971, WHCF, PPF, Rose Mary Woods, Name File, Box 18, NPM. Mainly because of the legal repercussions of Watergate, there have been heavy withdrawals of documents from the Rose Mary Woods files. The full text of the Hauser-Nixon memo just cited is one such casualty—its contents can only be guessed at from Hauser's cover note to Woods and from its title in the archive inventory. Also, at the time of my research (July 1995), the following boxes from the H. R. Haldeman files, SMOF, were among those that had been "withdrawn for review" in connection with the continuing Nixon estate lawsuits: Box 299, "1972 Campaign: Minorities and Affirmative Action"; Box 302, "Women and the Republican Party"; and Boxes 307 and 317, "Women and the '72 Campaign."

94. Memo, Ken Cole for Roy Morey, Apr. 18, 1972, WHCF, Subject Files, Human Rights, folder "[Ex] HU2-5 women 4/1/72–12/31/72," Box 2, NPM.

95. *Washington Post*, Dec. 3, 1970.

96. Quotations from, respectively, Hoff, *Nixon Reconsidered*, 102; Kissinger interview with the journalist Oriana Fallacci, early 1970s, text in Box 275, BSA; Jeannette Smyth (quoting Lucy Winchester on Kissinger's behavior in the early months of the first Nixon administration), "Guests Who's Coming to Dinner," *Washington Post*, Dec. 4, 1973.

97. Agnew quoted in Abzug, *Gender Gap*, 26; Nixon quoted and translated by Anderson in *Washington Post*, Dec. 3, 1970. Nixon was opposed to women's liberation and liked the idea of women "as wives and mothers," but also favored an enhanced role for them in government, according to Haldeman's paraphrase of a presidential address to a Girls Nation group: Haldeman Diary, CD-ROM, Aug. 30, 1971.

98. This theme is expounded in Robert Mason, "The New American Majority: The Challenge to Democratic Dominance, 1969-1977" (D.Litt. diss., Oxford University, 1997). But Mason argues that in the end Nixon failed to carry the Republican Party and, in 1972, ran for reelection as a president seeking an American majority, as distinct from a Republican majority.

99. "Dick Nixon" to Claire Giannini Hoffman, Feb. 11, 1969, and memo, "Female Equality," Erlichman for the president, Sept. 29, 1969, both in WHCF, Subject Files, Human Rights, folder "[Ex] HU2-5 Women. Beginning—12/31/69," Box 2, NPM.

100. Haldeman Diary, CD-ROM, Sept. 8, 1970, Jan. 10, 1971, paraphrasing Nixon, Feb. 8, 1971, Feb. 23, 1971, July 6, 1972.

101. Hoff, *Nixon Reconsidered*, 92–93, 99, 102, 110, 113; Graham, *Civil Rights and the Presidency*, 5.

102. Franklin, *M.I.A.*, 51–53. Stockdale later received the Medal of Honor. In 1992 he ran for the vice presidency on Ross Perot's independent ticket.

103. Memo, Finch for the president, Apr. 12, 1971, WHCF, POF, folder "April 1 thru 15, 1971," President's Handwriting, Box 10, NPM. In June 1970, Finch had resigned as secretary of health, education, and welfare because Nixon was dragging his feet in securing the desegregation of schools in the South: Ambrose, *Nixon*, 365.

104. Nixon quoted in Ambrose, *Nixon*, 470. In the 1972 presidential campaign, the Nixon staffers John D. Erlichman and Barbara Franklin organized special foreign-policy briefings for women appointees. The implication is that they were a potential loyalty risk because of their utter ignorance: Ehrlichman for [blank—template for "women employees"], Jan. 31, 1972, WHCF, Subject Files, Human Rights, folder "[Ex] HU2-5 Women. 1/1/72–3/31/72," Box 2, and memo, Barbara Franklin, for women employees, Oct. 3, 1972, WHCF, PPF, Rose Mary Woods, Name File, Box 18, both in NPM.

105. Kissinger quoted in Robert D. Schulzinger, *Henry Kissinger: Doctor of Diplomacy* (New York: Columbia University Press, 1989), 113.

106. George S. McGovern, *An American Journey: The Presidential*

Campaign Speeches of George McGovern (New York: Random House, 1974), 31. See also Alan Clem, "The Democratic Minority: George McGovern," in Herbert T. Hoover and Larry J. Zimmerman, eds., *South Dakota Leaders: From Pierre Chouteau, Jr., to Oscar Howe* (Vermillion: University of South Dakota Press, 1989), 315.

107. "Response by Senator George McGovern, Apr. 7, 1972, to WILPF Questionnaire," in folder "Vietnam Miscellaneous 1972," Box 26, McG; Swerdlow, *Women Strike for Peace*, 156.

108. McGovern, *American Journey*, 44.

109. Swerdlow, *Women Strike for Peace*, 156; Jeane Kirkpatrick, *The New Presidential Elite: Men and Women in National Politics* (New York: Russell Sage Foundation, 1976), 6, 430.

110. See Jeffreys-Jones, *Changing Differences*, 127–129.

111. Susan Tolchin and Martin Tolchin, *Clout: Woman Power and Politics* (New York: Coward, McCann, and Geoghegan, 1974), 54–56. See also Clem, "Democratic Minority," 325; and Theodore H. White, *The Making of the President 1972* (London: Jonathan Cape, 1974), 38.

112. Hoover, however, concentrated much more heavily on women, arguing that higher tariffs did not mean higher prices and that the Republicans were the party of peace: see Jeffreys-Jones, *Changing Differences*, 50–64.

113. Transcript of McGovern television address, Nov. 3, 1972, in folder "United Auto Workers 1972," Box 24, McG, published with permission of Princeton University Library; McGovern, *American Journey*, 212.

114. This was the Gallup estimate. According to the Harvard political scientist Ethel Klein, 38 percent of women's votes went to McGovern, compared with 32 percent of men's. See Abzug, *Gender Gap*, 39.

CHAPTER SIX Labor

1. Meany interview with Dick Cavett (ABC-TV, Dec. 19, 1974) reported in *Dispatcher*, Jan. 10, 1975.

2. Transcript, George Meany oral history interview, Aug. 4, 1969, by Paige E. Mulhollan, pp. 16–17, LBJ.

3. Robert Dallek, *Flawed Giant: Lyndon Johnson and His Times, 1961–1973* (New York: Oxford University Press, 1998), 64–65.

4. Joseph C. Goulden, *Meany: The Unchallenged Strong Man of American Labor* (New York: Atheneum, 1972), 353.

5. George Romney of the Automobile Manufacturers' Association, 1945, quoted in Nelson Lichtenstein, *The Most Dangerous Man in Detroit: Walter Reuther and the Fate of American Labor* (New York: Basic, 1995), vii.

6. See Kevin Boyle, *The UAW and the Heyday of American Liberalism, 1945–1968* (Ithaca, N.Y.: Cornell University Press, 1995), 208–210, 219.

7. Lichtenstein, *Dangerous Man*, 426.

8. Peter B. Levy, *The New Left and Labor in the 1960s* (Urbana: University of Illinois Press, 1994), 47, 50–51.

9. Goulden, *Meany*, 357; *Los Angeles Times*, Oct. 19, 1967; *Wall Street Journal*, Oct. 26, 1967.

10. Meany quoted in Goulden, *Meany*, 358.

11. *Time*, Nov. 3, 1967; *Los Angeles Times*, Oct. 27, 1967; *Washington Post*, Oct. 27, 1967; Charles DeBenedetti, *An American Ordeal: The Antiwar Movement of the Vietnam Era* (Syracuse, N.Y.: Syracuse University Press, 1990), 206.

12. Samuel C. May, "The Postwar Unemployment Problem in California, 1945–1947" (pamphlet, Berkeley: Bureau of Public Administration, University of California, 1945), pp. 1, 4, HI; Robert K. Arnold et al., *The California Economy, 1947–1980* (Menlo Park, Calif.: Stanford Research Institute, 1961), 15, 16, 247, 315. See also Sidney Lens, *The Military-Industrial Complex* (London: Stanmore Press, 1971), 100; Roger W. Lotchin, *Fortress California, 1910–1961: From Warfare to Welfare* (New York: Oxford University Press, 1992), xv.

13. Andrew Levison, *The Working-Class Majority* (New York: Coward, McCann, and Geoghegan, 1974), 160–161. See also Aaron B. Wildavsky, *The Revolt Against the Masses and Other Essays on Politics and Public Policy* (New York: Basic, 1971).

14. Levy, *New Left and Labor*, 51. Cf. Patrick Renshaw, *American Labour and Consensus Capitalism, 1935–1990* (London: Macmillan, 1991), 153, 162–163.

15. Michael Barone, "Our Country: The Shaping of America from Roosevelt to Clinton," in Byron E. Shafer, ed., *Present Discontents: American Politics in the Very Late Twentieth Century* (Chatham, N.J.: Chatham House, 1997), 36.

16. According to one survey, 14 percent of high school graduates served in combat in Vietnam, compared with 9 percent of college graduates; 7 percent of the progeny of high-income families fought, compared with 15 percent from low-income backgrounds: Lawrence M. Baskir and William A. Strauss, *Chance and Circumstance: The Draft, the War, and the*

Vietnam Generation (New York: Knopf, 1978), 9. See also James Fallows, "What Did You Do in the Class War, Daddy?" in Walter Capps, ed., *The Vietnam Reader* (New York: Routledge, 1991), 216.

17. See Christian G. Appy, *Working-Class War: American Combat Soldiers and Vietnam* (Chapel Hill: University of North Carolina Press, 1993), 24, 32.

18. George Gallup, "Union Members Split on Vietnam," *Washington Post*, Jan. 3, 1968; *New York Times*, Jan. 5, 1968.

19. *Dispatcher*, May 18, 1962, Feb. 8, 1974. Barry M. Silverman, research director of the ILWU, disputed the view that members of his union were special beneficiaries of the Vietnam War. He argued that (1) their work was not tied to the Vietnam Run, so they had other sources of income, and (2) shipping and warehousing for the run was geographically dispersed, so it was not possible for the ILWU to stop the war by going on strike. His second argument may have colored his first, in that he defended the union decision to exempt war materials in the West Coast waterfront strike of 1971: Author's interview with Barry Silverman, Sept. 25, 1975.

20. *Dispatcher*, Aug. 23, Nov. 1, 1963, June 12 and Sept. 18, 1964, Mar. 5, 1965, *Proceedings of the Sixteenth Biennial Convention of the International Longshoremen's and Warehousemen's Union* (Apr. 5–9, 1965), 58.

21. The Hawaii Local figures are for 1969. See *Procs. ILWU* (Apr. 5–9, 1965), 468; *Procs. ILWU* (Apr. 7–12, 1969), 152, 439–441.

22. *Dispatcher*, Sept. 3 and Oct. 15, 1965.

23. Levy, *New Left and Labor*, 48; and see Ronald L. Filipelli and Mark D. McColloch, *Cold War in the Working Class: The Rise and Decline of the United Electrical Workers* (Albany: State University of New York Press, 1995).

24. Philip S. Foner, *American Labor and the Indo-China War: The Growth of Union Opposition* (New York: International Publishers, 1971), 31.

25. Working-class respondents in Cambridge, Mass., were, however, more hawkish than their middle-class neighbors: Levison, *Working Class Majority*, 159–160.

26. Boyle, *UAW*, 221.

27. Victor Reuther made his allegations to Patrick Owens of the *Detroit Free Press* and Harry Bernstein of the *Los Angeles Times;* the quotation is from Owens's story and appears in Goulden, *Meany*, 377. According to the historian Philip Foner, revelations about the AFL-CIO-CIA relationship discredited the AFL-CIO's early support for the Viet-

nam War, encouraged the growth of opposition, and contributed to the Meany–Walter Reuther rift: Foner, *Labor and Indo-China War*, 15–16, 35 ff.

28. Noted in Joseph L. Rauh, Jr., "Writing the Democratic Platform," *New Republic*, Oct. 14, 1967, p. 12.

29. Victor Riesel, "Reuther Bolts Labor's Pro-Johnson Political Machine," typescript of syndicated column enclosed with memo, "For the President's Night Reading," by Joe Califano, Oct. 6, 1967, and memo, "Walter Reuther," by Doug Nobles for W. Marvin Watson, Nov. 28, 1967 (the memo, noting the May 1966 date of the Reuther-Meany split, listed the presidential committees on which Reuther served, a point carefully noted by LBJ in a further attached memo dated Dec. 5, 1967), both in WHCF, Name File, Reuther, Walter, 1/1/67–12/31/67, Box 111, LBJ.

30. *Los Angeles Times*, Jan. 20, 1967; William L. Abbott letter in *New Leader*, n.d., clipping in folder "Democratic Party: Democratic Peace Caucus, Sept.–Dec. 1967," Box 30, JLR; Levy, *New Left and Labor*, 56; Goulden, *Meany*, 356.

31. William H. Chafe, *Never Stop Running: Allard Lowenstein and the Struggle to Save American Liberalism* (New York: Basic, 1993), 265.

32. Joseph L. Rauh, Jr., "A Proposal to Maximize Support for an End to the War in Vietnam," undated typescript, in folder "Democratic Party: Democratic Peace Caucus, July–August 1967," Box 30, JLR.

33. Rauh, "Writing the Democratic Platform," 12; Gus Tyler, "The Liberal Crisis," *New Leader*, Oct. 23, 1967, pp. 3–4; Rauh to Richard Hudson (editor, *War/Peace Report*), Dec. 9, 1967, in folder "Democratic Party: Democratic Peace Caucus, Sept.–Dec. 1967," Box 30, JLR.

34. Mazey to Rauh, Sept. 7. 1967, in folder "Democratic Party: Democratic Peace Caucus, Sept.–Dec. 1967," Box 30, JLR.

35. Lichtenstein, *Dangerous Man*, 404.

36. Pre-delivery released text of LBJ speech, Dec. 12, 1967, folder "Vietnam 7E (3) 12/67–1/68. Public Relations Activities," Country File, Vietnam, NSF, Box 100, LBJ.

37. Dallek, *Flawed Giant*, 314–316.

38. *West Coast Sailors*, Aug. 9, 1968.

39. *West Coast Sailors*, Feb. 9, 1968.

40. *West Coast Sailors*, Jan. 19, 1968; author's interview with William S. Mailliard, Oct. 14, 1975.

41. *Seafarers Log*, Feb. 16, Aug. 2, Oct. 11 and 25, 1968.

42. Telegram, Harry Bridges and Louis Goldblatt to the president, Nov. 27, 1963, "GER" note attached to Walter Jenkins's draft of note on

behalf of the president, Dec. 19, 1963, Whitney Shoemaker on behalf of the president to Harry Bridges, Nov. 21, 1968, all in WHCF, Name File, Bridges, Box 453, LBJ.

43. Ackley quoted in Gareth Davies, *From Opportunity to Entitlement: The Transformation and Decline of Great Society Liberalism* (Lawrence: University Press of Kansas, 1996), 106.

44. Memo, "Preparing for Prosperity After Vietnam," Walter W. Heller for the president, July 12, memo, Joseph A. Califano for Gardner Ackley, July 16, draft memo, president for secretary of the treasury, director of the budget, and chairman of the council of economic advisers, enclosed with memo, Gardner Ackley for Califano, Aug. 1, all in 1966 and in WHCF, Name File, Califano, folder "Post Vietnam Planning," Box 57, LBJ.

45. Memo, Charles L. Schultze for Califano, Nov. 14, 1967, E. H. Rastatter's paper on Great Society programs and the war, Oct. 13, 1967, enclosed with memo, Califano for Schultze, Nov. 3, 1967, all in WHCF, Name File, Gaither, folder "Office Files of James Gaither: Facts and Figures: Vietnam," Box 290, LBJ; *The Potential Transfer of Skills from Defense to Nondefense Industries* (Sacramento: Department of Employment, State of California, 1968; a study prepared for the U.S. Arms Control and Disarmament Agency), 14.

46. Goulden, *Meany*, 362–364. Goulden's words.

47. Renshaw, *Labour*, 171; Boyle, *UAW*, 247.

48. *New York Times*, Oct. 17, 1968. See also the monitoring and endorsement of Humphrey's candidacy in the *Seafarers Log*, Oct. 11 and 25, 1968; and Goulden, *Meany*, 367; Boyle, *UAW*, 255; Theodore H. White, *The Making of the President 1968* (London: Jonathan Cape, 1969), 365–366; Jong Oh Ra, *Labor at the Polls: Union Voting in Presidential Elections, 1952–1976* (Amherst: University of Massachusetts Press, 1978), 129–130.

49. Labor's pivotal role in Nixon's foreign policy and reelection strategies was not lost on contemporary journalists and memoirists. See Rowland Evans, Jr., and Robert D. Novak, *Nixon in the White House: The Frustration of Power* (New York: Random House, 1971), 324; Elizabeth Drew, *Washington Journal: The Events of 1973–1974* (New York: Random House, 1975), 126; and William Safire, *Before the Fall: An Inside View of the Pre-Watergate White House* (Garden City, N.Y.: Doubleday, 1975), 584, 588.

50. Gregory Palmer, *The McNamara Strategy and the Vietnam War: Program Budgeting in the Pentagon, 1960–1968* (Westport, Conn.: Green-

wood Press, 1978), 24, 56; Henry Kissinger, *The White House Years* (London: Weidenfeld and Nicolson, 1979), 952; Lester A. Sobel, *Inflation and the Nixon Administration*, 2 vols. (New York: Facts on File, 1974), I, 9, 85.

51. Based on figures in Anthony S. Campagna, *The Economic Consequences of the Vietnam War* (New York: Praeger, 1991), 83.

52. Quoted in *Dispatcher*, June 3, 1970.

53. Robert W. Stevens, *Vain Hopes, Grim Realities: The Economic Consequences of the Vietnam War* (New York: New Viewpoints, 1976), 25.

54. *West Coast Sailors*, Aug. 8, 1969; *San Francisco Chronicle*, Oct. 20, 1969. See also Levy, *New Left and Labor*, 59.

55. Richard Nixon, *RN: The Memoirs of Richard Nixon*, 2 vols. (New York: Warner, 1979), I, 505–507; Stephen E. Ambrose, *Nixon: The Triumph of a Politician, 1962–1972* (New York: Simon and Schuster, 1989), 310.

56. Safire, *Before the Fall*, 542–596.

57. Sanford Gottlieb, "Probing the 'Silent Majority,'" *Sane World*, July 1970, p. 1.

58. Philip E. Converse and Howard Schuman, "'Silent Majorities' and the Vietnam War," *Scientific American*, 222 (June 1970), 24; Milton J. Rosenberg, Sidney Verba, and Philip E. Converse, *Vietnam and the Silent Majority: The Dove's Guide* (New York: Harper and Row, 1970), 18, 19, 77.

59. Harlan Hahn, "Dove Sentiments Among Blue-Collar Workers," *Dissent*, 17 (1970), 202–203.

60. Nixon, *Memoirs*, I, 506–507.

61. Under the caption "Scab Grapes—His Favorite Dish," the Oct. 28, 1968, issue of *Seafarers Log* displayed a photograph of Nixon grasping a bunch.

62. Printed slogan bearing union label, NLC.

63. Safire, *Before the Fall*, 584; Joshua B. Freeman, "Hardhats: Construction Workers, Manliness, and the 1970 Pro-War Demonstrations," *Journal of Social History*, 26 (Summer 1993), 725.

64. Appy, *Working-Class War*, 39–40.

65. Al Richmond, "Workers Against the War," *Ramparts*, 9 (1970), 31; Levy, *New Left and Labor*, 61.

66. *New York Daily News*, May 18, 1970.

67. Undated briefing memo, Colson for president, in folder "Building and Construction Trades Council Meeting with the President, May 26, '70," WHCF, SMOF, CC, Box 20, NPM.

68. *Scanlan's Monthly*, 1 (September 1970), 2–3. See also *Nassau Daily*

Review, Oct. 14, 1929; Harold Seidman, *Labor Czars: A History of Labor Racketeering* (New York: Liveright, 1938); Foner, *Labor and Indo-China War*, 88.

69. Levy, *New Left and Labor*, 61. Harry Bridges contended that, in inflationary times, workers could not afford time off to attend demonstrations: Bridges, "On the Beam," *Dispatcher*, Oct. 23, 1969. Cf. Foner, *Labor and Indo-China War*, 90.

70. Michael Rogin in the *New York Times Magazine*, June 28, 1970.

71. Freeman, "Hardhats," 726, 732, 735.

72. Quoted in Appy, *Working-Class War*, 40.

73. Harris poll cited in Levy, *New Left and Labor*, 61.

74. Nixon, *Memoirs*, I, 558.

75. Memo, Colson for president, in folder "AFL/CIO Council Meeting W/Pres., 5/12/70," WHCF, SMOF, CC, Box 20, NPM.

76. Undated briefing memo, Colson for president, in folder "Building and Construction Trades Council Meeting with the President, May 26, '70," WHCF, SMOF, CC, Box 20, NPM.

77. Charles W. Colson's paraphrases in his minutes of the meeting, reproduced in Colson, Memorandum for the President's File, Sept. 12, 1970, in folder "Building and Construction Trades Council Meeting with the President, May 26, '70," WHCF, SMOF, CC, Box 20, NPM. Nixon's father may have worked on the construction of his own home, but he was really a small businessman, a grocer: Stephen E. Ambrose, *Nixon: The Education of a Politician, 1913–1962* (New York: Simon and Schuster, 1987), 34–35.

78. Nixon to Gleason, May 27, 1970, in *Longshore News*, June 1970.

79. *Washington Post*, June 8, 1970; ILA poster, and memo, Colson for Michael Collins, June 22, 1970, in unmarked folder, and memo, Colson for Jeb Magruder, June 11, 1970, in folder "Hard Hats Participation," all in WHCF, SMOF, CC, Box 73, NPM.

80. In the Daniel Yankelovich survey commissioned by the *New York Times*, 43 percent of the respondents identified the war as the main issue facing the nation, with inflation second at 26 percent. The main local problems causing concern were drugs and crime, both at 19 percent: *New York Times*, Oct. 30, 1970.

81. *Malone* [N.Y.] *Telegram*, July 22, 1970. On Nixon's admiration for William Buckley, see Ambrose, *Nixon: Triumph*, 410; on his Republican registration, see Rowland Evans and Robert Novak in the *Hagerstown* [Md.] *Herald*, July 31, 1970.

82. On Goodell's claim to be one of Nixon's most loyal supporters on non-Vietnam matters, see the *Yonkers* [N.Y.] *Herald Statesman*, Aug. 20, 1970. On Goodell's "sharp turn to the left," see the *Batavia* [N.Y.] *News*, June 2, 1970.

83. Press release, "Javits to hold press conference on Cambodia and Vietnam," May 18, 1970, Box 46, JKJ.

84. *Oswego* [N.Y.] *Palladium-Times*, Aug. 29, 1970. There were complaints that the Democratic slate was entirely Jewish and African American and was drawn exclusively from New York City and that the Republican Goodell, too, had forgotten about upstate voters: *Riverton* [Wyo.] *Ranger*, and *Olean* [N.Y.] *Times-Herald*, both on July 22, 1970.

85. Kevin P. Phillips seminar talk, Department of History, University of Edinburgh, Apr. 29, 1997. In the 1968 election, Phillips was special assistant to Nixon's national campaign manager, John Mitchell. In 1969 he argued in an influential book that the construction of a Republican majority would need to be based on an appreciation of the "location and intensity" of old Democratic loyalties: Phillips, *The Emerging Republican Majority* (New Rochelle, N.Y.: Arlington House, 1969), 22.

86. Draft of Buckley speech dated "May, 1970," in file "1970 Speeches," Box 2, JLB. In an eve-of-election political advertisement, Buckley reiterated his message: "I want to go to Washington to speak out for the majority. America is under siege. I want to help our President lift the siege": *Cortland* [N.Y.] *Standard*, Oct. 29, 1970.

87. Draft of Buckley speech, in file "Long Island Association—6/25/71," Box 2, JLB; *New York Times*, Oct. 30, 1970.

88. Chamberlain, "Labor May Jump the Traces," *Lockport* [N.Y.] *Union Sun and Journal*, July 22, 1970. Further information on Maye in memo, Colson for H. R. Haldeman, Sept. 21, 1970, in folder "Labor Campaign," WHCF, SMOF, CC, Box 77, NPM.

89. *Hagerstown* [Md.] *Herald*, July 31, 1970; *Fort Myers* [Fla.] *News Press*, Aug. 20, 1970.

90. Memo, Colson for Haldeman, Sept. 21, 1970, in de-labeled folder, WHCF, SMOF, CC, Box 77, NPM.

91. Memo, Colson for Bud Krogh, May 28, 1970, enclosing Committee for a National Rank-and-File Conference press release, in folder "Jay Lovestone—AFL-CIO," WHCF, SMOF, CC, Box 78, NPM.

92. Memo, Colson for Murray Chotiner, July 28, 1970, in folder "Jay Lovestone—AFL-CIO," WHCF, SMOF, CC, Box 78, NPM.

93. Memo, Colson for Haldeman, Sept. 14, 1970, with Haldeman's

handwritten notes of approval in the margins, in folder "Labor Campaign," WHCF, SMOF, CC, Box 77, NPM. On Nixon's plan for maritime expansion, see *West Coast Sailors*, Nov. 7, 1969.

94. Memo, Colson for Murray Chotiner, July 28, 1970, in folder "Jay Lovestone—AFL-CIO," WHCF, SMOF, CC, Box 78, NPM.

95. "Republicans and Hard Hats," *National Review*, Sept. 22, 1970.

96. Memo, Colson for Haldeman, Oct. 22, 1970, in folder "Labor Campaign," WHCF, SMOF, CC, Box 77, NPM; *New York Post*, Oct. 30, 1970.

97. Drew, *Washington Journal*, 125.

98. Quotations in *New York Post*, Oct. 30, 1970; *Binghamton* [N.Y.] *Sun-Bulletin*, Oct. 31, 1970; James L. Buckley, *If Men Were Angels: A View From the Senate* (New York: Putnam's, 1975), 12.

99. *Sacramento Bee*, Oct. 15 and 22, 1970.

100. *Sacramento Bee*, Oct. 24, 1970.

101. *San Francisco Chronicle*, May 27, 1970. Northern California had been emphatically antiwar as early as 1965: poll commissioned by and reported in *San Francisco Chronicle*, Mar. 9, 1965.

102. Quoted in *Dispatcher*, June 3, 1970.

103. *New York Times*, May 20, 1970, quoted in Foner, *Labor and Indo-China War*, 100.

104. *Sacramento Bee*, Oct. 14 and 16, 1970.

105. *Sacramento Bee*, Oct. 18, 1970.

106. *Sacramento Bee*, Oct. 14 and 29, 1970; Ronald Reagan, *An American Life* (London: Hutchinson, 1990), 185.

107. *Baltimore Sun*, Nov. 1, 1970.

108. Memo, Haldeman for Jim Keogh, Nov. 25, 1970, and Walker paper, Nov. 30, 1970, both in folder "Labor," WHCF, SMOF, HRH, Box 129, NPM.

109. Memo, Keogh for Shultz, Dec. 4, 1970, in folder "Labor Campaign," WHCF, SMOF, CC, Box 77, NPM.

110. Memos, Colson for the president, Dec. 7, Colson for Haldeman, Dec. 8, Shultz for the president, Dec. 28, and Shultz for John R. Brown III, Dec. 30, all in 1970 and in folder "Labor," WHCF, SMOF, HRH, Box 129, NPM.

111. Memo, "Trouble on the Right," Patrick J. Buchanan for the president, Jan. 6, 1971, in folder "President's Handwriting January 1971," WHCF, POF, Box 9, NPM. Judging from Nixon's marginal notes on this memorandum, he reacted strongly to Buchanan's suggestion that the right was being badly handled by the White House. Addressing his com-

ments to Haldeman, he demanded more consultation with conservative gurus and an active policy against Reagan; he wanted to know whether his action on Cambodia was satisfying the right.

112. Buckley, *If Men Were Angels*, 4.

113. AFL-CIO executive council statements on foreign policy and on prisoners of war in Vietnam, transmitted by Lovestone, dated Feb. 19, 1971, and enclosed with memo, Colson for General Alexander Haig, Feb. 24, 1971, in folder "Jay Lovestone—AFL-CIO," WHCF, SMOF, CC, Box 78, and log entries for Mar. 3 and 6, 1971, WHCF, POF, Box 107, both NPM. Elizabeth Drew records AFL-CIO concerns about Brennan's appointment, although they may be a mid-Watergate expression of wisdom with hindsight: journal entry for Nov. 21, 1973, in Drew, *Washington Journal*, 126–127.

114. Nixon to Colson, Mar. 8, 1971, quoted in Safire, *Before the Fall*, 587; memo, Colson for president, Mar. 15 (referring to Nixon's letter of Mar. 8), 1971, in folder "January 1971–March 15, 1971," WHCF, POF, Box 9, NPM.

115. The quotation is Colson's paraphrase: memo, Colson for the president's file, July 26, 1971, in de-labeled folder, WHCF, SMOF, CC, Box 23, NPM.

116. Ambrose, *Nixon: Triumph*, 458–459.

117. Caption under photograph of meeting between Bridges and Nixon, in H. R. Haldeman Diary, CD-ROM version (Santa Monica, Calif.: Sony Imagesoft, 1994); telegram, Bridges to president, date unclear but possibly Aug. 18, 1971, and memo, Colson for Shultz, Aug. 19, 1971, both in folder "Jay Lovestone—AFL-CIO," WHCF, SMOF, CC, Box 78, NPM; Silverman interview; Goulden, *Meany*, 447–448; Theodore H. White, *The Making of the President 1972* (London: Jonathan Cape, 1974), 229, 348. Hoffa's release may have been an attempt to neutralize a bid for power within the Teamsters by the liberal vice president Harold J. Gibbons, a man whom Colson identified as an enemy of the Nixon administration: Lewis Chester, Cal McCrystal, Stephen Aris, and William Shawcross, *Watergate: The Full Inside Story* (London: Andre Deutsch, 1973), 224.

118. Wildavsky, *Revolt Against the Masses*, 37.

119. Included among the 456 top people in the Columbia survey were the heads of forty-one labor unions. Like all the other elite groups except "Republican office holders and politicians," they were dovish on Vietnam and defense spending: *New York Times*, Aug. 17, 1972.

120. Alan Clem, "The Democratic Minority: George McGovern,"

in Herbert T. Hoover and Larry J. Zimmerman, eds., *South Dakota Leaders: From Pierre Chouteau, Jr., to Oscar Howe* (Vermillion: University of South Dakota Press, 1989), 315; George S. McGovern, *The Great Coalfield War* (Boston: Houghton Mifflin, 1972), 1.

121. *New York Times*, Apr. 25, 1972.

122. *Milwaukee Journal*, Apr. 14, 1972.

123. *St. Louis Post-Dispatch*, June 25, 1972.

124. *Nation*, May 29, 1972.

125. *St. Louis Post-Dispatch*, June 25, 1972; *Dispatcher*, Aug. 23 and Nov. 1, 1963, June 12, 1964, Mar. 5, 1965; *Procs. ILWU* (1965), 58; unnamed critic quoted in Charles P. Larrowe, *Harry Bridges: The Rise and Fall of Radical Labor in the U.S.* (New York: Lawrence Hill, 1972), 377.

126. Clifton Caldwell and David Livingston to Fulbright, June 16, 1972; Fulbright to Livingston, June 30 and 31, 1972, all in folder "Vietnam Miscellany—I," Campaign Issues, Box 25, McG.

127. *Business Week*, July 29, 1972.

128. Text of McGovern's Sept. 4, 1972, address in George McGovern, *American Journey: The Presidential Campaign Speeches of George McGovern* (New York: Random House, 1974), 38.

129. AFL-CIO press release consisting of Meany's Sept. 18, 1972, address, in folder "AFL/CIO Convention (Meany) 11/19/72," WHCF, SMOF, CC, Box 28, NPM.

130. Nixon went on: "The same thing can be said of other groups or classes, including young, black, Mexicans, etc." Diary entry quoted in Richard M. Nixon, *Memoirs*, 2 vols. (New York: Warner, 1979), II, 163.

131. McGovern to Meany, Apr. 10, 1972, in folder "Meany, George," Campaign Issues, Box 17, McG.

132. *Washington Post*, Apr. 28, 1972; memo, Buchanan for Haldeman and Colson, Apr. 28, 1972, in folder "Jay Lovestone—AFL-CIO," WHCF, SMOF, CC, Box 78, NPM.

133. Colson paraphrase of the telephone conversation, June 5, 1972, in folder "Jay Lovestone—AFL-CIO," WHCF, SMOF, CC, Box 78, NPM.

134. Housewright quoted in *Business Week*, July 29, 1972.

135. Memo, Ehrlichman for president, Aug. 25, 1972, in folder "AFL/CIO Convention (Meany) 11/19/72," WHCF, SMOF, CC, Box 28, NPM.

136. Memo, "eyes only," Colson for Lovestone, Oct. 25, 1972, containing draft of Meany statement of the same date, in folder "Jay Lovestone—AFL-CIO," WHCF, SMOF, CC, Box 78, NPM.

137. Leslie H. Gelb and Richard K. Betts, *The Irony of Vietnam: The*

System Worked (Washington, D.C.: Brookings Institution, 1979), 286–287.

138. Glen Gendzel, "Xuan Thuy," in Stanley I. Kutler, ed., *Encyclopedia of the Vietnam War* (New York: Charles Scribner's, 1996), 645; Stanley Karnow, *Vietnam: A History* (New York: Penguin, 1984), 612.

Index

DS
558
.J44
1999